BENEATH
THE
SHADOW

John Griswold, series editor

JUSTIN
GARDINER

BENEATH
THE
SHADOW

LEGACY AND
LONGING
IN THE
ANTARCTIC

THE UNIVERSITY OF
GEORGIA PRESS
ATHENS

© 2019 by the University of Georgia Press
Athens, Georgia 30602
www.ugapress.org
All rights reserved
Designed by Kaelin Chappell Broaddus
Set in 9.5/13.5 Miller Text Roman by
Kaelin Chappell Broaddus
Printed and bound by
Sheridan Books, Inc.

The paper in this book meets the guidelines for
permanence and durability of the Committee on
Production Guidelines for Book Longevity of the
Council on Library Resources.

Most University of Georgia Press titles are
available from popular e-book vendors.

Printed in the United States of America
19 20 21 22 23 P 5 4 3 2 1

Library of Congress Control Number: 2018966792
ISBN: 9780820354958 (paperback)
ISBN: 9780820354965 (ebook)

Brief excerpt from "Berkeley Eclogue" ["Big subject.
Big shadow."] from *Human Wishes* by Robert Hass.
Copyright © 1989 by Robert Hass. Reprinted by
permission of HarperCollins Publishers.

FOR *ERIC*,
*FOR GETTING ME
ON BOARD THE SHIP.*
AND FOR *ROSE*,
*FOR STANDING BY ME
EVER SINCE.*

Big subject. *Big shadow.*

—ROBERT HASS

CONTENTS

*BENEATH
THE
SHADOW*

PROLOGUE

Growing up near the rundown coastal towns of Oregon, I used to walk the long, seagull-strewn docks on summer outings, mulling over the names of boats. Emissaries from the beyond—their riddles of small hopes brightly scrawled and broadcast to the bay. These were the little skiffs that trawled their nets near to shore, their lights at night bordering the sheltered coves.

But to christen a ship for the high seas must be another matter entirely. I've been told that to name a lifeboat at all is an ominous gesture: a provocation of the fates asea. Though for the larger vessels, especially the old wooden-hulled haulers that headed to the Antarctic for journeys of several seasons, one must have sought comfort in a name—*Resolution, Discovery*—chivalrous and steadfast, as brash and blustering as the men who sailed upon them. Or, in turn, proud and mythical ties—*Nimrod, Erebus*—sons of Cush and Chaos, bold prophets of some faraway place. Others invoking the celestial realm—*Aurora, Terra Nova*—the shepherding light one hopes to steer by. Some given, simply, a woman's name—*Jane, Cecilia*—that proper feminine noun the one delicacy such voyaging could afford.

What's in a name? Set your eyes on any map to make certain: a lot. For the Antarctic, perhaps more than anywhere else, what you'll find is a lexicon of salvation and despair, coastlines littered with the grand and unfathomable—Neptune's Bellows; Mount Terror; Bays of Hope and Bone; Capes of Longing, Fairweather, and Disappointment.

Amazing, given the fact that Antarctica was discovered less than two hundred years ago, and that it claims no permanent human inhabitants, how rich it is in peopled history. But stories are icebreakers only in the colloquial sense; like the ships themselves, they can be turned back, repelled, or lost at sea. If need be, they can also be trapped (*Belgica*), torn asunder (*Endurance*), or like the explorers themselves (Wilson, Bowers) put to a final and frozen rest.

=====

In February 2010, with the help of my friend Eric Guth, who works as a photographer and naturalist with Lindblad Expeditions (a *National Geographic*–sponsored educational cruise line), I boarded a ship bound for Antarctica and South Georgia. A stowaway of sorts, my passage was not assured until two weeks prior to sailing, as the number of registered guests inched up and down, before settling, finally, with an opening. Luckily enough, I was already in Patagonia, where I'd been backpacking on my own for most of a month and was a mere two days' travel to the port of Ushuaia. En route, I read—in shop windows, on T-shirts and postcards— slogans like "Patagonia, bottom of the world!" and "Tierra Del Fuego, farthest south," but the roads kept going, and beyond them I knew I would soon be heading.

CHAPTER 1

RESOLUTION
(1772–1775)

CAPTAIN JAMES COOK

The human tale of the Antarctic, like any great story, resists a straightforward chronology. We begin, as it were, in medias res. And by the time the first bundled sailor sets foot on that frozen stage, the world has already borne witness to many brave quests, to many competing sagas of ruin and origin. According to Maori legend, for instance, a Polynesian chief set off alone in a dugout canoe in 650 AD, sailing south from the island of Rarotonga, until he encountered a white island. In this telling, he became the first person to lay eyes on an Antarctic iceberg. Or maybe not. All efforts of navigation are dependent on the establishment of fixed points, and this holds true not just at sea or on land, but also with history. We have to locate our beginnings somewhere, even in the uncharted regions of the globe. And so, when it comes to the story of the last continent, most historians begin with the voyages of James Cook.

Commissioned by the British government to seek out "countries hitherto unknown," Cook's second expedition circumnavigated the globe at roughly sixty degrees south, pushing back the barrier, the outer limits of the unknown.[1] The *Resolution* was the first ship to cross the Antarctic Circle, a nautical feat that would not be repeated for close to fifty years. All told, the voyage spanned over seventy thousand miles—almost twice the distance of Cook's first expedition. And while Cook may have returned to London empty-handed—having been forced to turn back seventy-five miles short of the discovery he craved—his voyage put to rest a longstanding imperial fantasy of a temperate and bountiful southern land. What Cook thought surely to be a wall, however, was simply a doorway barred—with pack ice and katabatic winds—one of the only blockades he did not venture beyond.

If any one should have resolution and perseverance enough to clear up this point by proceeding farther than I have done, I shall not envy him the honour of the discovery; but I will be bold to say, that the world will not be benefited by it.[2]

James Cook, while perhaps the greatest seafaring explorer who ever lived, held no patent on boldness, nor honor, and in the decades that followed his demise—death at the hands of Hawaiian natives—the Southern Ocean trafficked in adventure; in greed; in sealing, whaling, and science.

It was not just hardened veteran polar explorers who headed south, but also green inlanders who'd never before laid eyes on snow; also expedition geologists, all of twenty, having completed just two years of college; also the restless merchant marine who would recite poetry to his crew; the recovering consumptive and ascetic doctor; the myopic recent Oxford grad who bought his way on board.

Yet if Cook couldn't foresee the dubious ranks of a dawning Heroic Age, how could he ever dream of the band of misfits and socialites who would lurk later in the wings—the advent of Antarctic tourism, shadow of that shadowy cast. Cruise ships full of retired lawyers with multi-thousand-dollar cameras they had no idea how to use; Filipino yoga instructors leading morning workouts in the lounge; recently divorced IT specialists from Nebraska; the card-carrying "away-school" dad, dragging his family along on another educational venture; and the itinerant adventure blogger, who bused down all the way from DC, checking in hourly on his Twitter feed.

Ah, but I am getting ahead of myself. A common enough occurrence in a region where one's sense of time is unmoored by the low angles of the sun, and where one's sense of distance is often tricked by a horizon that feels both infinite and near at hand. Besides, the Antarctic isn't a landscape to be taken in sequentially, but all at once—interweaving its grandeur, its science, its history. And the only way to gain access to such a place is to cross the world's most manic sea.

I shall therefore conclude this introductory discourse with desiring the reader to excuse the inaccuracies of style, which doubtless he will frequently meet with in the following narrative; and that, when such occur, he will recollect that it is the production of a man, who has not had the advantage of much school education, but who has been constantly at sea from his youth.[3]

The second of eight children, Cook was born to a Yorkshire farm laborer in 1728. Prospects for social advancement in eighteenth-century Britain were bleak, but Cook was fortunate enough to receive a basic education at a village school, before first venturing to sea at the relatively late age of eighteen. Offered a three-year apprenticeship, Cook served on a coal-hauling brig christened the *Freelove*. This was hardly a fitting ship's name for Cook, who—in all his years of exploring—is said to have remained always faithful to his wife at home, even as they were never to live together for longer than a year at a time. The men under his charge, however, were not known for practicing a similar restraint. The "trade in nails" had been well established prior to Cook's sailings to the southern hemisphere, as Tahitians in particular came to prize such hardware above all else, realizing how superior nails were to stone or bone tools for building. As one scholar puts it, "In order to pay for sex, sailors from the *Dolphin* [the first European ship to visit the island] had extracted so many nails from the framework of the ship that not only was there nowhere to hang a hammock, but also the vessel itself was in danger of falling to pieces."[4] Cook attempted to curb such trade, and while he managed to keep the ship's fasteners largely intact, he knew there were limits to even a captain's control of his men. Venereal disease ran rampant among his crews, who spread infections among the islanders, and in his first visit to the tropics, three sailors went so far as to run away just prior to departure, hoping to stay permanently with their "Tahitian wives," and had to be dragged back on board.

When it came to alcohol, Cook's abstemious nature also stood in stark contrast to those of his crew, who were generally allotted eight beers a day, along with their highly prized ration of grog—a mixture of brandy, sugar, and water that was distributed daily with some ceremony in barrels set out on the foredeck. Holidays were a particularly rambunctious time, and the rough weather of the high latitudes often occasioned an extra ration of booze to keep spirits (as well as ships) afloat. The captain no doubt disapproved of this lasciviousness, holding himself at some distance from the men under his charge. Still, Cook was no stranger to friendship, and he maintained a lifelong correspondence with John Walker—the Quaker shipowner who was Cook's benefactor as a young man.

I should hardly have troubled you with a letter was it not customary for Men to take leave of their friends before they go out of the World, for I can hardly think my self in it so long as I am deprived from having any Connections with the civilized part of it, and this will soon be my case for two years at least.[5]

While rarely reaching full-on sailor proportions, my pal Eric has never been known for turning down a beer—"clever but liking grog," as Cook was apt to claim.[6] Convenient, as in exchange for getting me on board, I'm likely to be buying this man drinks for the rest of my days. Backpacking domestic partners of sorts, Eric and I have been joining up for wilderness trips for over a decade now. Since graduating from college, we have probably spent more time together in the backcountry than in the front one, so it always feels a little odd when we set eyes on each other against the backdrop of a city. Both aspiring artists (poet and photographer), when we aren't way off in the woods together, we've tended to travel in parallel streams—often on the move, frequently single, seasonally unemployed, and always trying to spend about as much time as possible in the outdoors.*

We make plans to meet up at the southernmost Irish pub in the world. This is an endeavor that requires some deliberation—and maybe a compass bearing—as the port of Ushuaia actually houses two Irish pubs less than a block apart. This town was founded as a prison colony back in 1873, in an attempt to secure Argentine sovereignty, and much of the town was actually built by prisoners, with timber from the surrounding forest. Pair with that inauspicious beginning a few generations of castaway sailors— along with the more recent surge of adventure travelers—and it comes as no surprise that the town doesn't lack for drinking establishments. Eric's ship docked only a couple of hours ago, and the bar is crowded with passengers and crew. With him is Kendra, a friend from the ship whom I already know and like, the three of us having gone backpacking together once back in the States. Kendra is in her late twenties, with long brown hair tied back. She has a serious, "cut-the-bullshit" demeanor that has no doubt been honed through years of being employed in an industry domi-

---

*For the record, I have—for the last several years—worked as an adjunct English instructor, which may well be the contemporary, landlocked, academic equivalent of the navy seaman.

nated by men. Like Eric, Kendra has worked her way up in the company, from steward to deckhand to her current position as the assistant expedition leader. What this means is that she is the point person for all 150 of the guests throughout the duration of the trip—"the hardest job on the ship," Eric claims, and I don't doubt him. Apparently, she pulled a few strings herself to get me on board, and I happily buy us a round.

It's standing room only, so we huddle up to a small table where their friend Stefan has saved us space. Tall, wiry, brooding—shaped less by muscle than by forty years of experience at sea—Stefan hasn't always plied the tourist trade. He is an experienced shiphand (in addition to naturalist, author, and photographer) who once worked for seven seasons on a Swedish ice vessel helping to establish two scientific stations on remote Queen Maud's Land in East Antarctica. Stefan is a father figure toward Eric, encouraging his photography and helping him to secure work over other, more established people in the field. "Ah, so this is the poet," Stefan begins in a rough, moody English, shaking my hand. "Well, good. For Eric, you write some ice poems to go along with his photographs. Then, you make a book together." Seems easy enough. "Not long poems," he adds, waving his hand away with a tinge of disgust. "Not too many words, just enough to pair with the images."

"I'll see what I can do," I offer, and right away I know I like the guy.

As the evening goes on, I meet several others from the staff—the whale expert, the dive specialist—in addition to them all being friendly and intelligent, they strike me at the moment as being pretty much the luckiest people in the world.

Lands doomed by Nature to perpetual frigidness; never to feel the warmth of the sun's rays; whose horrible and savage aspect I have not words to describe. Such are the lands we have discovered; what then may we expect those to be which lie still farther to the south?[7]

Luck, like beauty and jealousy of course, often lies in the eye of the beholder, and while James Cook was almost universally respected in his time, he did not lead a life that many would envy. Unlike Eric and his colleagues, who generally work a schedule of three months on, then three off, Cook sailed for years at a time, in cramped quarters to unknown lands, braving endless trials of weather and navigation. While Cook would wind up transforming western Europe's knowledge of over half the world, the English public gave him up for dead on his first voyage, after his absence stretched on to three years. Of Cook's six children, three were born when he was at sea—two of them dying before he got back. The captain's fame may rest, chiefly, on the wealth of what his expeditions found in warmer climes, but from his journals it is clear how fixated he was on the discoveries that eluded him in the south. When Cook sent out boats to collect ice from the drifting bergs, upon melting it they found the water perfectly drinkable and free from salt—an indication of solid land, they wagered, if only they could reach it.[8] Three times he ventured beyond the Antarctic Circle, though each time he was turned back by the pack, without answer or reward.

I, who had ambition not only to go farther than anyone had been before but as far as it was possible for man to go, was not sorry at meeting with this interruption, as it in some measure relieved us, at least shortened the dangers and hardships inseparable from the navigation of the southern polar regions.[9]

In preparation of my own foreseeable hardships, I have—after consultation with Eric—purchased exactly three items:

  1) a fifth of Old Smuggler's whiskey,

  2) a bottle of O'Malleys Irish Cream (the poor man's Baileys), and

  3) a new dress shirt.

The lack of an open bar paired with a shortage of funds necessitated the first two purchases, and the first night's captain's dinner (evidently a somewhat frilly affair) brought along the third. The next morning, after a few hours of sleep at a cheap hostel, I meet up with Eric again down at the docks. Checkpoints, armed guards, ID badges—if it wasn't for Eric's goofy, bearded grin I'd feel like we were entering a military compound. We make our way down narrow wood-planked corridors, dwarfed by a line of filthy freighters and the occasional luxury cruise. Our ship, the *Explorer*, is easy to pick out given the gold *National Geographic* insignia rectangle emblazoned across its blue hull. On board, we stop first at Eric's room, where he loans me a pair of slacks to go along with my new shirt. On their inner lining I see the word "Guth" penned in black Sharpie. "This is nice," I say. "Did your mom do this for you before you left home?" Eric laughs, "It is just something they do with the staff's laundry. Here, try these on too." Eric hands me a pair of knee-high, fleece-lined rubber boots he'd set aside from the previous voyage. A necessity for shore ventures, such boots cost hundreds of dollars, though most guests don't bother to pack them up upon their return.

About half the size of half of a dorm room, Eric's bunk is well equipped with a small desk, a bathroom the size of a normal shower, a built-in cabinet with a few drawers, and a fold-down bed—standard ship lodging I'd wager, though granted I've never before been on much of a ship. Next, we head to my room, and right away it becomes clear that, in addition to buying Eric the occasional beer, I probably ought to throw in my firstborn child. It's bigger than any hotel room I've ever stayed in, and there are a nice wooden table and chairs, twin beds, a refrigerator, an armchair, a full bathroom, a large closet hung with plush white robes, and a television that is currently showing underwater footage with the accompaniment of bad jazz. "What is this shit?" Eric asks, muting the sound. "They redesigned all the guest rooms last year and put in these televisions," he tells me. "The staff was opposed to it, but at least there's no satellite. They show a couple movies each night, and guests can tune in to the evening lectures and recaps if they don't want to attend." Eric had hoped to upgrade himself to this cabin, but it turns out there is another stowaway who will be bunking with me instead. A friend of the ship's hospitality supervisor, Eric says, though he doesn't know anything more than that. Eric glances at the clock and says he'd better get going. They are about to start general boarding, and all of the staff helps to carry luggage and show people on board.

With Eric gone, I take a few minutes to unpack, then head out for a look around. Apart from a handful of ferry rides and an afternoon of halibut fishing out of Homer, Alaska, over a decade ago, I've never been on a ship before, and certainly not one as grand as this. From the bow, I can survey the entire harbor and see that the *Explorer* is clearly the pride of the docks. At roughly 350 feet long, it is small by even the most modest of cruise line standards, accommodating 150 guests at full capacity, along with 50 staff members, and another 100 or so among the mostly Filipino crew. Still, it has six impressive viewing decks and seems built, almost entirely, out of an unbroken line of expansive windows.

When Lars-Eric Lindblad first chartered an Argentine naval ship to take a group of tourists to the Antarctic in the 1960s, he pitched the experience as part of a scientific undertaking, requiring each of the guests to read a list of books before departure. In this, Lindblad owes quite a lot to the legacy of James Cook, as the entire vision of this company is modeled after his three voyages. Cook was known as the first scientific explorer. His expeditions identified thousands of new species, employed professional artists and astronomers, and established a tradition of interdisciplinary research that would become a trademark of the Royal Navy's trips to the Antarctic. On Cook's first expedition alone, the ship's botanists returned to London with so much exotic flora that they expanded the number of known plant species in the West by a quarter. Cook even went so far on this first voyage as to share his personal cabin with the ship's chief naturalist, Joseph Banks. Fifteen years younger than the taciturn captain, Banks was a vibrant, promiscuous man who had already inherited a vast estate and paid £10,000 (close to $1 million in today's terms) to join the expedition. Banks was not only well educated but also accustomed to opulence, and he saw this venture as a sort of trumping of high society's Grand Tour—a status and motivation not dissimilar to the ones guiding your typical cruise ship ecotraveler.

I should probably just come clean on this right from the start: for a twenty-day voyage to the most remote continent in the world, for the three gourmet meals a day, the trips to shore, the Zodiac rides and use of kayaks, the nightly lectures, and the espresso bar and high teas each afternoon, I am paying just over $50 a day—or, as Eric pointed out last night, about $25,000 less than the standard fare. *Twenty-five thousand,* a figure I would like to claim is the equivalent of a year's income for me, though that would require both (a) having a job, and (b) keeping it for a full year—neither of which I've been known to excel at.

Ship accommodations were much more of a spartan affair in Cook's day of course, and this led to some tension between the captain and his most famous onetime passenger. Banks had intended to sail again on board the *Resolution*, arranging with the Admiralty to build a new deck large enough to accommodate an entourage of seventeen—including two horn players and six servants. Cook initially consented to these demands, though when the expansion resulted in making the ship dangerously top-heavy, he ordered it torn down and had Banks replaced.

The man who wants to lead the orchestra must turn his back on the crowd.[10]

Though it is commonly attributed to Cook, I can find no record of this quote inside his journals, nor in any of the biographical materials I've read. While the sentiment seems like one he would agree with, the statement itself reads as a touch too smug and epigrammatic for a person of Cook's constitution. Apart from a few colorful passages that lament the lack of findings in his forays south, Cook's journals tend to read like a business affair—detailing the ship's stores and preparations, the troubles of navigation, the endless daily tasks of seafaring. Whenever possible, he leaves himself out of the story entirely, and, taken as a whole, his journals make no reference to family or home. For her part, Cook's widow burned all of his letters to her upon his death, so apart from his official writing obligations Cook remains in large part a mystery.

In any case, the phrase above was most likely coined by the businessman James Crook, a near contemporary of the great captain, who made his fortunes in the first half of the nineteenth century in Upper Canada. Cook, on the other hand, for playing his part near the center of modern exploration, was paid a mere six shillings a day, though it is claimed he still outfitted his personal cabin with brass doorhinges at his own expense. Such lavishness is almost nonexistent inside his journals, which reveal a character far too reserved to indulge much in descriptions of either self or scenery.

Friday, 16th. The most part fine, Clear weather. Punished Henry Stevens, Seaman, and Thomas Dunster, Marine, with 12 lashes each, for refusing to take their allowance of Fresh Beef. Employed taking on board Wine and Water. Wind Easterly.[11]

After making my first full circuit of the deck, I climb up to the window-lined library, where I find—among a few hundred volumes of Antarctic exploration and scientific texts—a whole shelf dedicated to Cook's voyages. His collected journals may be far from a literary masterpiece, but they have long held the interest of anthropologists, historians, and scientists. To point to one recent development, Cook's detailed records of weather and ice conditions have helped to map out climate changes in the high latitudes of both polar regions. Still, the library is not a natural environment for Cook, whose intellect veered more toward the practical and systematic, and he would have felt more at ease downstairs in the chartroom, with its map-covered tables and walls.

Cook largely taught himself mathematics, surveying, and astronomy while serving for most of a decade off the coast of Canada and was still virtually unknown outside navy circles when the Admiralty selected him to lead the voyage to observe the transit of Venus in 1769. The Royal Society hoped that an accurate observation of this rare astronomical event from different regions of the globe would enable scientists to calculate the earth's distance from the sun. Later astronomers would declare the entire exercise a failure, as the instruments of the day were not precise enough to fulfill the task; nonetheless, this scientific undertaking resulted in the big break of Cook's life, leading him to a series of bold adventures. Over the span of his career Cook sailed over two hundred thousand miles—the rough equivalent of circling the equator eight times or voyaging to the moon. He was the first to use triangulation to establish land outlines and was responsible for mapping out over five thousand miles of previously unknown coastlines. His official maps were so great in detail and scale that many were still used into the twentieth century.

All that more impressive when one takes into account that in Cook's time, the world's mapmaking was still governed by equal parts knowledge and myth. The Greeks, in their love of symmetry, had argued for the existence of a great southern land to balance what was known of the north. *Antarktikos* means "opposite the Bear," and refers to the constellation Ursa Major, which hangs over the northern sky. But the Greeks' geographical theorizing had turned into nightmare and farce by the Middle Ages, where the uncharted south was seen as a place of terror, of monsters "unknown to the sons of Adam"—sea beasts with many heads; eaters of raw flesh; a tribe whose eyes grow beneath their shoulders, their mouths inside the cavity of their chests.[12] Even into the early nineteenth century, such tall tales were commonly confused with science. American captain John Symmes, for instance, theorized that a great gaping hole of six thousand miles at the South Pole opened into another earth. And, back in Britain, Cook's famed rival Alexander Dalrymple argued that "the number of inhabitants in the southern continent is probably more than 50 millions [*sic*]. . . . There is at present no trade from Europe thither, though the scraps from this table would be sufficient to maintain the power, dominion, and sovereignty of Britain, by employing all its manufacturing and ships."[13] Dalrymple never forgave Cook for being chosen over him to lead the southern voyage, and he goaded Cook upon his return, claiming that if he had been chosen, "[he] would not have come back in ignorance."[14] Quite likely— as Cook must have known—if Dalrymple *had* been chosen, he would not have come back at all.

I hear voices, and not just from dead explorers, but also from arriving guests. I circle back to my room and, upon entry, startle my roommate— just out of the shower and donning one of those white robes. Short and stocky with thick glasses and thinning gray hair, Bill greets me with a booming voice, shaking my hand forcefully. Given the fact that he is hardly dressed, I feel a little awkward with the introduction, and—not knowing where else to turn my gaze—focus mostly on his bushy and rather wayward eyebrows. I haven't had a roommate since my freshman year of college, and even when I go backpacking with people, I stay in my own one-person tent, so I feel rather out of practice. We exchange pleasantries about the Northwest (Bill lives in Seattle) and I ask about his job (a vague adminis- trative position that sounds like a front). Eventually, I excuse myself to get cleaned up, and afterward we walk down to dinner together.

Every innovation whatever tho ever so much to their advantage is sure to meet with the highest disapprobation from Seamen, Portable Soup and Sour Krout were at first both condemned by them as stuff not fit for human being[s] to eat. Few men have introduced into their Ships more novelties in the way of victuals and drink than I have done; indeed few men had the same opportunity or been driven to the same necessity.[15]

The first night, I have the lamb, though I am tempted to try the duck. The lady sitting next to me (an exuberant middle-aged woman from Wich- ita, whose husband owns a chain of Western Outfitter stores) chooses the duck, and I consider asking whether she wants to share plates, though this strikes me as perhaps a custom reserved for the lower tax brackets. Also at our table are a quiet couple from New England and naturalist Peter Carey—a New Zealand–based zoologist with a remnant of red hair and a friendly beard. This is the season's last sailing, and the ship will be routed up to the Arctic after we disembark. Peter tells us, however, that he will both be leaving the ship a little early and staying in the region a lot longer to conduct research. Apparently, we will be dropping him off at an uninhabited island near the Falklands that he has purchased, along with three other nearby islands, through the nonprofit organiza- tion he heads, in an attempt—among other things—to rid them of rat in- festation. For two months he'll be there all by himself, mostly killing and dissecting rats, from what I gather, though he doesn't go into too much detail, perhaps not wanting to spoil the meal. Over the years, an array of invasive animals—some introduced deliberately—have spread across many of the Antarctic and subantarctic islands. Rats, rabbits, reindeer, mice, and feral cats are among the most widely distributed, as well as some of the most harmful. The continent itself has proven a much less accommodating host for such species, though rising temperatures along the peninsula (both on land and in water) will likely complicate this in the decades ahead.

Our waiter comes over with dessert (some sort of chocolate torte with fresh berries), and the Wichita lady—who has already informed me that this is her fourth time sailing with Lindblad—leans over to assure me that the food is always this good. For the last month, I've been subsisting mostly on cheap backpacking meals that probably held more in common with the standard fare of Cook's men than anything I'm likely to eat while on board.

A partial log of Cook's supplies reads as follows: "59531 lbs of biscuit, 7637 pieces of salt beef, 14214 pieces of salt pork, 1900 lbs of suet, 19 tons of beer and 1398 gallons of spirits."[16] As well as an unusual assortment of antiscorbutics—"Sour krout, salted cabbage[,] . . . marmalade of carrots, and inspissated juice of wort and beer"—that were all meant to ward off the common ship's plague of scurvy.[17] During the Age of Exploration, between 1500 and 1800, it has been estimated that scurvy killed at least two million sailors, yet over the course of his three sailings Cook lost only one man to the disease—an unprecedented total in his time. This likely had more to do with his insistence on fresh meat whenever available (petrel soup, boiled penguin), and on his determination to supplement their meals with edible plants (a nice perk to having naturalists on board) at every island stop, than it did with his ninety-eight barrels of sauerkraut that he threatened to flog sailors over if their daily rations were refused. Fresh bounty, however, was not always available, which sometimes led to other questionable ingenuities. At one point in the *Resolution*'s sailing, after Cook himself was "taken ill of the bilious cholic," the naturalist Johann Forster sacrificed his beloved dog for consumption. While this event took place long after they had turned to the north, the tale serves as a grim foreshadow of southern expeditions to come.

We had no other fresh meat whatever on board; and I could eat of this flesh, as well as broth made of it, when I could taste nothing else. Thus I received nourishment and strength from food which would have made most people in Europe sick. So true it is, that necessity is governed by no law.[18]

Cook was an Englishman through and through—concerned with colonialism and empire—but he found much to praise in the lifestyles of the native populations he encountered, often voicing critical judgments of the materialism of his homeland by comparison, which he found needlessly complicated and even antithetical to real happiness. Nonetheless, Cook's voyages among the Pacific Islanders would lead to the most appalling impacts on their way of life—from disease to conflict and transformation of societies. By some estimates, their collective numbers plummeted from eighty thousand to just eight thousand over the span of the next fifty years. The peopleless lands of Antarctica—even if Cook had managed to get there—should have spared him a similar infamy, yet Cook's reports of vast populations of fur seals on islands such as South Georgia would soon lead to a different form of massacre.

All this history is enough to turn one to drink, and with the meal gone, our table turns its focus more fully to the wine. Peter asks whether any of us are feeling nervous about the next two days' passage across the Drake. The Drake Passage has the largest ocean current in the world, with six hundred times the flow of the Amazon, as well as some of the most incessant winds. According to Peter, this has to do with the Coriolis effect, and something called "infinite fetch"—which, to my surprise, has nothing to do with a border collie. Basically, the Drake is the only place on earth where the wind circulates the globe without ever touching land, lending itself to legendary gales and towering waves. I'm the only greenhorn at the table, though none other than Peter have crossed the Drake before, and we've all heard stories. Despite his chosen profession, Peter admittedly struggles with the high seas. In fact, as he tells us, on their last return trip to Ushuaia, he wound up having to give a lecture while lying down. The Drake has wreaked havoc on far more than scientific talks, however, and it is estimated that some eight hundred ships have met their fate in these waters, with over ten thousand seamen perishing. Tonight shouldn't be a problem, as we will stay in sheltered waters till we round Cape Horn; somewhere in the middle of the night, though, we'll hit the "roaring forties" and "screaming fifties," and all bets will be off.

After dinner everyone gathers in the lounge for a toast from the captain and more mingling. Oliver Kruess hails from Sweden, and in a thick accent he tells us that he has been plying Antarctic waters for close to twenty years. He is tall and well kept, dressed in full white captain's attire with shouldered epaulets. According to Eric, Kruess is the ideal commander for a voyage such as ours. An incredible spotter of wildlife, with a strong knowledge of natural history, Kruess is also always willing to try new landing sites and has "a lead foot when it comes to pushing deep into pack ice." What seems clearest to me at the moment is that he also possesses a strong stage presence. His English may be impeccable, but the guy makes sly use out of his accent, allowing him to slip in a harsh judgment or crude joke every now and then. Cook, on the other hand—judging from the few historical portraits available—seems to have been a rather unassuming man, with little in the way of a sense of humor. Though he did possess a trademark accessory—a single black glove he wore to conceal an ugly wound he'd suffered as a young man.

I raise my drink and take another look around—a cocktail party with equal parts Gatsby, Ahab, and Crusoe. I feel a bit overwhelmed and out of place. As with any roomful of people, some seem eccentric, others refined, some humorous, and some dull and vain. The average age is probably pushing sixty, and that is taking into account the two adolescents from the away-school family, the thirtysomething adventure blogger, and the young couple on their honeymoon from Chicago, whom I rather like. I spot Eric at a table across the room surrounded by guests and decide to head out to the deck to watch the birds crisscrossing our wake in the evening light. Petrels and albatrosses—sooty, black-browed, and wandering. The birds' companionship over the next three weeks would prove almost constant, as they ride effortlessly the winds and air currents at the back of ships.

These birds are the real voyagers. I've read that they even sleep on the wing—that after a wandering albatross fledges from its nest, it won't return to land for up to five years. One of the scientists on board the *Resolution*, William Wales, would go on to teach the English poet Samuel Coleridge while at Cambridge, and it is thought that his descriptions of the landscape and the ghostly soaring of the birds was the inspiration behind the *Rime of the Ancient Mariner*. We take our revelations, I suppose, wherever we are fortunate enough to find them—even when they are relayed to us secondhand, even when they are included as part of a guided tour.

The sublime, as a literary concept, was brought into prominence by Cook's British contemporaries. The word itself is derived from the Latin *sublimis*, a combination of *sub*, meaning "up to," and *limen*, meaning "boundary" or "threshold." Coleridge used the term to speak of something that points to-

ward the unimaginable, and it is often meant to signify an aesthetic quality in nature largely distinct from beauty. Some of the first treatises to develop the term were written by Englishmen who had recently traveled to
the Alps, finding in those famed mountains "an agreeable kind of horror"—
something much more wild and unbound than the foggy moors of their
homeland, though perhaps the concept's true home is the eerie icescapes
of the far south.[19]

Off in the distance, the Martial Mountains loom large over the outskirts
of Ushuaia. For most of the past week, I've been up in those mountains—
crossing snowy passes, traversing a few glaciers—but nothing I've seen,
on this trip or any other, has prepared me for where we are headed next.
I'm excited of course, but I still can't help feeling a touch of sadness as we
round the outlying islands—watching these last stretches of land fade from
view. When will I see a tree again? The lighted window of a house? Imagine leaving it all for a year or more, without knowing, even, whether you'd
ever make it back. Cook saw one hundred men desert before the *Resolution* sailed (more than half the crew), and the fate of those who did come
must have weighed heavily on his mind as they drifted into the unknown.

*For I firmly believe that there is a tract of land near the pole which is the
source of most of the ice that is spread over this vast southern ocean. . . . It
would have been rashness in me to have risqued all that had been done
during the voyage, in discovering and exploring a coast, which, when discovered and explored, would have answered no end whatever.*[20]

Upon his return in the summer of 1775, Cook accepted a post overseeing
the Royal Hospital at Greenwich—a facility for aging sailors. After twenty
years of service in the navy, having become one of the first men in British
history to rise through the enlisted ranks to assume command of his own
vessel, Cook was retiring. Now forty-six, with a comfortable stipend, and
his wife and children close at hand, Cook had misgivings almost immediately. "My fate drives me from one extream to a nother," he wrote to his old
benefactor. "A fews [*sic*] Months ago the whole Southern hemisphere was
hardly big enough for me and now I am going to be confined within the
limits of Greenwich Hospital, which are far too small for an active mind
like mine."[21] Within months Cook abruptly changed course, agreeing to
captain another journey, this one aiming to discover a Northwest Passage.
But the other side of the globe would prove no more welcoming, and after
being repelled once again by heavy pack ice Cook returned to Kealakekua

Bay in Hawaii. Only a month before, Cook and his men had been greeted like gods here, lavished with gifts and elaborate feasts. And that's more than just a figure of speech: these islanders may actually have mistaken Cook for a deity, as they had never before seen white people or such grand ships, and the Englishmen's first visit coincided with their annual celebration of the fertility god Lono. This cloak of immortality soon faded, however, after one of Cook's men died of a stroke, and upon their return from the north, they were greeted with open hostility. Cook, as was his custom in dealing with natives, returned this hostility in kind, making the fateful decision to try to take their king hostage after the theft of one of their boats.

Cook's death was a gruesome one—pelted by stones and struck by a club as he and his men retreated to a waiting boat. Dashing into the shallow surf, only ten yards from safety, Cook was stabbed in the back with an iron dagger—a gift he had bestowed on the islanders only a month before. "It is a sublime death in all respects," wrote the German Romantic Johann Wolfgang von Goethe, "and it is also beautiful that the majesty of the untamed world has claimed its rights on him."[22] This is a bold statement to make— one that, through the critical lens of colonialism, hints at a fearful symmetry and justice. Cook traveled the world declaring possession of countless lands in the name of Britain, and here those roles are reversed. After all, Goethe is not saying simply that the Hawaiian natives had a rightful claim on their own land, but rather that they had one on Cook himself. There is a lesson here—about overreach, about the self's relationship to the wild. And while Cook may have escaped the untamed world of the Antarctic, his death offers a warning to those who would follow him into the ice.

Back in the lounge, no one seems interested in turning in early. Laughter and stories fill the small tables, everyone in good spirits, though on a trip up to the bar I find Stefan, sulking a bit in a corner.

"Ah, so now you see us for what we really are," he begins. "We are not scientists. We are not sailors. We are social-boys."

CHAPTER 2

VOSTOK

(1819–1821)

CAPTAIN THADDEUS BELLINGSHAUSEN

Antarctica: in many ways it is a land of plenty and excess, though we associate it most commonly with what it lacks. It is a desert after all, the driest of the entire globe, even if as much as 70 percent of the world's fresh water is thought to be locked inside its vast ice sheets—their immense weight having caused the continent to sink over three thousand feet into the earth's crust. On most of Antarctica, it never rains and rarely snows. Though the continent accounts for roughly one-tenth of the earth's land surface, its only substantial river—the Onyx—is less than twenty miles in length. By current estimates, 98 percent of its landmass is covered in ice. Yet while its interior extends for thousands of frozen and seemingly flat miles, hidden as much as fifteen thousand feet beneath the polar plateau are mountain ranges taller than the Appalachians. It is not just the driest continent, but also the coldest, the windiest, and the tallest (with an average elevation of over seven thousand feet above sea level). It is a landscape that seems built straight from the stuff of myths and dreams, and it has held a central place in our collective imagination since long before we even knew it was there.

Sadly, I am not much of a dreamer, at least not in the slumbering, subconscious sense. Almost as a rule, my dreams are annoyingly banal—no flying or dismembering, nothing in the least bit surreal. Perhaps this is why I've never ventured into the world of fiction-writing—though if my REM plotlines tend to veer toward the mundane, they are often literary in a different sense. When I have been up late reading, I tend to dream in the voice, the style, even the syntax of the book at my side. It comes as no surprise, then, that so many of my travels have proved likewise bookish, that my experience of a new place is commonly tied up with the written texts of those who came before and pointed the way. It is as though I am always arriving on the scene too late or uninvited, left with little else to do but scrawl the footnote to some epic tale.

The world had to wait over forty years before Cook's greatest journey found its rightful heir. And when it did, it came at the hands not of the English gentry, but of the Russian elite. Thaddeus von Bellingshausen was born in the remote province of Estonia in 1779, the same year as Cook's untimely death, where he served as a naval cadet from the age of ten. When Bellingshausen was summoned to St. Petersburg to assume command of the expedition, his overland journey across the empire took over a month. Russia's czar Alexander I—since coming into power after the assassination of his father—had doubled the number of domestic universities (from three to six) and was noted early in his reign for actively encouraging science and the arts. As his rule continued, however, Alexander fell increasingly under the spell of religious mysticism, and it is rumored that the true purpose of this voyage around the world—far from the realm of science—was to seek out the "Book of Life," said to be hidden in a cave on a Caribbean island guarded by spirits. If there is a line of truth to this, then the daydreaming czar had appointed the wrong man for the job. Bellingshausen was no mystic treasure-seeker. Like Cook, he was a skilled cartographer, and he held the rank and file of the British Navy—and Cook in particular—in such high regard that it verged on adulation. From 1803 to 1806, Bellingshausen had served as an officer on the first Russian voyage around the world. Along the way, their ship called at Hawaii and visited the site of Cook's murder, which left an indelible impression on the young man. Bellingshausen modeled his entire trip after Cook's second voyage—from the diet of the crew to the standards of cleanliness to the laconic style of his prose. This is not to say that he intended to duplicate Cook's journey, and, in fact, Bellingshausen went to great lengths to ensure that his own sea route seldom overlapped with Cook's. His intention was not to replicate, but to bolster the Englishman's findings through pairing them with his own. Yet there was at least one area of their respective journeys where—due to no fault of his own—Bellingshausen fell well short of his forebear, as the two

German naturalists who were enlisted to join the expedition stood him up upon his arrival in Copenhagen. This was no mere indulgence, as science was meant to serve a vital function on their voyage. Russia had already learned from its exploits in Siberia and Alaska that there was money to be made in the far corners of the globe. Animal species might prove commercially valuable, and prized rock samples could lead to mineral extraction. Beyond all this, Bellingshausen wanted to leave his mark, to make some worthwhile contribution to human understanding. But the staff vacancy remained unfilled, even after Bellingshausen paid a London visit to the long-since-retired Joseph Banks.

In this way our hopes of making discoveries in the field of natural history were dashed to the ground and we had to console ourselves with the intentions of doing our best to collect all we could find and, on our return, to submit it to specialists to distinguish between the known and the unknown.[1]

Even after its discovery, and all its subsequent exploration, Antarctica is still commonly referred to as "the unknown continent," though the dividing line between its ecosystem and the rest of the known world takes place long before you reach land or the ever-shifting pack. The Antarctic Convergence delineates this boundary, where the subantarctic waters meet the colder surface waters from the south. Ships crossing this line encounter a noticeable drop in temperature, often a sudden fog bank or a line of turbulence, and almost always a great congregation of sea birds. Though in our case—and in the case of most vessels crossing the Drake—the vast majority of people on board are already fast asleep. Ships commonly cross the Convergence with little more than a bump in the night, but it represents a far more challenging boundary to most other forms of life. Antarctic krill, for instance, would perish in the relative warmth to the north. These tiny crustaceans weigh in at just over a gram and can gather in swarms as dense as thirty-five thousand per cubic meter, each casting its own light with photophores protruding from the sides of its abdomen. As such, they can make for easy targets, and krill are feasted upon by most everything down here—from penguins to squid to large baleen whales. It is said that an adult blue whale can consume up to five tons of krill in a single day, and still the ocean is rife with them. During the lean times, an adult krill even has the capacity to regress in size, degenerating its own sex organs as a means for reentering adolescence and conserving energy. A coping mechanism that, I'll admit—without going into all the maudlin details—I might just as well have used myself over these last couple of years. At least we, of the human subset, can still drown our heartbreaks in beer and voyaging, while the only available recourse for krill is to gorge themselves on the slime that coats the underside of sea ice.

Tossing and turning with such thoughts, I rise to greet the day . . . and then lie immediately back down.

The vessel laboured dreadfully and dangerously because a heavy swell was running from west-south-west, meeting and uniting with the seas coming from the east, and rising into appallingly high breakers from which the wind blew the seething white foam and carried it through the air.[2]

As a child, I never could stomach anything more than the most innocuous of fair rides, and ever since getting stuck in a typhoon over a decade ago, on a flight between Korea and Japan, I struggle to fly. In recent years, it seems that even the gentle swaying of a porch swing can cause me some level of discomfort, so I'm not sure what made me think this crossing would be easy. If the waves were only metered—an iambic slowness to pattern the laborious rise and fall—there might be some hope for me. But no, out of sync—inexorably free-versed—the ship lurches forward, tripping over the uneven crossties of the sea.

Bellingshausen's journey predates the steam engine, of course, and their only means for navigating the ship was to man the sails from aloft. All the more difficult in an Antarctic squall, when the seas are heaving, and sleet and snow are freezing the riggings so the ropes handle like wires.

At 5.0 A.M. the main topsail and the main and mizzen staysails suddenly split. The position of our ship was such as only those who have experienced it can imagine. . . . Sea and air seemed to mingle and the labouring of the ship drowned all other sounds. We remained now under bare poles at the mercy of the furious gale. I ordered some of the sailors' hammocks to be hoisted on the mizzen shrouds in order to keep the vessel to the wind.[3]

No thank you. In all likelihood, I'd be one of those poor saps (more numerous than you might first imagine) who get hurled overboard in the night's storm, never to be heard from again. But as is—heroically and unsteadily—I pull on pants, make my way quietly across the room so as not to stir my roommate, and venture off to breakfast.

Out in the hall, a rope has been strung up over the full length of the ship as a sort of makeshift handrail. Two determined couples inch their way along as if in some geriatric conga line. While I might have youth on my side, this arrangement is evidently old hat to them, as they calmly reach one hand in front of the other pulling themselves forward with the rope, and I soon realize that I'm holding up the ranks. All the more so once we get to the breakfast bar and the others begin to nimbly fill their plates while the ship continues to pitch and roll. Feeling queasy, with my legs repeatedly shifting to counter the ship's pulse, I finally manage to shovel a few spoonfuls of egg onto my plate and sink down at an empty table nearby. Waves smash up against the bow, dramatically spraying the windows, and a kind Filipino server somehow makes the rounds with a thermos of coffee. In a few minutes, I am joined by a man in a Hawaiian shirt who seems entirely too cheerful under the circumstances. His cliché cruise ship attire feels more than a little out of place given our location, but it turns out he is actually from Hawaii, and that he's spent much of his life at sea. I don't feel capable of maintaining a conversation, though he proves more than happy to fill in the available gaps. Not surprisingly, this ship is full of bucket-list travelers—all seven continents, one hundred different countries—but this guy's dream is evidently to run a marathon in each of the fifty states. He tells me he just ran number forty-one last month in Arizona, which surprises me a little, as he hardly has the build of a distance runner and is currently devouring a breakfast plate that consists almost entirely of pastries. I, on the other hand—chronically skinny and coming off a rather frugal month in the backcountry—would gladly consume a whole platter of doughy goodness, if I could only keep the bile from creeping up the back of my throat.

I excuse myself, interrupting the marathon runner as he's listing off the states he still has to go—Delaware, Nevada, Alaska—and make my way back to my room via the rope of shame. By now, Roommate Bill is awake, and I mumble a few short responses to his well-meaning questions before lying down. In an hour or so, Eric pays a visit, doing his best to conceal his amusement at my condition, and convinces me to head out on the deck for some fresh air.

A two-day crossing is one thing, but Bellingshausen and his crew were away for over two years—rarely in protected waters or in sight of land. Their ship, constructed of unseasoned pine boards, was horribly ill suited for polar sailing, causing them to retreat to Australia and some of the surrounding islands for winter. There they fixed their leaking ship and resupplied. They also gathered quite a menagerie before returning to the Southern Ocean.

Altogether we had eighty-four birds on board the Vostok. They all made a great deal of noise; some of the parrots knew a few English words; the other birds screeched and whistled in their native way. We also had a kangaroo, which ran about loose, was very tame and clean, and often played with the sailors.[4]

In the long term, however, none of the animals would prove fit for the polar climate, and one by one—the black cockatoo, the green turtle dove—they began to die off, leaving the men with nothing to distract themselves with from the monotony of days.

A marsupial may be unfit for the Antarctic cold, but the region hosts its own intricate web of species that have evolved with the climate over millions of years. The vast majority of these animals take their cues for breeding, feeding, and migration from the annual formation of sea ice—the greatest seasonal event to take place on earth, with roughly nine million square miles of pack ice appearing and disappearing each year. While Antarctic sea ice has, thus far, proved more stable than that of the Arctic, it has started to decline on the western end of the peninsula, and the long-term effects this will have on ice-dependent species could prove catastrophic.

We last left our bachelor krill, if you'll remember, philosophically munching on subaquatic slime. And krill is, without question, the life force of the Antarctic. In fact, there is a greater biomass of krill—about 600 million tons—than that of any other species (our own included) on earth. But krill larvae are dependent on sea ice, as are the more picture postcard–friendly species of the Adelie and emperor penguins. Given its high salt content, the sea freezes at 28.8 degrees, and even a minor shift upward in water temperatures can have a gigantic effect on both the total extent and duration of sea-ice formation. Adding to the concern, many nations now consider krill worth harvesting. Rich in vitamins and consisting of about 50 percent protein when dried, krill is especially appealing in regard to farm fish and livestock. Krill fisheries are now a growing business, with China announcing plans to increase its annual harvest to as much as two million tons. The Antarctic is the last substantially intact marine ecosystem in the world, though how long this will continue to be the case is a dangerously open question. The Southern Ocean communicates with all other oceans—which gives it a poetic significance but also highlights its interconnection to all areas of the planet. If our oceans continue to acidify at their current rate, pH levels will eventually decrease to a level where invertebrates such as the Antarctic krill can no longer form shells, and by then the flood of wholesale changes to the ecosystem will be well out of control.

The cold rushes over us as we step out on the deck. The breeze does feel good, as does the ocean spray and the heavy drizzle from above, though I'm still sweating, still nauseated in any position other than on my back. Eric advises me to focus on the horizon—the gray sea blending with the gray sky—but that seems only to emphasize how much the ship is swaying. I hear the propeller churn in the vacant air before we smash back down on the back of another wave. A couple of low-flying seabirds hover, gloatingly, nearby. I try to fix my attention on them, the soothing span of their near motionless wings.

A few snow-white and polar petrels, also some storm petrels, flew near the ship. These latter we found in all latitudes from the equator to the ice regions and called them, during the voyage, "Jews of the Sea," because, like the Jews on land, these birds have no abiding place but roam over the ocean in all latitudes.[5]

My current thoughts, unfortunately, are all longitudinal in nature, as in supine, as in the desire to crawl back in bed and stay there for the next forty hours. Eric accompanies me back to my room, sharing the story of his worst personal crossing of the Drake. "We were heading north after a ten-day peninsula trip," he begins, "with a forecast of eighty-five-mile-per-hour winds and thirty-foot swells." I don't even bother to ask what we are facing now, as I know it doesn't compare. "Only a few miles into open water, and our ship's tracking system picked up another vessel taking a very odd course up ahead," he continues. All the tourist ships down here keep in regular contact and share itineraries as a way to stagger trips to shore and maintain the air of total isolation for the guests. This other vessel, however, was clearly in some trouble, and as the *Explorer* got closer, they were able to make out the broken message of a distress call. "A large wave had taken out their bridge windows and short-circuited much of their electrical system," Eric says, "around the same time that one of their engines failed. They were hove-to, going a mere four knots and struggling to keep their bow into the swell." In those conditions, there was nothing that could be done as to rescue, but the Lindblad crew did manage to catapult a satellite phone over so the other ship could regain communication with the coast guard up in Ushuaia. This was a dangerous process that involved steering close enough for one of the deckhands to launch the sealed phone across with what Eric calls "a rocket line," while braving hurricane winds from the top of their ship. "Just be glad I didn't sneak you on board for that trip," Eric adds with a grin.

In all likelihood, Francis Drake would have been just fine with this legacy. Britain's most feared "Sea Dog," Drake began his career as a slave trader, moving on to make his living by preying on Spanish ships in the New World. In 1581, he was knighted by Queen Elizabeth after becoming the first Englishman to circumnavigate the globe. Over two years before, Drake's ship—the *Golden Hind*—got caught in a storm as they arrived at the Strait of Magellan. They were pushed down the Fuegian coast, out past Cape Horn and over fifty-seven degrees south into the passage that would bear his name. What moved Drake to exploration was not science or cartography, but gold. He returned to Britain as the world's richest pirate, with a huge bounty on his head, and the Spanish nickname "El Draque" (the dragon).

Antarctica itself is shaped roughly like a dragon, or maybe a giant lopsided stingray, with the knobby and mountainous nine-hundred-mile tail of the peninsula extending northwest toward South America. Its mountains are actually an extension of the Andes connected by the Scotia Ridge that runs under the Drake Passage. Forty million years ago, the Antarctic split from South America, joining the Pacific and Atlantic Oceans and dramatically cooling the continent as it drifted toward the South Pole (at the rate of a few centimeters per year). Due to the variety of its terrain, the wealth of its summer wildlife, and its relative accessibility, the peninsula is often claimed to be the most majestic region of the continent. Yet the air temperatures of the peninsula, always the warmest region of Antarctica, have spiked by more than five degrees over the past fifty years, which is at a rate about ten times faster than the average for the rest of the world. So, like a lot of the world's majestic places, this one is rapidly changing.

The next day and a half pass me by in a daze. Eric—God bless the man— brings me my meals, which I manage to nibble at, having to set the plate down and lie flat on my back between each bite. On the second evening he hangs around for a while, mostly chatting with my roommate as I'm lousy company. Tomorrow, Eric assures me, we will move into more sheltered waters off the peninsula and I'll feel better.

I wake early, my body impatient with all this sleep, and sure enough the motion of the ship has mellowed into slow, even swells. I throw on layers and, still cautious, walk out to the deck just as a large tabular berg sails past on our right. Ghostly, regal—"like floating reveries" as one writer described them.[6] This berg must be well over fifty feet tall, its leveled top dwarfing the mast of our ship. I'd like it—or else us—to slow down so that I could study it more fully—the waves lapping up against its sloping walls—but already in the dawn light I can see two more ahead drifting near. Now I have traveled as far away from my life as I can get, I say to myself. Am I supposed to take pride in this? To wear it as some badge of honor? As a child, I always felt drawn to the stories of people who ventured far into the wild places of the world. Though, as I got older, it started to seem less about *toward* than *away*, less a location than a way of holding myself apart. Like a hunk of ice cast out, adrift, at ease in its own slow melting.

Icebergs are prominent in Arctic waters as well, but these tabular bergs—formed by breaking off the continent's ice shelves—are found only south of the Convergence. As impressively large as this one seems to me now, it is dwarfed in all comparison with the largest bergs on record, some of which are so immense that they develop their own weather patterns. When the b-15 iceberg broke off the Ross Ice Shelf in 2000, it was measured to have a surface area of over four thousand square miles, nearly the size of the state of Connecticut. After b-15 collided with the Drygalski Ice Tongue, Antarctic maps had to be redrawn. I follow the berg to the back of our ship and look to the horizon—no sign yet of the continent, though it could be there, enshrouded still in the dawn sleet and fog.

Words cannot describe the delight which appeared on all our faces at the cry of "Land! Land!" Our joy was not surprising, after our long monotonous voyage, amidst unceasing dangers from ice, snow, rain, sleet and fog. . . . The land discovered by us gave us reason to hope that there must surely be other land in the vicinity, because the existence of only one island in that vast extent of water seemed to us impossible.[7]

This was the first land ever spotted inside the Antarctic Circle—still four or five hundred miles further to our south, in the middle of this sea that now bears Bellingshausen's name. One of the world's most inaccessible islands, it wasn't seen again for ninety years. Bellingshausen named it Peter I Island, after Russia's greatest czar, though at a mere sixty glacier-covered square miles (roughly the size of Staten Island), and set nearly three hundred miles away from the mainland, it remains nothing more than a blip on any map you're likely to set eyes on. This was back during the "Little Ice Age," as it was called, and even at the height of summer, drift ice made it impossible for the ship to get within fifteen miles of shore. No doubt the crew felt their collective hearts sink a little, as they turned back to meet the horizon's empty gaze. A week of pushing north through ice-filled seas, and they discovered another island on the southern end of Marguerite Bay, where our ship will arrive later today. This land Bellingshausen named after Alexander, and for over a century it was thought to be a part of the continent itself, though it is actually the world's second-largest uninhabited island, separated from the mainland by an ice-covered sound to the east. After a week more of sailing the *Vostok* stumbled upon an even more improbable sight.

At 10 o'clock we entered the strait and encountered a small American sealing boat. I lay to, dispatched a boat, and waited for the Captain of the American boat. The lead did not touch bottom at 115 fathoms. Soon after Mr. Palmer arrived in our boat and informed us that he had been here for four months' sealing in partnership with three American ships. They were engaged in killing and skinning seals, whose numbers were perceptibly diminishing.[8]

Thus ensued one of Antarctica's most bizarre instances of international diplomacy. At least Bellingshausen had heard reports back in Australia of sealers being active in the area, whereas Nathaniel Palmer—a twenty-one-year-old New Englander sailing a forty-five-ton cutter named the *Hero* through uncharted waters—had no reason to think he wasn't alone at the bottom of the world.

Such illusions, of course, can no longer be harbored in our day. Ecotourism is one of the fastest-growing branches of the industry, and it is estimated that four to six million Americans alone travel overseas for nature each year. Antarctica sees only the smallest fraction of these travelers, though the numbers have grown from about three hundred annual visitors in the early 1970s to over twenty-five thousand landed visitors for much of the last decade, most hailing from the United States, and all traveling on ships that burn upward of three and a half gallons of fuel per minute. I'm doing my best to not dwell on all of this right now, though the early-morning breakfast queue extending into the hall serves as a rather inescapable reminder. The human inchworm crawls ahead, and I pile eggs, potatoes, bacon, and biscuits high onto my plate—no pastries to be found (perhaps the marathon runner ate them all). Feeling social, I sit down at a crowded table with the expedition leader, Tom Richie, seated at its head. Tom is the company poster child. Wearing a wide grin and full white beard, he looks half seasoned adventurer and half jovial Santa. Now in his sixties, Tom is a carryover from another era, a time when expedition travel went almost totally unregulated. A time, just a couple of decades ago, when they basically just took boats wherever they wanted, making up itineraries as they went, letting animals on board in the Amazon as they floated downstream. Tom is an easy conversationalist with an encyclopedic mind; half an hour with him is enough to pique the interest of even the most ardent homebody.

Mr Palmer told me that the above-mentioned Captain Smith, the discoverer of New Shetland, was on the brig Williams, that he had succeeded in killing as many as 60,000 seals, whilst the whole fleet of sealers had killed 80,000. As other sealers also were competing in the destruction of the seals there could be no doubt that round the South Shetland Islands just as at South Georgia and Macquarie Islands the number of these sea animals will rapidly decrease.[9]

James Cook may not have found Antarctica, but his reports on the abundance and potential usefulness of fur seals was enough to spur an industry. On May 21 in 1820, a ship sailed into Stonington, Connecticut, with a cargo of seal skins—they sold for an astounding $22,146—and the frenzied race in Antarctic waters was officially on. Fur seals were highly prized by the Chinese, who used their pelts for slippers, and their numbers were decimated over the span of twenty years. It was a grisly affair—men would club hundreds a day, skinning and salting the hides all along the bloody shores. They killed the adults and left the abandoned pups to starve without their mother's milk. The sealers' purge was so relentless that the species was soon thought extinct, though a small colony luckily survived, undetected, on isolated Bird Island that would eventually repopulate their species to the astonishingly estimated 200 million alive today.

While Bellingshausen's evident concern did nothing to quell the tides of the sealers' rampage, this entry is quite possibly the first recorded opposition to environmental degradation in the Antarctic. To the young Nat Palmer, however—who'd later go on to run guns for Simon Bolivar—such reckless bloodletting was all just part of the game, and any protestations were certain to fall on deaf ears. But if the personas of these two men—the young ruffian seeking adventure, and the stoic captain soon to draw his own journey to a close—seem diametrically opposed, they achieve a sort of symmetry in the man sitting across from me this morning. In one story, Tom laughingly tells about the guest who was attacked by a howler monkey they'd brought on board; in another, he recounts the time a female passenger tried to sneak away across the headland of an uninhabited island, planning to write her memoir as a season's castaway in the Antarctic, only to be dragged back screaming to the ship. There was a popular saying among early sailors down here: "Beyond forty degrees south there is no law. Beyond fifty degrees south there is no God." This was a prideful statement, of how out of bounds exploits were at the bottom of the world. Talking with Tom, one gets a similar sense (without all the gory destruction) for what expedition travel must once have been like. And while this makes me glad to be sitting with him now, it is hard not to find myself wishing I could have traveled with him thirty years ago.

What do I see and what do I hear from a boy in his teens: that he is commander of a tiny boat the size of a launch of my frigate, has pushed his way towards the Pole through storm and ice and sought the point I in command of one of the best appointed fleets at the disposal of my august master have for three long, weary, anxious years, searched day and night for.[10]

Here is an example of what we might charitably call another misappropriation. This account of Bellingshausen's comments came about over two decades after his meeting with Nathaniel Palmer, and from a man named Frank T. Bush—a confidant of Palmer's who wasn't even there. The Russian captain's own account is much more cursory, and it is hard to imagine Bellingshausen was overawed by the blustering commander of the diminutive *Hero*.

Kendra's voice comes on the loudspeaker, announcing that the mainland has just come into view. There are still a few hours of sailing before we land, but our breakfast group—along with most of the other guests—ventures out to the portside deck to see for ourselves. The debate over who first laid eyes on the continent—whether it was Bellingshausen or Palmer, or even the British sailor Edward Bransfield—boils down to who saw what and when, as well as whose account one is willing to believe, and it remains a contentious issue to this day. In any case, it is hard to care much about it when you find yourself staring out at this coast for the first time. Heavy cloud cover and a bit of rain still hover over our ship, but the sun has broken through on the horizon, shining down on a long line of snow-covered peaks—the nunataks breaching the thick ice.[11] This, as I would come to learn in the weeks ahead, is the trick of the sky down here—to illuminate only what is out of reach, to pile gray upon gray and counter it, on the far horizon, with a thin band of hopefulness. No wonder the early explorers kept pushing south, kept holding out faith. While I can claim no epic voyage for myself, it sure feels good to have arrived.

We had been absent for 751 days. During that time we had been at anchor in different places 224 days, and had been under sail 527 days. Altogether we had covered 57,073½ miles—a distance equal to more than 2¼ times the equatorial circumference of the earth. During the course of our voyage we had discovered twenty-nine islands, two of these were in the Antarctic, eight in the South Temperate Zone, and nineteen in the Tropics. One coral reef and lagoon were also discovered.[12]

Bellingshausen—it should probably be added—has been ill-served by posterity. He completed the greatest sea journey since Cook, but his journals had to wait over a decade to get published and received little attention even then. This was a troubled and uncertain time in Russian history. The failed Decembrist uprising in the wake of Alexander's death in 1825 had triggered a more insular turn for the country, which became highly policed and skeptical of the world beyond its borders. It would take over a century for Russia to turn its gaze back to the Antarctic, and while Bellingshausen's exploits remain at the center of competing claims for discovering the seventh continent, Nathaniel Palmer didn't bother to remember his name. It is even said today that Bellingshausen's family home back in Estonia has been converted into a mental asylum. So if this last sentence of his log makes it sound as though he was left clinging to straws—*one coral reef, one lagoon*—in the hindsight of history, this proves quite accurate.

As for the first Antarctic landing, historians say it happened in February 1821—several months after Nat Palmer swaggered on board the *Vostok*. Another American sealer party, led by Captain John Davis, was having no luck. All the known sealing grounds were either already devastated or swarming with competitors. Their small ship, *Cecilia*, sailed south through the Bransfield Strait to what is thought to be Hughes Bay on the peninsula. Davis sent a small boat to shore, where they found no seals and soon returned. Their whole trip was becoming a disaster; a snowstorm blew up, forcing them back to open water. So much of the history of exploration seems predicated on the idea of legacy—of leaving a mark on the world that will stand for all time. Yet the ship's logbook from the day reads simply: "Sent her on Shore to look for Seal at 11 A.M. the Boat returned but find no sign of Seal at noon our Latitude was 64°01' South Stood up a Large Bay, the Land high and covered intirely [*sic*] with snow. . . . Concluded to make the Best of our way for the Ship I think this Southern Land to be a Continent."[13]

From this entry, one can assume that the last person to first set foot on a continent was, like Davis, a sealer from New Haven, Connecticut though—beyond this—we have no idea who that person was.

CHAPTER 3

BELGICA
(1897–1899)

DR. FREDERICK COOK

Fittingly, perhaps, in the annals of polar exploration, the first man to show any real literary promise was also its most infamous liar and a confirmed rogue. Frederick Cook, the son of German immigrants, was born in a hamlet of upstate New York in 1865. His father, a country doctor, died when he was only four, leading the family to relocate to Brooklyn under considerable financial hardship. Cook would go on to follow the family vocation, earning his MD from New York University. Marriage and a budding medical practice appeared to have settled him into a prosperous and contented future, but when his young wife died in childbirth Cook set off, impulsively, on an adventure that would forever change his life's course—signing on as a surgeon for Robert E. Peary's first expedition to the Arctic. The two men initially formed a successful partnership, though they would become bitter rivals decades later over disputed claims for reaching the North Pole. The controversies surrounding Dr. Cook, however, all lie in the northern latitudes, and before disgrace laid him low, he was to play an honorable part at the onset of Antarctica's Heroic Age.

To consent by cable to cast my lot in a battle of the south, with total strangers, men from another continent, speaking a language strange to me, does indeed seem rash. But I never had cause to regret it. The Antarctic has always been the dream of my life, and to be on the way to it was then my ideal of happiness.[1]

While the cosmopolitan crew of the *Belgica* may have lacked a common language, everyone on board our ship seems to speak an at least passable English. Still, there are plenty of other ways to feel disconnected from fellow travelers, a fact I am reminded of as I file into the mud room to disembark for the mainland. An icy drizzle has been falling through heavy fog all morning, and the other guests are outfitted in identical blue, full-length expedition coats (evidently, if you fork over twenty-five thousand bucks they give you a free jacket). Lacking the team uni, I wait patiently for my turn to go ashore. A wind has risen, worsening the already choppy seas. Kendra, with clipboard in hand, oversees the hatch, checking off our names as we edge forward and don small inflatable vests. Naturalists pilot the Zodiacs, the engines of the small rubber crafts blaring as they drift close. A short British lady directly in front of me seems to have about eight layers on underneath her jacket, with a red wool cap and thick matching mittens that remind me of a child setting out into her first snow. She hesitates before taking the hand of a crewman whose job it is to help lower passengers into the boats, and turns back to me, shouting into my ear, "Is my hood on?"

Is my hood on? It takes me a moment to process this, making sure it isn't some kind of trick question. I spot Kendra out of the corner of my eye cracking a smile, and finally answer, "Yes, ma'am, it is." She nods in affirmation, then steps out to brave the elements.

Despite all the talk of extremes, summer temperatures off the peninsula—referred to by some hardy polar veterans as the "Banana Belt"—can be quite moderate, generally hovering right around freezing. Overcast skies paired with the usual gusting winds can chill you to the bone, but if it is calm and the sun is out, it can be downright comfortable. I step down into the Zodiac, where seven other guests have already huddled into place, and Jason—the ship's resident geologist—stands stoically in the back. We will be landing at a place called Red Rock Ridge, down at the southern end of Marguerite Bay, where an Adelie penguin colony is still finishing breeding—"All those dumpy little birds shitting on the beautiful rocks," Jason adds drily. "At 68'17," he tells us, "this is the furthest south our ship has ever been." Two fur seals, sprawled on drifting ice, look up as we float near, then lay back their heavy heads: unimpressed. Jason brings us close and shuts off the engine so that guests can take pictures. A giddy enthusiasm pervades the small boat, and while I feel it too, I'm still struggling to come to terms with the guided-tour nature of it all. Dr. Cook called the Antarctic the dream of his life, and history is full of tales of those who lost their fortunes, if not their lives, in coming to this place. Who am I to be joining them? Surely, even among my fellow passengers there are many who have sacrificed more than I, have dreamed longer of this arrival.

One says, "Now I am nine thousand, nine hundred and eighty-nine miles from home. It is noon, but at home they are just taking breakfast." Another says, "Everybody that I love is nine thousand miles over our starboard quarter. They are just entering upon the duties of the day." . . . To-day we know the exact spot on which we are being thrown about by a great unknown sea of mystery, and this knowledge seems to bring us nearer home because it offers us something tangible with which to make comparisons. In reality, however, we are as hopelessly isolated as if we were on the surface of Mars, and we are plunging still deeper and deeper into the white Antarctic silence.[2]

Before Jason can steer us on toward the mainland, we are greeted by another guest, rising up this time from below. The leopard seal may lack the cuddly quality of the more common fur seal, but its solitary and reptilian profile elicits its own wave of awe. This one seems to have taken issue with our arrival, as it opens its wide jaw, revealing a harrowing set of teeth that it promptly sinks into one of our boat's inflated tubes. A regular enough occurrence, I guess, as it doesn't appear to overly concern Jason, who spins us around so passengers on the other side can take in the view. I have a cheap point-and-shoot camera in the pocket of my raincoat, though I'm more interested in getting a clear sense of this creature just now than in claiming any photographic keepsakes. It slinks back under us, then puffs out air from its flaring nostrils as it resurfaces. Leopard seals are the apex predator down here, growing up to thirteen feet in length and weighing as much as eleven hundred pounds. While they feast heavily on krill, leopard seals are best known as penguin-killers, with studies suggesting they kill off between 1 and 5 percent of a given rookery. I see three or four penguins up ahead, porpoising through open water—leaping into the air in a series of short, shallow arcs to breathe as they travel—and like to think we're doing our part by running interference. A band of guests already on shore crowd the rookery perched on rocks. From this distance—given the uniformity of dress and the abundance of layers—it looks like one species of penguin infiltrating another.

Over a century ago, Frederick Cook—along with the other eighteen men on board the *Belgica*—traveled all along this coast, making at least twenty landings as they worked their way south at the tail end of summer. Baron Adrien Victor Joseph de Gerlache de Gomery, one of the overly long-named officers of the Belgian Navy, captained the bare-bones crew, which made up the first fully scientific expedition to Antarctica. This was a grass-roots voyage, funded in large part by private donations. Belgium, as a nation, had little interest in the Antarctic at the time, and de Gerlache had no polar experience. Presumably he did not inspire a great deal of optimism in the crew, as several members deserted at their last port of call in Punta Arenas that December. Those who remained celebrated Christmas in the Beagle Channel, near Cape Horn, and de Gerlache gifted each of the officers and scientists with novels he had selected, tailoring to individual tastes. This was, for all intents and purposes, one of the last useful things he would do for the expedition. Nevertheless, the *Belgica* was assured its share of posterity, for, in addition to Dr. Cook, there was another member on board who would soon carve his place near the icy center of polar history. Roald Amundsen was a young and adventurous Norwegian who was looking to make a name for himself. He had little to contribute to the ship's scientific agenda, but he offered his services as the first mate, free of charge, because of how eager he was to gain experience in the polar regions.

There was nothing remarkable in the appearance of this land upon which we were about to embark. It was a heap of hard rocks, mostly granite. The northern exposure was bare, the ravines were still leveled with winter ice, and the southern point had on it a small ice-cap. We afterwards saw a hundred others of similar nature, and all will pass under the same description.[3]

If you have a hundred landings, why then sure, I can see Cook's point—and for this spot too, his commonplace description will suffice—but what an experience it is to first step foot on these shores. By this point in my life, I've traveled widely across four continents, and I can't claim to remember first touching down on any of them, but my heart leapt as I stepped out of the Zodiac into the shallow surf. A large part of this has to do with arriving by boat, of course—as well as knowing right away how unlikely it is that I would ever make it back. I add my life vest to a small pile resting on the rocks, though some of the guests have opted to leave theirs on—an added safety precaution perhaps, or just too eager to start taking photographs. These birds—unlike most of the world's native populations, I'd wager—couldn't care less about having their picture taken. Their loud squabbling and comically threatening gestures are all geared toward each other, and you'd be inclined to say they treat people as indifferently as they do rocks, except that—having nothing else to make their nests with—rocks are actually the dominant currency in these parts. Not that there is, in any observable sense, a barter system at play. "Communal but uncooperative" is how a penguin rookery was described in last night's lecture, and along with the stench and noise, that's the first thing you are likely to tune into. Thus a penguin, long coveting a neighbor's stone that, to the undiscerning human eye, looks pretty much identical to all the others, sets off to rob a nearby nest, leaving his own momentarily unattended, and setting off a chain reaction of opportunistic theft and flipper bashing. The chicks, long nurtured by this societal greed, manage to go one better. When a parent returns from the high seas—just another voyaging Odysseus who has been away too long—it can no longer recognize its child's call, and while this parent too would no doubt like to sneak back home unattended in rags, it is immediately set upon by a mob of hungry youths aiming to filch a gullet full of krill. The adult flees in a mad dash (chivalry be damned), hoping that eventually all but its rightful heir will tire out and turn back, and the feeding—which looks oddly as if the adult bird were about to munch off the chick's head—is allowed to take place. The whole scene is enough to make you reconsider having children, or—for that matter—to avoid playing with anyone else's. Still, the collective frenzy of a penguin colony makes for hours of entertainment.

If Cook, for his part, started to grow impatient with the repeated landings, quite possibly it had to do with how late in the season it was, and a feeling of unease as the Belgian captain kept pushing them further to the south. Near the end of February, they had several close calls with the pack, yet de Gerlache stubbornly kept course—unswayed by the objections of several members of his crew. Finally, it was too late, and on March 4 they found themselves locked—for the next eleven months—in a moving sea of ice.

If our vessel should be destroyed no one at home could possibly know the location of our wanderings, or the site of our final destruction, and with our equipment we could not navigate the Cape Horn seas to a land of human habitation. Our faith then is pinned on the Belgica; our life is linked with hers. If she gains freedom our liberty is assured; if she sinks, we shall all go to an icy grave.[4]

Belgica antarctica—named after the ship whose crew discovered it—is the largest purely terrestrial animal on the continent (measuring in at a whopping two to six millimeters in length). A flightless midge that is also Antarctica's only endemic insect, Belgicas can survive the freezing of their own body fluids and reside at the top of a food chain that has only two links. While they have no predators, the Antarctic itself preys on most everything down here, and it is thought that the midge's flightlessness may actually be an adaptation to prevent the incessant winds from blowing them to their death in the unforgiving sea. The bug-eyed scientists on board the man-made *Belgica* could only hope they would face the challenges of the Antarctic winter with a similar fortitude. For now they were the ones at the mercy of the violent gales that caused the pressure of the floes to constrict dangerously around the ship. Pack ice, under the heavy force of winds that commonly gust up to 150 miles an hour down here, can travel as far as 10 miles a day, and the crew could do nothing to help chart their course.

Historians are split over the true intentions of de Gerlache—whether in fact he had been determined all along to captain the first expedition to winter inside the Antarctic Circle. But there can be no doubt they were ill prepared: lacking sufficient clothing, provisions, lamps. The ship's hyposulfite supply was also insufficient, and knowing that exposed photographic plates could not be taken across the torrid zone, Dr. Cook set about trying to find a chemical substitute that would allow him to continue with his photography. He succeeded, though this transformed his hobby into a dangerous pursuit.

In an old copy of the British magazine Answers there was a brief mention of the use of prussic acid as a fixing solution for daguerrotypes. Here was hope, but it was to be a play with the shadow of death.[5]

For this crew, the shadow of death would extend far beyond the darkroom. Anxiously, they continued with preparations: making clothing out of blankets, piling snow high on the foredecks to preserve heat, and storing seal and penguin carcasses before the wildlife fled for winter. Dr. Cook instigated most of these activities, having brought with him a wealth of knowledge from his winter with Peary in the north. Amundsen proved his most eager student, and the young Norwegian soon came to place the ship's doctor on a higher pedestal than he did its captain.

Set back on a higher bluff, a few solitary penguins gaze down at the squalor of the rookery. They look like mini tuxedo-wearing slumlords, though actually they are molting—their bodies puffed up from the blood of new feathers piercing their skin. Polar penguins are insulated from the extreme cold by the densest feathers of any bird on the planet, with up to 250 per square inch, but these feathers cannot be replaced at sea. For several weeks these adults—which routinely lose up to 40 percent of their body mass during molt—will keep their distance from the others, without eating or waddling about. Apart from dying, molting is the one activity that penguins prefer to do alone.

Flying in low circles overhead, a pair of skuas patrol the neighborhood. These dirty birds are the real slumlords of a rookery, possessing a hooked beak and predatory guile that defies their classification in the seagull family. A healthy adult Adelie penguin weighs twice as much as one of these birds and brandishes a beak sharp enough to poke out an intruding eye, so skuas often work in pairs—distracting a nesting adult long enough for another to swipe at an unattended hatchling or egg. Through sheer ruthless cunning, a pair of skuas will frequently devour a full third of an Adelie rookery's eggs and chicks.

Along with the elusive emperor penguin, Adelies are the only species that breeds exclusively in Antarctica. Their numbers are in decline across the region, however, and they are increasingly pushing further to the south. Until recently, this bay had too much ice and not enough open water to accommodate an Adelie rookery, but this entire coastline is rapidly changing. If the trend continues, Adelies could wind up retreating far below the Antarctic Circle to breed, and since they hunt chiefly by sight, the lack of winter light in high latitudes may further diminish their numbers.

After a short walk along the rocky shore, we are shuttled back to the comforts of the ship to await our own first Antarctic night. The sky now has cleared, almost entirely, and while a strong wind makes the evening uncomfortable, I linger out on the foredeck to watch the familiar sun set over the strange bergs. It is all so new to me still that my eyes shift constantly away from the horizon to the backdrop of the continent, as if to reconfirm to myself that I'm really here—or, rather, *near here*, as the separation of our ship from the actual place feels inescapable in the fading light. Having always preferred spending my time in the outdoors alone, or with those few individuals with whom I came, I avoid campgrounds like the plague, choose dispersed camping far into the backcountry whenever possible, and tend to travel in shoulder or off seasons to avoid crowds. Eric has even joked that I should hike with a shirt that reads, "Not for Navigational Purposes," and just point to it whenever another hiker asks me how far it is to the next camp or summit, given how annoyed I get with those questions. An experience like this, then, falls well outside the realm of my wilderness travel aesthetics. "Can I see nature under such conditions?" famed naturalist John Burroughs wondered, as he set off on a similar venture, albeit on the other side of the globe—on board the 1899 Harriman Expedition up in Alaska.[6] Yet what other choice do you have, if you long to see a land that is so difficult to access? Today may have marked our arrival, but I still feel like I'm stuck on a sort of threshold—with the real place stubbornly out of reach. Frustrated, perhaps, by a similar urge to narrow that gap, Cook ventured off the ship one night to sleep out on the ice with only a sleeping bag.

At first my teeth chattered and every muscle of my body quivered, but in a few minutes this passed off and there came a reaction similar to that after a cold bath. With this warm glow I turned from side to side and peeped past the fringe of accumulating frost, around my blow-hole through the bag, at the cold glitter of stars.[7]

In a few hours (the temperature hovering around negative four degrees), Cook woke to find his hair frozen solid to the hood of his bag, and slept indoors from there on out. I've got my own sleeping bag on hand, as well as my tent, but nights ashore are strictly off limits. The lights of the lounge behind me shine warmly against the dark, telling me it is time to go in.

The sun set on the crew of the *Belgica* on May 16 and would not return for seventy days. For a little while—at least when the sky was clear—a midday flash of color would linger in the north. On moonlit nights, when the wind was calm, members of the crew—starved of exercise and suffering from the monotony of life on board—would set off on skiing excursions to the surrounding bergs that had been locked with them in the pack. As the darkness took hold, morale began to sink, depression, paranoia, and lethargy set in, and men took to their beds for days at a time. Through it all, Cook's energies were unwavering. Amundsen, writing years later about those months, had only praise for the expedition's doctor: "He, of all the ship's company, was the one man of unfaltering courage, unfailing hope, endless cheerfulness, and unwearied kindness. When anyone was sick, he was at his bedside to comfort him; when any was disheartened, he was there to encourage and inspire. And not only was his faith undaunted, but his ingenuity and enterprise were boundless."[8]

Boundless, I soon learn—upon reentering the lounge—is also an apt description of our ship's supply of Guinness. Evidently they overpurchased, and seeing as how this is the season's last voyage, the overstock is selling at half price. I find Eric, where I left him an hour ago, sitting at a table with Abby and Mason (the young newlyweds from Chicago), and Steven and Kenji—a middle-aged couple Eric and I had sat with at dinner. An odd but adorable pair: Steven is from a small town in South Dakota, where he works as a computer programmer, and Kenji is from Okinawa, where he still lives. The two of them met on a Lindblad cruise over a decade ago, and—from what I gather—their visiting one another's homes is complicated, due to visa restrictions and the conservative backdrops of their two, otherwise wildly different, cultures. Consequently, they go on a lot of trips together, and while neither of them seems in any way outdoorsy or adventurous, they are a great pair to share a drink with. As for Abby and Mason, they are both witty and outgoing, and they also have a clear intellectual curiosity that I like. They may be here on their honeymoon, but they are also decidedly here to learn. Despite the gulf between us in regard to social standing (she works in advertising, and he in the stock market), we hit it off really well. If I was bound to fall in with a few of my fellow passengers, I'm happy to cast my lot with this group, amidst the warm light of these crowded tables.

The moonlight comes and goes alike, during the hours of midday as at midnight. The stars glisten over the gloomy snows. We miss the usual poetry and adventure of home winter nights. We miss the flushed maidens, the jingling bells, the spirited horses, the inns, the crackling blaze of the country fire. We miss much of life which makes it worth the trouble of existence.[9]

All through the winter, existence on board the *Belgica* teetered at the edge. Dr. Cook knew the importance of fresh meat in warding off scurvy, but de Gerlache developed a paranoid aversion to the flesh of both penguin and seal, going so far as to forbid the crew from eating them. While it was not known at the time, scurvy is caused by an acute lack of vitamin C, which humans—unlike most species—cannot synthesize for themselves and must therefore get from what they eat. Fresh foods were known to help, though there were also medical theories at the time focused on bacterial infection, popularizing the notion that a diet of "untainted" tinned foods would suffice. Untreated, scurvy is fatal, and in addition to physical ailments like bleeding gums and loosening teeth, the disease can cause depression, delusions, and other altered mental states. The men turned increasingly to the ship's doctor for help, both for real and imagined troubles. To cure what Cook termed "polar anemia," he ordered the men to spend hours at a time staring in at a blazing stove. For lethargy and depression, he sent them out to walk scheduled laps around the ship, forming what became known as the "madhouse promenade," and, indeed, Cook treated at least two men on board for the onset of insanity. Yet the worst was still to come.

June 5—Today we have to record the darkest page in our log—the death of our beloved comrade, Danco. It has not been unexpected, for we have known that he could not recover, but the awful blank left by his demise is keenly felt, and the sudden gloom of despair, thus thrown over the entire party, is impossible of description.[10]

Emile Danco was the expedition's geophysicist, and his death of congestive heart failure couldn't have come at a worse time, with the Antarctic midnight still weeks away, and the collective hope of getting through running dangerously low. The very presence of the body in their midst was too much for them, and after sewing his remains into a bag of sail-cloth, they kept it outside on the ice, packed into a sledge, until they came up with a burial plan. They searched for a crevasse big enough to serve as a grave, and once this failed, they cut a large hole with axes and chisels through the ice in a recent lead—one they had to hold open constantly, while the service was read, and the others lowered the body, laden with two heavy weights, into the frigid sea.

Back in my room, I sink gently into bed, pulling the covers high even though the room is quite warm. Eric and Mason were pushing for another round, but I've promised myself to wake up at five each morning, when most of the ship is still in bed, and spend a couple of hours up at the library, trying to write.

Writing, after all, was supposed to be the chief motivation for this trip, how I rationalized taking a semester off from teaching to head south. And the results thus far have been underwhelming—a lot of stray notes, a few new drafts of poems. It is hard to polish off much work when you are stringing together weeklong trips in the backcountry, with no desk or chair, putting in big miles over rough terrain and carrying everything on your back. It has been wonderful, though hardly as productive as I had hoped. I'll still have several months to fill with writing once I get back to the States, but I'm hoping that over these next couple of weeks, with a bit of a routine, and most of the creature comforts, I'll have more to show for myself. Though it is the show itself down here that I want to make sure I'm not missing. A familiar refrain for me, I am afraid, as I always seem to struggle to fit writing in.

Once, about five years ago now, I took a proper writing vacation—renting a snowed-in cabin in northern Ontario for three months. It was there that I wrote the poems that got me into graduate school, and that I first learned how much I loved the solitude that comes with ice and snow. On calm nights, after having sat working at my table for most of the day, I'd venture off with snowshoes out onto the lake—cramming the woodstove full as I left. To combat the cold—and it was cold, *damn cold*, though not as bad as the negative forty-five degrees that the *Belgica* measured that winter—I'd travel fast, nearly running, which was no easy task with the long wooden snowshoes that came with the cabin. By the time I circled back an hour or two later, I'd always stop outside the full window, and stand there peering in at that little table, my typewriter, the stacks of books and papers glowing in the cabin light. Though I was tired and ready for warmth, and though I doubted plenty about myself—my writing, some of the choices I had made—it always felt gratifying just to stand there looking in on that life: "To be there, inside, and not be there," as Ray Carver once wrote of a similar moment.[11] And it didn't bother me at all to know I was borrowing this meditation from one of his poems; in fact, if anything, this heightened it.

Perhaps Cook and some of the other men felt a similar glow, as they'd circle back on skis, in the moonlight, to gaze on their ice-shrouded ship—a feeling of *being there*, fully in one's life, even if the prospects looked grim. Solace and encouragement, after all, were in alarmingly short supply right then. To help with morale, one of the sailors had brought with him from Europe a kitten whom they christened Nansen—after the famed Arctic explorer. Throughout their journey, the entire crew became inordinately fond of him—yet once winter settled in, the cat became irritable, lashing out at anyone who tried to touch him. He stopped eating. They brought in a pet penguin in hopes of cheering him up, though to no avail.

Altogether "Nansen" seemed thoroughly disgusted with his surroundings and his associates, and lately he has sought exclusion in unfrequented corners. His temperament has changed from the good and lively creature to one of growling discontent. His mind has wandered and from his changed spiritual attitude we believe that his soul has wandered too. A day or two ago his life departed, we presume for more congenial regions.[12]

After the cat's death, things just about bottomed out. Another sailor went crazy, announcing as he stormed off the ship that he "was going back to Belgium." De Gerlache and Lecointe (the second-in-command) both penned their wills and took to bed, leaving Cook and Amundsen in control of the ship. Immediately they changed the crew's diet, began serving penguin and seal, and saw gradual improvement. In the evenings, they'd gamble huge sums of imaginary money in card games to help raise the collective spirit. Then, on July 22, they ventured out together to watch the rising sun.

I am certain that if our preparations for greeting the returning sun were seen by other people, either civilized or savage, we would be thought disciples of heliolatry. Every man on board has long since chosen a favorite elevation from which to watch the coming sight. Some are in the crow's nest, others on the ropes and spars of the rigging; but these are the men who do little travelling. The adventurous fellows are scattered over the pack upon icebergs and high hummocks.[13]

A makeshift and unreliable worshipper at best, I watch the sun come up through the sheltering windows of the library and manage—for the first time in weeks—to pen a full draft of a poem. "At that age," Graham Greene wrote in one of his stories, "one may fall irrevocably in love with failure."[14] And success for me, however moderately defined—a book of poems, published—once seemed entirely within reach. But it was further away than I knew, and not moving noticeably closer. A year had passed—a year full of course prep and student work. Then on to the second, and I wasn't writing. I lost the thread, I guess. It can be hard to keep playing the role of the aspiring young writer as you get older. Well, I'm hardly the first person to travel to this faraway place in search of something.

That morning, after breakfast, they set up a station for kayaking. The inky water of the bay is entirely peaceful, but a combination of too much coffee and too little exercise spills over, and I paddle needlessly hard across the glassy surface, spraying water up on myself. Doing a few laps, I work up a decent sweat in the full sun. Small bergs and translucent shards float at my side. A booming rumble startles me, and I turn to shore just as a hanging ice shelf calves into the sea—the continent casting adrift what it has harbored close for thousands of years. Exclamations from a few guests floating nearby bring me back to where I am—tagging along on this expensive cruise—but I no longer feel so bothered by that. In fact, I feel genuinely happy at the moment to see my own wonder mirrored back in these ageing faces. What bargain with the world does one have to make to grow old gracefully? I hope I'm still kayaking into my seventies and finding new challenges and joys beyond that. I hope this sense of wonder doesn't leave me.

For the crew of the *Belgica*, that new dawn must have seemed, collectively, like a new lease on life. Spurred on by the sun and the change in their diets, the men began to travel further away from the ship; Cook and Amundsen, with their eyes already turning to future ambitions, were the first to try man-hauling sledges across the Antarctic ice. Here again, the ship's doctor led the way, developing a new tent design that held up better in the harsh polar winds, as well as an improved style of snow goggles. Both of which Amundsen would go on to incorporate in his future voyages.

As the spring progressed, the crew took wagers on when their ship would finally break free from its hold, only to watch, with rising fear, as the estimated dates proved too soon. Instead of the jovial Christmas they had been envisioning, the unthinkable had to be considered: that the ship might not be freed, and they'd be forced to spend a second winter right there. Even Cook, the most optimistic and resilient of the crew, felt certain that another winter would do them in.

Then, on New Year's Eve, they saw open water over two thousand feet away—a possible escape if they could only reach it. They conducted experiments with dynamite but failed to break up the ice. Finally, after much deliberation, Cook convinced the men that they must take it upon themselves to get free, rotating in shifts around the clock with three four-foot saws to cut a canal from the open water back to their ship. To many of them, it must have seemed an impossible task. Given the need to saw two parallel lines, and the cross sections necessary to form the canal, a distance of over a mile and a half would have to be cut. They were able to clear the upper sheets of ice with shovels and picks, though this still left solid ice of three to four feet thick for the saws. On top of that, the water they were aiming for wasn't even the open sea, but rather a small basin surrounded by more ice.

I have had little time to write for one week. Eight hours daily with a heavy saw, and the spine twisted semi-circularly, is not conducive to literary ambitions. It is, however, a capital exercise. Everybody is being hardened to the work and developing ponderous muscles. Our skin is burnt until it has the appearance of the inner surface of boot leather.[15]

By the first of February they had managed to carve the canal to within one hundred feet of the ship, but the remaining ice was so thick as to be almost impenetrable. In one spot they sawed for eight hours and cut less than five feet. Then the wind shifted, undoing all their hard work and blowing the canal closed. Two weeks passed like this until—unexpectedly, and on Valentine's Day no less—the canal reopened, extending all the way to the ship. For the first time in over eleven months, the *Belgica* was afloat, though this presented its own host of obstacles—literally so, as icebergs, also afloat, threatened nearby. Once again, it was Cook's ingenuity that may have saved the ship, as he ordered the crew to drape the hull with penguin skins to serve as bumpers against the ice.

That afternoon, we gain some sense of what this must have been like, as we sail north into the famously ice-chocked channel known as Lemaire. Our hull, of course, is fortified with steel, and needs no penguin skins to cushion the blows. The ice pops and crumbles as we plow our way through— "bergy bits" and "brash ice" in the vernacular of Antarctic sailors. All hands on deck to witness the show. And the Lemaire is a stunningly beautiful channel, less than a mile wide in some parts, as it stretches between Booth Island and the continent. Commonly referred to as Kodak Gap, this is one of the most photographed stretches of the whole Antarctic, with cascading glaciers descending on both sides. All is texture and angles, each sculpted surface a composite of refracted light. Presiding over the scene are the peninsula's giant snow-clad peaks. Two of these towers, Eric tells me as we approach, are known informally as Una's Tits, after a ribald tale of a sailor's exploits while on shore. Not these shores, of course. But understandably a lonely sailor's memory is long in such regions, and these two peaks do look like breasts, at least a little, with twin caps of ice topping the crests of basalt.

The *Belgica* was the first ship to sail through this channel, and de Gerlache chose to name it after Charles Lemaire, the famed Belgian explorer of the Congo. This was a less affable association than a shore-leave romance, as Belgium's brutal colonial presence in the Congo, killing an estimated five million indigenous Congolese over the span of just twenty years, was rapidly becoming an international scandal. Dreams of colonialism and power, of empire and fame—this was the "heart of darkness" that Joseph Conrad would soon explore in his mythical tale of Kurtz. But did the same motives that led Lemaire to the Congo lead some of the Heroic explorers here? It is easy to think of the Antarctic as a world apart, but we bring our demons just as surely as we bring our ships.

Here, within sight of the open sea, we were again imprisoned by the closely packed ice for thirty days, but at last, when we had almost abandoned all hope of escape and were preparing for work during a second winter night, a gentle southerly wind drove us with the sea ice out beyond the line of icebergs, and then we were free to seek the world of life in our own way.[16]

For each man on board the *Belgica*, after all their perseverance, the future just then must have seemed unfalteringly bright. Making our own way out of the channel, we sail north into the serene waters of Gerlache Strait, a clear sign that—for all his evident shortcomings—the Belgian captain was still celebrated as a hero upon his return. Sailor Knutsen, on the other hand, was left broken by the long winter, and died shortly after their return. Another Norwegian sailor named Tollefsen, though he initially recovered, would soon have a mental breakdown, living out his final days in an institution for the insane. Amundsen, for his part, was not yet through with the ice, and his greatest chapter in a life of exploring was still to be written.

As for Cook, all of thirty-two at the time—the same age as I—*the world of life* had a great deal in store for him, though it proved to be rocky sailing. Seven years after his heroics on board the *Belgica*, Cook made an outrageous claim that he was the first to summit Mt. McKinley. A cropped photo of his companion standing triumphantly at the top of the world was later exposed as a fraud—the small promontory where the photo was shot (over fifteen thousand feet below the McKinley summit) is now known as Fake Peak. With the fame he'd garnered from his McKinley hoax, Cook then set out to claim the North Pole, returning with a triumphant story in the same year as Peary did. Cook was seen as the likeable and romantic underdog who'd already conquered the highest peak in North America, and now braved the journey to the pole largely on his own; by comparison, Peary was known for his hot temper and gruff demeanor, and his strong financial backing had allowed him to enlist a small army of natives to help claim the prize. Initially, the public was on Cook's side, but when Peary and his backers began to pick apart his McKinley story—eventually presenting a signed affidavit from Cook's climbing partner admitting the photo was a sham—Cook's reputation was in tatters. As one commentator at the time put it, "Cook was a gentleman and a liar; Peary was neither."[17]

Historians today actually believe that both men fabricated their stories, though the general consensus is that Peary made it much closer to the pole (perhaps within sixty miles). In any case, he did not have to suffer the same indignity as Cook, as Peary was never exposed as a liar in his lifetime. Cook's reputation would soon take a further blow, after he became involved in the Texas oil business, and was convicted of fraudulently using the U.S. mail to overstate the prospects of his company. So the man who was credited by all on board as being the savior of the *Belgica* would wind up serving six years in prison as a charlatan. Amundsen, for his part, stood by his old friend, and visited him several times in jail. There could be no question then as to the level to which Cook had sunk, but Amundsen also knew firsthand what sort of person he had once been, and he felt certain that he owed his life to this man.

That night, after the evening lecture, one of the staff brings in a block of glacier ice that had been gathered earlier from the bay. Passing the ice around, it seems a shame to hold such ancientness in our hands, then to break it further with a blade, and stir the shards thoughtlessly in a whiskey glass, over brave talk of what little we've seen and done—though we still do.

CHAPTER 4

DISCOVERY

(1901–1904)

DR. EDWARD WILSON

At the turn of the twentieth century, the British Empire found itself at a crossroads. Germany had begun to threaten its political and economic dominance on the continent, and though they held claim to the strongest navy in history, with over four hundred million people still under British rule, many at home began to warn of imperial decline. A series of failed colonial ventures across Africa was culminating in the disaster of the Boer War, and, increasingly, polar exploration was seen as an opportunity to revive national confidence and restamp Britain's dominance on a grand scale. The Sixth International Geographical Congress had been held in London in 1895, where Royal Geographic Society president and polar enthusiast Clements Markham helped to launch an ambitious resolution among the major powers of Europe to pursue scientific exploration in Antarctica. The only two expeditions to take up the challenge thus far, however, were both led by foreigners. Markham was adamant that the British should now step to the fore. It had all begun with James Cook, after all, and had been furthered admirably by the likes of Weddell and Ross, so it befell a new generation—spoiled by wealth and ease—to plant the Union Jack in its rightful place at the South Pole. And upon this scene of bravado and empire arose a most unlikely man.

"If you knew him," fellow explorer Apsley Cherry-Garrard would one day write of Edward Wilson, "you could not like him: you simply had to love him."[1] From all accounts of those who had the fortune of voyaging with Wilson, that is just what they did. Known affectionately on board as "Uncle Bill," Wilson was a self-taught artist who began drawing at the age of three. By nine, he was already collecting butterflies and flowers, determined to pursue life as a naturalist. Like Frederick Cook, however, Wilson was also the son of an accomplished physician, and he too pursued the family vocation. A Keatsian explorer of sorts, Wilson chose to finish his doctor's training at a mission in the slums of London. It was there that he contracted tuberculosis, and there, also, that he met a similarly devout Christian named Oriana Souper. Three weeks after they were married, and still struggling to regain his health, Wilson set sail with Robert Falcon Scott on board the *Discovery*.

If the climate suits me I shall come back more fit for work than ever, whereas if it doesn't I think there is no fear of me coming back at all. I quite realize that it is kill or cure.[2]

This was no airy bluster, as Wilson had failed the trip's medical exam and was authorized to head south only at his own risk. Hardly a thrill-seeker by nature, Wilson had a penchant for viewing hardships as gifts from God, and it was this, perhaps more than anything, that drew him to the Antarctic.

Guiding motives, or even talk of a "calling," is to be expected. After all, even today Antarctica is no easy place to get to—nobody simply winds up down here. My friend Eric is no ascetic, and rather than dreams of hardship or adventure, I like to think it is beauty that has led him here—his pursuit of beauty through art. In this, he is certainly not alone on board. Each morning, when I'm up writing in the library an hour or two before sunrise, I see Stefan already making the rounds—a cup of coffee in hand, and always with his camera dangling from his neck. Unlike most photographers, Eric tells me, Stefan takes very few pictures—sometimes no more than a dozen or so for an entire voyage. By comparison, Eric guesses that most days he takes a hundred or more shots, and whenever he sees Stefan lifting his camera, Eric doesn't hesitate to turn away from whatever he is looking at to follow Stefan's gaze—a testament to how much he trusts his friend's artistic sense. While I've only had a couple of conversations with the guy,

I find myself placing my trust in Stefan as well. He has a sincerity that doesn't translate easily into small talk. Clearly, he loves the Antarctic, loves the high seas, but he tires of the big meals, the loud guests, the good wine. He has a wife at home, Eric tells me, who is quite sick, enough so that he almost didn't make it down this season. At least now there is the internet, and the use of a radio-phone when necessary, so one isn't dependent solely on the annual delivery of mail.

Dear girl, it has remained fresh in my mind ever since, the happy sight of you in your grey dress and black hat waving your hanky to me till you were a mere dot in the tossing little launch altogether. And so we at last were really off, and I on board, and Ory on land, left for three years. . . . May God keep us for one another, and we shall be ever more happy then.[3]

Unsurprisingly, most of the men who sailed on the *Discovery* were bachelors, and Wilson (at age twenty-nine) was not only one of the oldest on board, but also the only man with no military training. This separateness was nothing new for Wilson, as the intensity of his religious devotion had often set him apart. Each Sunday, he held his own mass up in the crow's nest, where he claimed to most feel the presence of God. Back home, he had always found society burdensome, and had sometimes resorted to taking sedatives before attending gatherings. Now, he was almost always in the company of others, yet he thrived.

While Wilson was qualified in medicine, his love for nature and art were so strong that he often felt himself pulled in too many directions. In fact, part of the appeal of joining the *Discovery* expedition was the opportunity to fuse the, at times, disparate passions of his life.

Medicine and Surgery form a work that one should either give up one's whole and undivided attention to from the first, or else leave strictly alone in practice: and I'm afraid I have done neither, for I have squandered my energies over various hobbies instead of making my profession my one object in life.[4]

What can I say except that I relate, that I often question whether I am dedicating enough of myself to my own chosen pursuit. "It was hard to be a great writer," Hemingway once said, "if you loved the world and living in it and special people. It was hard when you loved so many places."[5]

That's a tension I have always felt, though I also know that pursuing writing has provided me a sort of alibi to go through life in the manner I desired, to spend as much time as I have alone and in the outdoors. So has art been, for me, the reason, or merely the excuse? Wilson doesn't offer an answer for himself, at least not in his journals, which are largely dedicated to recording the small details of his days. He considered them to be written mostly for his wife and would make carbon copies of each page to send home whenever he had the chance. In reading them, it is hard not to feel moved by how close he became—almost from the outset of the expedition—with a young and boisterous product of the merchant marines named Ernest Shackleton. Contrasting characters in many regards—and separated by nearly a decade in age—they shared a philosophical disposition and an almost boundless energy for the journey at hand. They formed a standing order between them to wake each other whenever there was a worthy sunrise, animal sighting, or anything else of note. They'd often stay up late in conversation when one of them was assigned watch, and Shackleton—a voracious reader since his youth—regularly read aloud his favorite poems to Wilson as they sailed south. As eager as they both were to reach the Antarctic, they also bonded through reminiscing often about home, and about their loved ones (Shackleton was newly engaged) that they had left behind.

The pianola is a perfect godsend. I spend some time at it every day. We have only a few very good pieces, but Chopin's Ballads in A flat one never tires of. We have also Chaminade's Autumn, the Last Rose of Summer, All Soul's Day, all old friends, and many others. I made old Shackle very home sick today, and myself nearly as bad, but it soon takes the form of an intense joy at the thought of coming home again. We have now been away a full month and all of us are seasoned sailors.[6]

For our own part, we have traveled south largely without musical accompaniment, though relics of old Britain still abound. A fact made particularly clear this morning, as we disembark at Port Lockroy, nestled in a narrow channel off Anvers Island, and watch the red cross of St. George flapping wildly in the wind, beneath a backdrop of stunning, snowy peaks. In truth, the flag feels like overkill, as the entire base, known simply as Base A, is decked out in Britain's colors—the bright red shutters and trim looking more than a little out of place among the landscape's immense grays and whites.

Base A was originally established back in World War II as part of a secret naval operation named Tabarin, after a favorite Parisian nightclub. Operation Tabarin was backed by Prime Minister Churchill and aimed to keep tabs on German shipping. After the war, several of the bases were turned into meteorological stations, supplying foundational readings that have proved essential for charting climate change here at the peninsula. Piloting our Zodiac, Tom Richie tells us that the British abandoned Base A in 1962 and adds his own small part in its history: "We came here in the late seventies and rediscovered the place, then lobbied for the British government to restore it and make a museum out of it." Operating for only the five-month cruising season, the base welcomes over fifteen thousand visitors a year—a number that would have seemed inconceivable not just a century ago but as recently as twenty years back. To be honest, the number seems inconceivable to me even now, as we have seen neither ship nor soul since departing Ushuaia. They are out here though—the flocks of upper-class expedition tourists—even now at the end of the season.

When the twelve original signatory nations drafted the Antarctic Treaty in 1959, they made no mention of tourism, as the first commercial visit to the Antarctic had occurred only three years before. As the industry has advanced, the Treaty coalition has had to scramble to keep up and put necessary regulations in place to handle the surge in visitors. The main building of Base A is large enough to host only a couple of dozen guests at a time, though the astonishing number of nesting gentoo penguins that share the island would outnumber even the largest tour groups.

"When we laugh at the penguins, we laugh at ourselves"—a saying allegedly coined by a French sailor. And penguins are, without question, one of the most human of animals: dithering and self-important. Right now, the chicks are fledging, and many of them sport odd patches of scruffy down, appearing like members in a punk band or awkward teenagers. "Gentoo" is the archaic word for "Hindu," and the name was decided upon for this breed by early British explorers who thought the triangular white patches above their eyes were reminiscent of a turban. By this stage in their lives, each chick's demand for food is so great that both parents have left to forage at sea, and the abandoned young cluster together instinctively in what are known as "crèches"—the word means "crib" or "day nursery"—where they struggle to keep warm and ward off the dive-bombing skuas. Penguins' mating rituals also seem oddly human. While the bull elephant seals

hold their annual blood bath each spring, the penguin method of woo-
ing is limited to a lot of strutting, near-constant chest puffing, and—when
deemed necessary—the occasional flipper-bash. Full of piss, vinegar, and
krill paste, penguins are also known for their boastful clucks (sounding re-
markably like a squeaky dog toy), which can set a tidal wave of near identical replies rippling across a colony. It was Wilson who first described this
behavior as "ecstatic"—a term still in use today—though surely the scene is
too comical and undignified for that. He first laid eyes on a penguin rookery when visiting the subantarctic island of Macquarie.

*Closer and closer we came to this main island, until about two or three
o'clock in the afternoon, when I told the Pilot that I would give him a bottle of liqueur if he could persuade the Skipper to allow us to land here for
collecting. Off he went like a shot and soon after came up and told me he
wanted the liqueur.*[7]

Like many explorers, Wilson remarked in his journals on how easy the
birds were to capture and kill. Having evolved without terrestrial predators, penguins have no natural fear of humans. A docility, it should be
mentioned, that has not spared them any of our abject cruelty. In truth, the
Discovery was lucky to find any penguins at all on Macquarie, where hundreds of thousands had been rendered into oil in the mid-nineteenth century—many of them infants who were herded on ramps and forced to leap
into cauldrons of oil. Sailors on board the *Belgica* had their own preferred
method of harvesting, as they discovered that penguins would respond
with curiosity whenever they heard a cornet play, and so saved themselves
the trouble of hunting birds far out from the ship.

*At the very spot where we landed there lay a big brown seal fast asleep. Out
came cameras, hammers, guns, rifles, mauser pistols, clubs, and sketch
books, till the poor beast woke up and gazed on us with its saucer-like
eyes. . . . The poor beast was sacrificed in the interests of science.*[8]

After such stops, Wilson would devote days to processing specimens—
working long hours at skinning, then turning quickly to paint the birds'
heads and feet before the colors began to fade. "A duty much against the
grain," as he phrased it, though he placed high value on the work.[9] "It
seemed a terrible desecration," Captain Scott wrote in his own journal, "to
come to this quiet spot only to murder its innocent inhabitants and stain

the white snow with blood."[10] In truth, Scott must have been as surprised as any of the men to be venturing out to these far-flung shores. As a lieutenant in the navy, Scott specialized in torpedo work, which would hardly prove a transferable skill in the Antarctic. Scott was here, in large part, because Royal Geographic Society (RGS) president Clements Markham had taken an interest in him as a young man, after witnessing Scott show a dash of courage in winning a hard-fought cutter race in the West Indies, and had recommended him for the post. Scott was thirty-one at the time of the *Discovery* voyage, his dark hair already beginning to thin, and aiming for promotion to secure a firm financial footing to help take care of his widowed mother and his two unmarried sisters. While Scott was very much a secular man, he shared with Wilson a versatile mind, with interests that extended far past his formal training. For this reason, he developed a stronger personal commitment to science than did either Shackleton or Amundsen—his two biggest rivals of the Heroic Age. Perhaps for this reason as well, he would prove to be a better writer. On the other side of the coin, Scott appears to have battled depression for most of his life, was riddled with self-doubt, and struggled with a bad temper—none of which made him a natural leader of men. Scott also suffered from a pronounced queasiness at the sight of blood, and he had a deep-rooted sensitivity toward animal suffering that long predated his voyages to the Antarctic. His cousin Bertie would later recount how Scott had—without success—attempted to curb this character trait as a young man, through visiting a local slaughterhouse.[11] Now, even at this early stage of the trip, Scott was learning that the Antarctic too was no place for the faint of heart.

An important annex to the Antarctic Treaty protecting Antarctica's fauna and flora was adopted in 1964, giving protection to all native plants, birds, and mammals south of sixty degrees latitude (with the glaring exception of whales). Even so, this doesn't mean that all is smooth sailing. These gentoo penguins, for instance—which are slightly larger than Adelie penguins, allowing them to dive to a greater depth for krill—are actually a subantarctic species that has infiltrated the polar ecosystem. What is startling about this migration is how quickly and fully it has taken place, over the span of only a few decades. As the American scientist Bill Fraser, who has studied penguins for over thirty seasons on the Antarctic Peninsula, has warned, "this is foretelling the future across major parts of the planet. All those places we cherish are going to change."[12]

In a sense, the ecosystem of Antarctica has an affinity with poetry: fewer words, greater meaning; fewer species, greater consequences. Where a more diverse and manifold ecosystem may have the ability to adapt to the loss or displacement of any single species, a more minimalist ecosystem can prove susceptible to collapse. In this sense, while the Antarctic continent covers over five million square miles—and the density of wildlife down here is truly astonishing—it may have more in common with the ecosystems of small islands that are highly sensitive to disturbances.

Inside the base, images of penguins adorn postcards, sweatshirts, hats, and coffee mugs. The museum gift shop funds the base's upkeep and staffing, though the more interesting displays are dedicated to explorer rations and old photographs. Some of the shelves are also stocked with more recent supplies—rusting tins of "Hunter's Steak & Kidney Pudding," magazine pinups of Doris Day. Having intentionally left my wallet on board, I flip through a book of Wilson's watercolors, lingering over many of the iconic scenes—emperor penguins at Cape Crozier, the red glow of smoke rising from Mt. Erebus during their first winter. While this base is rich in Antarctic history, the real epicenter of British operations in the Heroic Age took place over two thousand miles west of here, beneath the shadow of that billowing volcano. Wilson was the last painter to accompany an Antarctic expedition as the person in charge of recording topography, and Scott claimed he could match Wilson's drawings to his own maps with astonishing accuracy. On the way south, Wilson built a bad-weather sketching box that he hung around his neck, allowing him to draft while aloft in the many storms. The conditions only got worse once they arrived on the continent. Working at halt camps, or at brief pauses along the march, Wilson would make quick field sketches in pencil—"slipping his hands out of his mitts for a minute or two at a time"—making notes as to color and tone that he would attend to back at the ship.[13] Even there, and especially during winter, he struggled with poor lighting, and was forced to work in cramped quarters, sharing the ward-room table with the frequent meals and nightly card games (unlike the others, Wilson took no interest in cards). Some of his most fascinating sketches were drawn outside in winter, his pencil digging hard into the paper to leave a visible mark. Humble about his artistic ability, along with most everything else, Wilson would often grow frustrated by his failure to do justice to his surroundings, discussing openly the wonders a painter such as Turner would have been able to produce.[14]

These days are with one for all time—they are never to be forgotten—and they are to be found nowhere else in all the world. . . . One only wishes one could bring a glimpse of it away with one with all its unimaginable beauty.[15]

There is a tendency in our portrayal of the old explorers to sketch incomparable beings—without blemishes, hesitancies, or contradictions. It is a shame really, as this only emphasizes their distance from us—not just in time, but also in spirit. The truth, thankfully, is more complicated than that. Among the *Discovery* crew there were dreamers, drunks, and dropouts. There were heroes, and there were failures. They made all kinds of mistakes. In their first season in the Antarctic, they had trouble with stoves, with skis, with handling dogs and packing sledges. They wildly misjudged distances, ate the wrong food, and wore the wrong clothing. These were no experts—not as scientists, nor as adventurers. Many had never spent a night in a tent before. Some of the men were no doubt selfish and foolish. Some were aspiring artists. Some traveled here because they had felt defeated everywhere else. One man, George Vince, died while trying to walk back to the ship in a blizzard, blundering over a cliff at the edge of the Barrier. Another man, Clarence Hare, became disoriented in the same storm, and stumbled back to base two days later, having slept out without shelter under a snowdrift. Like each of us, they were, by turns, courageous and filled with self-doubt. While we can flip through matted books of Wilson's watercolors now, it is worth noting that he died without ever having seen a book of his in print.

Yet if it is important to resist the urge to idealize the early explorers, we must also avoid the other extreme: the impulse to be overly critical and judge them on the basis of what we know now, or what was learned only after much trial and error. Taken as a whole, the British teams that headed to the Antarctic at the turn of the century are sometimes dismissed as bumblers, incompetent amateurs who were foolishly resistant to learning from other nations. This is, in large part, a cultural judgment of the English—and certainly there is plenty of history to back it up, especially in light of the waning empire and its stubborn Edwardian sense of manliness and martyrdom.

Cultural preconceptions such as these die hard, if at all. I happen to be a soccer player, or I once was anyway, and I still put some energy into following the European game, where pundits of the British league often praise its physical intensity—its macho, hurly-burly football style. Critics from the continent, on the other hand, tend to lament the league's lack of beauty and technique—its fixation on mindless running. Of course, this has less to do with individual players, who come from all over, and more to do with a perceived cultural mindset. As one journeyman footballer phrased it to an interviewer who asked him to compare the different leagues, "in England there was a general groan about players who didn't chase a lost cause, but a roar for anyone who'd gallop after an opposition player to contest a meaningless throw-in."[16]

Useless heroism, chasing a lost cause: this is one way that the British Antarctic expeditions of the Heroic Age are sometimes depicted. One of Scott's harshest critics, historian Roland Huntford—sounding more than a little like a surly armchair sports pundit himself—put it this way: "Only in Britain do we revere the man. . . . Elsewhere in the world, Scott is seen as rather second-rate—an incompetent loser who battled nature rather than tried to understand it."[17] It is important to bear in mind, however, that the *Discovery* expedition marks the first-ever attempt to penetrate the Antarctic interior. All the existing literature on polar travel was centered on the Arctic. Dogs, at least with experienced handlers, had been quite successful there, but could smooth and largely level surfaces be expected in Antarctica? No one knew this as of yet, and the men of the *Discovery* would have to provide the base knowledge that other expeditions would build on. Moreover, if there was an insular British mindset at play, Captain Scott went some distance to reach beyond this, traveling to Scandinavia before both of his expeditions south to seek council from experienced polar explorers like Fridtjof Nansen. The British brought dogs, as well as skis (both of which Nansen encouraged), though certainly their lack of expertise with both presented a handicap. In the end, I'd wager that if Scott's first expedition did travel south with a firm "British mindset" that it probably helped them as much as it hurt them, though—as Wilson was quick to point out—their party was representative of only half the equation.

Men don't improve when they live together alone, cut off from all the better half of humanity that encourages decency and kindness. Some of our mess have quite dropped the mask and are not so attractive in their true colouring.[18]

The two British women working here at the museum are both young and attractive. Their work is centered on the visiting tourists (an average of two ships a day). They stock shelves, work the cash register, and handle the mail (the base also functions as a post office—processing an astounding seventy thousand pieces of mail each season). Still, one of the obvious perks of the job is a great deal of free time. "What do you girls do for fun down here?" asks an unintentionally creepy passenger in disbelief. "We read a lot of books," one of them responds, eliciting—for some reason—a wave of laughter. Theirs is just a seasonal job, though I wonder whether, given the chance, they'd opt to stay for the winter. I wonder whether I would. Of the roughly two hundred scientific stations in Antarctica, only about thirty of them stay open year-round, and even those operate with a rotating crew. The annals of Antarctic lore are full of crazy winter tales— the Soviet who killed a companion with an ice axe during a chess match; the Argentine staff doctor who, at the end of autumn, burned down the base where he was stationed to force his own rescue; the American admiral who brought with him two coffins and twelve straightjackets to see the winter through.

The *Discovery* crew was not free of tension and minor turmoil over their first winter, though they fared better than most did. All had various official duties to keep them busy, and Wilson and Shackleton took on the added project of publishing the *South Polar Times*. The two friends built up an "editor's office" in one of the holds of the ship, arranging cases for seats and a small table for Shackleton's typewriter. Wilson handled the artwork, and Shackles oversaw the rest—writing many of the articles himself and soliciting work from others. With only one copy of each edition ever printed, distribution took care of itself. Each issue was thirty to fifty pages long and included cartoons, weather reports, caricatures of the officers and men. The crew used the ship itself as their winter quarters, though the hut they'd constructed on shore for storage also served as a theatre for regular productions of plays. They even held weekly debates on a wide range of topics. Collectively, they may have been an ill-bred and undereducated group, but they possessed a range of cultural knowledge that would put most any society nowadays to shame.

After dinner we had a Tennyson v. Browning competition, which resulted from a discussion as to their respective merits yesterday at dinner. Shackle upheld Browning and Bernacchi Tennyson. Each had to choose a passage from his own author on various subjects such as love, science, philosophy, wit, art, beauty. They read these out to us and we sat in judgment and voted.[19]

That evening, back on board the ship, Stefan treats us to our own performance—with equal parts personal history, scientific lecture, and art treatise—as he talks us through a series of his own photographs. As with Wilson, Stefan may lack some tolerance for society at large, but that hardly means he can't command a room. And, also like Wilson, all his assorted devotions and disciplines seem to form a harmonious whole—the life feeding the science feeding the art. "The divorce rate among emperor penguins is 85 percent," he declares gruffly after clicking to a panoramic shot of a rookery, "but imagine you just got back from a season on the high seas, and you walked into Yankee stadium to find thousands of almost identical and available partners calling out to you, 'Darling, Darling, I'm yours! I love you! Come to me!'" A quick, and uncharacteristic, imitation of a waddling penguin garners a round of laughs.

In one moody, twilight shot there is a close-up of two Adelie penguins, their lone tracks edging out of the frame in a fresh dusting of snow. To set this up, Stefan tells us, he positioned himself behind a small rise just off from the rookery. He wanted the unbroken whiteness of the snow, so he brought along a pocket brush to dust away the particles of ash and cover his own tracks. Next, he needed solitary birds, and clean ones—not soiled in the shit and regurgitated krill of the colony—so he laid flat on the ice behind the ridge and started mimicking a penguin's call, hoping to intercept a few inquisitive birds just coming to shore. Stefan positions his hands at his mouth and offers us three measured and muffled calls punctuated by long pauses. More laughter. "Funny now, yes," he says, seemingly annoyed by the response, "but consider that I'm out there freezing."

My ignorance of Browning is formidable, and I haven't read Tennyson in years, though I do think of Yeats—

> A line will take us hours maybe;
> Yet if it does not seem a moment's thought
> Our stitching and unstitching has been naught.[20]

Which is to say that what I took away most from Stefan's talk—which was also what I learned from my best writing professors in college—is the necessary role that obsession plays in art.

As for Wilson, with his first year in the Antarctic winding down, he became increasingly fixated on the emperor penguin. It was the bird that
held the most mystery, having barely been encountered by earlier expeditions. It was also widely thought at the time to be one of the planet's most
primitive birds. Yet just as with the *Belgica antarctica*, a penguin's flightlessness is actually an ingenious adaptation. When the ice sheet began to
form some thirty-four million years ago, penguins evolved to fill an open
niche in the bounty of the Southern Ocean. Back in Wilson's day, evolution was understood more as a one-way track—for birds, an adaptation
from solid to hollow bones, but never in reverse. For this reason, Wilson
hoped that studying emperor penguins would reveal the evolutionary link
between birds and reptiles. A German evolutionist named Ernst Haeckel
had recently popularized the theory of recapitulation, positing that a study
of developing embryos could reveal traces of an organism's evolutionary
history. Wilson was so committed to this pursuit that after a spring sledge
party had stumbled upon the emperors' breeding site at Cape Crozier, on
the western end of Ross Island, he was almost sorry to have been chosen to
accompany Scott and Shackleton for a push south across the Barrier, as it
precluded his hope of journeying to Crozier that season himself.

I am afraid this long southern journey is taking me right away from my
proper sphere of work to monotonous hard work on an icy desert for three
months, where we shall see neither beast nor bird nor life of any sort nor
land and nothing whatever to sketch.[21]

The Great Ice Barrier, now known as the Ross Ice Shelf, was discovered
by their fellow Englishman Sir James Clark Ross in 1841. Ross's two ships,
Erebus and *Terror*, had successfully navigated the pack ice that had turned
back all other attempts at approaching this side of the continent. Now in
a huge open sea, Ross had hoped to sail as far as the South Magnetic Pole,
yet he was stopped by an immense wall of ice, what he called "the Barrier."
In truth, it was far bigger than he dared imagine—larger than all of France
and averaging over two thousand feet in thickness. Turned back finally at
McMurdo Sound, Ross established a new farthest south, and discovered
what would become the launching pad for the race to the pole. At the time
that the *Discovery* arrived on the scene sixty years later, there wasn't even
certainty as to whether Antarctica was a continent, as opposed to just a collection of islands, but Scott and his scientists correctly identified the Barrier as a shelf of floating ice. They eventually calculated a rate of movement

for the ice of roughly one mile every three years toward the sea (or between five and ten feet per day), where it breaks off, eventually, into large tabular bergs. Ross called it the Barrier, of course, because it impeded his progress to the south, but in a more accurate sense, Antarctica's ice shelves function as buttresses that stabilize the great glaciers behind them. The Ross Ice Shelf is the largest in the world and has, to date, proved much more stable than others on the continent, such as the rapidly diminishing Larsen Ice Shelf up here on the peninsula. An ice shelf's rate of collapse and melting is highly erratic and difficult to predict. Fissures and cracks appear over time, weakening the integrity of the shelf until it reaches a point of irrevocable decline. From there, things move with alarming rapidity. The 1,250-square-mile sector of the Larsen shelf that collapsed in 2002, for instance, which had been stable for at least ten thousand years, vanished in the space of about a week.

Collapsing ice shelves were on nobody's mind when the three friends left their base at Hut Point near the end of 1902, though they had plenty else to fear, and all wrote farewell letters to their loved ones at home before setting off (Scott, who was still unattached, wrote to his mother). They left on the second of November, with nineteen unruly and largely untrained dogs, along with nearly a ton of food, instruments, and supplies. By this time, they had been in the Antarctic for close to a year, and had learned much from past mistakes—how to set up a tent in a gale, how to work the stove properly to cook their hoosh.[22] Other things were still being experimented with; in their first sledge journeys, for instance, they had donned odd sleeping gowns in place of sleeping bags, and later they would try sharing a single three-man bag—sacrificing what little they had of individual comfort and privacy for a few degrees of added warmth. Regardless, and no matter how tired they inevitably were, sleeping was always difficult.

None of us thought we had slept at all, but from listening to the others snoring we knew that everyone else had. This is generally the case on these cold journeys. One sleeps and gets a good amount of rest without ever knowing it, but one is certainly awake most of every night and I think one never gets an hour's sleep without waking. . . . One dreams a great deal, and these are really the only evidence one has of having been asleep, for one knows one could not have thought so irrationally when awake. And moreover they are vivid dreams of home and warmth and England, far more vivid than any waking thoughts.[23]

While hardly having grounds for complaint, I must admit that my current sleeping arrangement is not ideal. Our lodging may well be far larger than a tent, but increasingly I find myself avoiding the room during waking hours. Roommate Bill, on the other hand, seems to be spending more time there than ever, and most all of it in his bathrobe. Tonight, for instance, I could have sworn I saw him up in the lounge less than five minutes earlier, but when I head back briefly to the room, he is already dressed down—the open V of the robe's neck revealing more gray chest hair than I'd care to see. I assume there are boxers on under there, but there's no way to be certain. "I just get so sweaty in clothes," he remarked to me the other night, as he flopped onto his bed. This would seem to make life outside of a luxury cruise a tad difficult. Only six days into our three-week cruise and already my relationship with my roommate appears to be headed south.

On their sledge journey across the Barrier, Wilson brought a copy of Darwin's *The Origin of Species*, and the three explorers took turns reading aloud each night as they huddled in their tent. Since its publication in 1859, Darwin's seminal text had been at the center of competing evolutionary theories across Europe. Given Wilson's religious devotion, Darwin would seem like a strange fit at first, though Wilson didn't see it this way. "All my religious ideas," he wrote, "are founded on the principle of evolution driven to its logical conclusion."[24] And with a Hegelian sort of spiritualism, he believed that each person's life advanced toward perfection, fulfilling the purpose for which it was created.

Like many with a liberal arts background, I first read Darwin as part of a freshman core class. A bit of a slog for eighteen-year-old me, who had already determined a course of study centered on literature. What a world away from that classroom, how much more alive that text must have seemed to those three men—on a vast plain of uncharted ice—as they lay side by side, awaiting sleep. Bedtime reading for Roommate Bill and me, however, will have to wait, as Eric and Kendra are taking me out to the weekly crew party down at the lower deck.

From the looks of things, Lindblad is a great company to work for, and from all I've heard the ship's employees get along wonderfully well, though there is an obvious division between the staff and crew. They sleep on different decks, they eat separately, they get paid separately and work different schedules, and above all else they look different. The staff (made up of the naturalists and essential ship personnel) are basically all Caucasian,

Americans and Scandinavians for the most part, while the crew, as I've already said, is almost exclusively Filipino. The appeal of this arrangement, from the industry's standpoint, seems obvious: English is the national language of the Philippines, and contracting with an overseas labor company no doubt helps to skirt minimum-wage laws and avoid various forms of taxation. Hiring a block of employees from a single country also likely helps to build a sense of camaraderie, and Eric tells me that one night near the end of our trip there will be a special menu of Filipino fare. I'm looking forward to it, for while the meals have been consistently excellent, there's a bit more of a western bias than I'm used to, having spent close to two years of my life in Asia. In the end, however, and despite the evident sense of goodwill on all sides, the racial dynamic of the ship carries a troubling sense of "the help" that is hard to ignore.

Darwin's theory of natural selection—it should be added—was causing reverberations not just inside the scientific community, but also throughout British society at large, revealing its own western bias. By the turn of the century, Darwin's writings had increasingly become associated with controversial ideas of social reform. Darwin himself was a longtime abolitionist, though his cousin Francis Galton—who served for over forty years as an influential member of the RGS Council—founded the eugenics movement, championing the cause of selective breeding, and waging an ideological battle against what he referred to as the decline of the British race. The RGS oversaw and was the main source of funding for polar expeditions such as Scott's, and Galton openly promoted his ideas of racial superiority among the explorers. Unfortunately, one does not have to look far to find evidence of such attitudes spilling over into the expeditions themselves. Look over the handful of issues of the *South Polar Times*, for instance, and you will find articles written in mocking dialect, as well as pictures of the "Dishcover Minstrel Troupe"—outfitted with blackface and tattered clothing for the amusement of the men. The group even named their most ill-tempered sled dog Nigger, which Scott later remarked "wholly failed to convey the grandeur of his nature."[25] Far from an exclusively British phenomenon, similarly offensive remarks are found in the journals of most explorers of the day.

White men on a white continent. While the three explorers marched slowly to the south, there is no indication that any of them felt it would ever be any different. At least Wilson showed signs of being a little less ra-

cially smug and myopic than many with whom he traveled, penning the
following in a letter to his wife:

*My mind is much occupied with a hope that we shall be able sometime to go
to Japan together. I have a longing to sketch there and see the country and
the people more than any other place in the world. They are the only really
naturally artistic race living, and I am sure one would learn much from
them.*[26]

Down at the crew mess hall, tables have been cleared out to make space
for dancing, while several others have been pushed together to house an
assortment of food and open bottles. In true Filipino fashion, a karaoke
machine has been set up, and people are already taking turns with the mic.
I've spent about three months in the Philippines, split up over two trips
a couple of years apart. For a time, I was even trying to convince a few
friends to move with me to a tucked-away mountain town I'd stumbled
upon in my travels through northern Luzon, though it never panned out.
Still, it is a country I would happily return to, and I don't think I've ever
experienced a more musically inclined culture. Everybody sings there, and
most everyone sings well. Even in the most remote villages up in the rice
terraces, there was always a guitar being strummed, always a group of kids
gathering at night to sing the same familiar songs.

Not surprisingly, it is quite unusual to have a guest of the ship attend a crew
party, but Eric and Kendra are obviously well-liked among the group—in
part from having both worked as stewards in the past—and they cleared it
with the crew ahead of time. A few of them I've already gotten to know a
little. Carlos is the old man who runs the espresso bar early in the morning, and since I'm usually his first customer, we tend to talk a bit. Nadine,
the yoga instructor, is from the remote northern island of Batan, where I
once spent most of a month on my own, and I've enjoyed hearing her stories of the place. Soon the karaoke machine is put on hold, and the crew—
worn down from a long week of serving, cleaning, and cooking—is ready
to dance.

*Hard day's work. 15 miles covered to make 5 miles southing. Dogs getting
very tired and very slow. We were at it from 11.30 a.m. till 9.30 p.m. and
now at 11.15 p.m. we are at last in our sleeping bags. Surface worse than
ever, with a thick coating of loose ice crystals like fine sand. We pray for a*

wind to sweep it all off and give us a hard surface again. This is wearing us out and the dogs, and yet we cover no ground. And the exertion of driving the poor beasts is something awful.[27]

After the Southern Party covered decent ground for the first couple of weeks, things started to unravel for them. Increasingly, the route was covered with deep sastrugi—the wind-furrowed ridges drawn by the driven snow—that wrecked the surface for sledging, especially when paired with a soft crust heated from the sun. The dogs began to weaken substantially, with Wilson surmising that the dried fish that served as the dogs' sledging ration had been spoiled during the sea voyage south. They switched to night marches in hopes of a better surface and more energy from the dogs outside the heat of the day. Air temperatures rarely got above freezing, but the radiating heat off the snow was intense enough for the dogs to overheat and the men to suffer repeatedly from sunburnt eyes—a condition also known as "snow blindness." (This was especially true for Wilson, who regularly took off his goggles to make sketches at camp.) Their noses and lips were horribly cracked, and their faces—otherwise blackened from the smoke of their paraffin stove—throbbed with open sores peeling from the sun. Shackleton had also developed a persistent cough that was keeping them awake in the tent. A strong and proud man, Shackleton had a tendency to push himself too hard in life. He had also been diagnosed with asthma at the outset of the expedition, and quite likely he was already struggling with some form of a heart condition. As his close friend, Wilson had advocated for his inclusion on the Southern Journey with Scott, yet he also expressed some misgivings about Shackleton's health in a letter home before their departure.

I feel more equal to it than I feel for Shackleton; for some reason I don't think he is fitted for the job. The Captain is strong and hard as a bull-dog, but Shackleton hasn't the legs that the job wants; he is so keen to go, however, that he will carry it through.[28]

The amount of shouting and beating that was required to move the dogs was, in Wilson's words, "soul-sickening," even after they'd switched to splitting loads—relaying the team so they traveled three miles for every one to the south. After the first month, the men started reduced rations to extend their journey. The pole itself was no longer entertained as a possibility, but Scott was determined to set a record of as far south as he could. Still on the

Barrier, they had hopes of at least reaching solid land, and turned course to the southeast, where an impressive coastline of snow-covered peaks had come into view. The weakest dogs began to collapse in their traces, and while Scott made the order, he couldn't stomach the act, so Wilson handled the butchering throughout.

The dogs seem a trifle better in health for the pieces of their companion, whom I cut up and distributed among them. Not one refused to eat it, indeed most of them neglected their fish for it. There was no hesitation. "Dog don't eat dog" certainly doesn't hold down here, any more than does Ruskin's aphorism in Modern Painters that "A fool always wants to shorten space and time; a wise man wants to lengthen both." We must be awful fools at that rate, for our desire is to shorten the space between us and the land. Perhaps Ruskin would agree that we are awful fools to be here at all, though I think if he saw these new mountain ranges he might think perhaps it was worth it.[29]

Many of the crew members with Eric's company come back year after year, so they must find the job worthwhile. Though no doubt they too wish they could shorten the space between themselves and the land they crave. While they make more money here than they can make at home, the sacrifices are real, and generally they see their families for only three months of the year. Most of them are also city people—having lived all their lives in Manila or Cebu. Eric tells me that he and a few of the other naturalists are always trying to convince them to join the shore parties, to participate in the hikes and Zodiac rides and kayaking trips. A handful of the crew have taken them up on this—occasionally, and when their work allows—though most prefer to stay on the ship. This is not their landscape, not their culture or climate, and while much the same could be said for all of us on board, they are here for different reasons, having never sought this place out to begin with. Perhaps, then, some people really do just wind up down here. And while I can understand their remove, I must admit that it seems a shame to travel to this remote and fascinating place without taking the opportunity to fully see it.

From start to finish today I went blindfold both eyes, pulling on ski. Luckily the surface was smooth and I only fell twice. I had the strangest thoughts or day dreams as I went along, all suggested by the intense heat of the sun I think. Sometimes I was in beech woods, sometimes in fir woods, sometimes

in the Birdlip woods, all sorts of places connected in my mind with a hot
sun. And the swish-swish of the ski was as though one's feet were brushing
through dead leaves, or cranberry undergrowth or heather or juicy blue-
bells. One could almost see them and smell them.[30]

This was from two days after Christmas; the night before, one of Wilson's
eyes was so painful from snow blindness that he resorted to dropping co-
caine into it repeatedly, and finally took a dose of morphia to get to sleep.
They had tried to celebrate the holiday—eating three much-needed hot
meals, as well as a small tin of blackberry jam that Wilson had smuggled
into their stores, and a small plum pudding Shackleton had hidden in one
of his socks. Nonetheless, the mood was far from festive. On Christmas
Eve, Wilson had detected signs of scurvy in all three of them. This did not
come as a surprise, for a spring sledging party had already been forced to
return to base after recognizing early symptoms in themselves. The men's
diet back at the ship relied enough on fresh seal meat that short sledging
trips such as that one should not have run into any problems, but cooking
the meat too long can drastically reduce the levels of vitamin C transfer;
likewise, if parts of the animal, such as the liver, are avoided for consumption, the scurvy-preventing component of the meat is further mitigated. Of
course, none of this was known at the time (even the discovery of vitamins
was still more than a decade away), and much of scurvy prevention was essentially guesswork.

By this time, the Southern Party had been without fresh meat for sixty
days, and the longer they stayed out the more susceptible they were to the
disease. They were also running short on rations and oil, and the eleven remaining dogs were all but worthless. On the last day of the year—now 380
miles from Hut Point, and still another 500 miles away from the pole—
they turned back. Wilson's watercolor sketch from this day shows a red
skyline and a low fog through which the vast transantarctic peaks stand
out in the distance—a formidable boundary that would somehow have to
be crossed if they were ever to reach the pole. Some claim this picture is a
wistful composition, as though a new day was dawning, beckoning them
further to the south, though to me, the mountains just look far away—
beautiful but unobtainable. In any case, their energies were now all focused on getting back alive.

One of the dogs dropped dead in harness today. Several others look as though they would like to.... I now save half a biscuit from supper to eat when I wake at night, otherwise I simply can't sleep again. I have never experienced such craving for more food before.[31]

It feels great to dance, to sip whiskey from paper cups, to feel young and foolish and poor again, after a week of high luxury. I have also really been craving exercise. There are trips every day now to shore, and small hikes, but apart from the quick sweat I worked up on our kayak outing the other day, the only perspiring I've done has been due to seasickness. The ship actually has a small gym, with a stand-up bike and treadmill, but even when we are anchored in a calm bay, I find myself getting nauseated after running for more than a few minutes. A night of dancing, a night clear of guests and official duties, is a welcome respite for everyone here. Kendra seems particularly appreciative, as there have evidently been a handful of especially difficult guests on this sailing. Eric tells me that she is also dealing with some personal turmoil—a long-distance relationship that may be on the brink. In truth, her relationship isn't as long-distance as you would expect, as the guy happens to be less than twenty miles away from us at the moment—at the American research base of Palmer Station, just the other side of Anvers Island, where he maintains their fleet of Zodiacs. Kendra was actually hoping that he'd be able to spend tonight on board with us, but something with his scheduling has gotten in the way, and while I hardly know Kendra, I can see clearly that this past week has taken a toll on her.

Since the last blizzard Shackleton has been anything but up to the mark, and today he is decidedly worse, very short winded, and coughing constantly, with more serious symptoms which need not be detailed here, but which are of no small consequence a hundred and sixty miles from the ship, and full loads to pull all the way.[32]

This is Wilson's entry from January 14, their having just arrived at their first depot, after some difficulty locating it in a storm. Here the last of the dogs was killed. One of Wilson's most well-known sketches commemorates the sad event—two sets of tracks (human and canine) lead to the foreground of the picture, where a scalpel has been left gently in the snow, and only the human tracks turn back toward the distant sledges. The man walking away from the scene doesn't look back, though you can sense a clear weight to his shoulders, a slowness to his step. The months of cruelly driving the dogs—of watching them rapidly deteriorate until, by the end, unharnessed but still faithful, they did their best to trudge on to the next camp—was enough to make all of them vow to never do it again.

After abandoning what little could be spared, they had whittled their load down to 525 pounds. This was a mass they had man-hauled reasonably well in the past, but they were much weaker now, and soon enough Shackleton's condition sunk to such a level that he could no longer do his share of the work. Stiffness of muscle joints, exhaustion, and shortness of breath are all early symptoms of scurvy, though additional undiagnosed ailments may have compounded the problems for Shackleton. While his worrying condition didn't fully present itself until the return journey, Scott still placed a disproportionate part of the blame for the party's turning back on Shackleton. Owing to his "constitutional" weakness, as Scott termed it, and going so far as to mockingly refer to Shackleton as "our invalid" in his book—a perceived slight that Shackleton would never forgive him for.[33] In truth, they were all at great risk, each suffering with early symptoms, and the party was lucky that the condition didn't reach such a crippling stage in all three of them. For weeks Shackleton had hardly slept, coughed continually, and regularly spit up blood. Wilson and Scott hauled the loads, and Shackleton did his best to keep up.

The crew party goes on for hours. By the end, I am worn out and noticeably slurring my speech. Kendra is at least as tipsy as I am, and Eric does his best to keep the two of us quiet and upright as he leads us back to our rooms. We may be anchored off the coast of the loneliest continent, but the night winds up feeling more like a bender back in college.

Shackleton, still very seedy, went his own pace on ski. We then did 5 hours more and camped at 8 p.m. having done some 15 miles in the day. Our main object now is to get Shackleton back to the ship before we get caught in another blizzard. He has been very weak and breathless all day, but has stuck to it well and kept up with us on ski.[34]

On February 3, after an absence of ninety-three days, the three men staggered back to Hut Point. By some accounts, Scott and Shackleton had a bitter falling-out on the march, though their journals supply little evidence of this. While rest and a fuller diet may have been all that Shackleton needed to return to health, Scott ordered him home a year early on the relief ship, against Shackleton's protests and those of the second-in-command.

Despite the late night, I take my usual seat up in the library at dawn. I'm supposed to be writing, though it seems enough this morning to stare out at the ghostly shapes of the surrounding bergs. "You never forget your first one," Stefan had told me, on the night we set sail from Ushuaia. But I don't know. So much of my past has simply floated away, the structure of my life like that of a ball game, too many innings sectioned off into lineups of home and away. Wasn't I supposed to be further along than this by now? Stitching together people and places to be—one day, perhaps—a chapter, a foothold, a life.

Some say your past is everything you've failed to be. Some say that Shackleton wept on his return home, that already he was hatching a plan to return to the ice. Wilson, for his part, turned his attention back to the emperor penguins—reading everything he could get his hands on that winter, devising his own theories, concocting his own ambitious plans. And when his spring trip to the rookery at Cape Crozier proved too late in the season to find live eggs, he was not dismayed, even knowing then what a harrowing task obtaining such specimens would entail.

A party of three at least, with full camp equipment, should traverse about a hundred miles of the Barrier surface in the dark and should, by moonlight, cross over with rope and axe the immense pressure ridges which form a chaos of crevasses.[35]

Obsession, through which most that has been memorably done was conceived. It seems so easy at times to not risk that part of yourself—to not wager it all on your own doubtful vision of your work. Wilson must have felt he was called by God to attempt such an unlikely feat—and the rest of us?

The whole work no doubt would be full of difficulty, but it would not be quite impossible.[36]

CHAPTER 5

TERRA NOVA

(1910–1912)
WINTER JOURNEY

APSLEY CHERRY-GARRARD

Polar exploration is at once the cleanest and most isolated way of having a bad time which has been devised. It is the only form of adventure in which you put on your clothes at Michaelmas and keep them on until Christmas, and, save for a layer of the natural grease of the body, find them as clean as though they were new.[1]

Being a kind, considerate, and about equally impoverished friend, Eric offers to turn my laundry in under his free account. Now, and for years after (I don't shop much), the inside tag on the lining of my shirts/pants/ underwear will all have "Guth" scrawled across them in permanent pen. An excessive reminder of my old pal's generosity as I step each morning into my clothes. But as the author of the above passage would no doubt claim, there are far more consequential ways to feel yourself marked by those with whom you've traveled.

Apsley Cherry-Garrard—known by all simply as "Cherry"—was the heir of English landed gentry, and an Oxford graduate with a degree in classics. In many ways, he would have felt at ease among the luxury crowd of our ship—well educated, born into money, with a conservative and entitled worldview. Aware that on sledge journeys each man would have to take a turn as the cook, Cherry—who had been waited on his entire life—panicked, making a rare foray into the kitchen of his estate to receive a lesson before setting sail. The two and a half years he spent on his journey south, however, would change him utterly from the sheltered man he was, and—in several ways—haunt him for the rest of his life.

Over eight thousand people applied to join Scott's second expedition on board the *Terra Nova*. Scott's old comrade-turned-rival Ernest Shackleton had returned from Antarctica the year before to a hero's welcome. His was an expedition of bold firsts and farthests—an ascent up Mt. Erebus, a sledge journey to the South Magnetic Pole, and, most importantly, the discovery and traverse of the Beardmore Glacier that got his four-man team of man-haulers within one hundred miles of the geographic pole. In addition to all of this, Shackleton had turned the Antarctic into a commercial venture—promoting his expedition in books, lectures, newspapers; he even turned his ship, the *Nimrod*, into a makeshift museum and charged admission. Volunteering for an Antarctic voyage had never been so enticing, so likely to result in fame and prestige—especially with the continent's biggest prize so clearly within reach. Cherry's application was initially rejected, as he had no relevant training or experience, but when Cherry offered a £1,000 donation all the same (the equivalent of about £75,000 today), the gesture caught the attention of Scott, especially as Cherry had the personal backing of Scott's right-hand man, Edward Wilson. At twenty-four, Cherry was one of the youngest of the crew, and had been enlisted, on Wilson's discretion, as the "assistant zoologist." It was a running joke among the officers that Cherry had earned this title because he knew a lot of Latin. By the end, however, Cherry wound up sledging more than any of them—three thousand miles, all told—more even than the four men who were selected by Scott to accompany him to the pole.

When I went South I never meant to write a book: I rather despised those who did so as being of an inferior brand to those who did things and said nothing about them.[2]

A hesitant though exceptionally capable writer, Cherry took ten years to pen his account of the *Terra Nova* expedition. This was after he had been invalidated from World War I, where, among other ailments, he suffered a brief psychotic episode. Battling depression for the remainder of his life, and what—in contemporary terms—was likely post-traumatic stress disorder, Cherry claimed, "My own writing is my own despair."[3] And his book—the best ever written about the South—reads as much like a testament to friendship and personal loss as it does an explorer's tale. *The Worst*

Journey in the World—whose title was suggested by Cherry's neighbor and first reader, the esteemed Irish playwright George Bernard Shaw—benefits from the split-self nature of its narrative. We are given both Cherry as a young man experiencing the often unnerving events that take place, and the older man reflecting back with clear regrets and a great deal of affection. Whereas the majority of explorers' accounts often wind up sounding like a victory speech, Cherry's tone is less certain and more rewarding than that; what he gives us are the layers and contradictions of a narrator struggling to make peace with his past.

There is after the event a good deal of criticism, of stock-taking, of checking of supplies and distances and so forth that cannot really be done without first-hand experience. Out there we knew what was happening to us too well; but we did not and could not measure its full significance.[4]

This morning I have breakfast with Roommate Bill. I can tell he has been feeling lonely, and figure it is my place to try to help. First, he tells me about his wife, their two dogs. The longer he goes on, though, the clearer it becomes that there is something else he is talking around. From previous conversations I know he used to work for a cruise line such as this, centered in the Galapagos, that this was his connection with the hospitality supervisor and how he found his way on board. What he tells me now is that somewhere in that previous life he got a young woman pregnant, that he panicked and broke things off, never seeing her again. Years later, he tells me, he wrote to her—after she'd given birth to their son overseas, after he'd married and settled down in Seattle—because he wanted to pass on his contact information, in case their son ever wanted to get in touch. "I've never heard from him," he says, looking me squarely in the face. "In truth, I figure he's probably about your age."

This is a lot to take in, and from a man I can't particularly claim to know or like. The dining hall has pretty much cleared out by this time, and we are both sipping the last of our coffee and looking awkwardly out the big bay windows. Why is he telling me all of this? What is it I'm supposed to say in response? Maybe I should trade places with Eric, who has never met his father. Maybe the two of them could don bathrobes together and play catch all day on the foredeck. Though, in truth, I probably won't mention any of this to Eric, who recently tried to connect with his own father, sending him a letter after tracking him down online and seeing pictures of him with a family somewhere in the Midwest. Eric was raised alone, his mom never marrying. "What got me as much as anything," Eric told me, "was that I had a brother and sister I didn't even know." Eric also told me how many times he read over that letter, how seriously he took even the decision of what stamp to place on the envelope. And, as of yet, nothing—no response.

So many of the old explorers grew up without a father—Amundsen, Bowers, Oates, Frederick Cook—while others, through their early deaths, would leave behind children who would never know their own. I have not always been close to my father, though we are now, and I can't imagine what it will be like to continue on in the world after he is gone. Will I make some bold plan, change my life's course? It almost seems as though that's no longer fashionable in this day and age, though just as surely we can become orphaned, rudderless, unmoored.

Cherry, for his part, lost his father at the age of twenty-one. Major-General Apsley Cherry-Garrard had served with distinction in the Indian Mutiny and in the Kaffir and Zulu Wars in Africa, and it is thought that one of Cherry's motivations in journeying south was to somehow prove himself equal to his old man. Ever since he was a boy, Cherry suffered from crippling shortsightedness, which his father regarded as an insult to the family name, and which greatly limited his involvement in sports. He was a rower though, and he had a slight but muscular build that lent itself to the hard work of sledging. In the year after his father's death, Cherry met Wilson—a fatherly figure without a son, who took him under his wing from the outset. Of Cherry, during their first year down south, Wilson wrote, "I really never have seen anyone with such a constant expression of 'this is what I have been looking for' on his face."[5] Scott recognized this as well, giving the young man his own stamp of approval: "Cherry-Garrard has won all hearts; he shows himself ready for any sort of hard work and is always to the front when the toughest jobs are on hand. He is the most unselfish, kind-hearted fellow, and will be of the greatest use to the Expedition."[6]

In the six years since the *Discovery*'s homecoming, Scott's own life had seen drastic changes. He was returning to the ice as a new father, leaving behind a young wife and an infant son back in Britain. He had been married for less than two years, to a sculptress of some regard named Kathleen Bruce. Bold, independent, and pursued throughout her life by doting men, Kathleen had studied with Rodin in Paris, where she formed an exotic cohort of friends that included the avant-garde dancer and bohemian Isadora Duncan. Quite what Kathleen saw in the reserved and formal captain is something of a mystery, though Scott's journals do reveal an artistic disposition at times, and Cherry was not the only person to remark on a special aura he had, even as it spilled over into something of a judgment.

I have never known anybody, man or woman, who could be so attractive when he chose.... But few who knew him realized how shy and reserved the man was, and it was partly for this reason that he so often laid himself open to misunderstanding. Add to this that he was sensitive, femininely sensitive, to a degree which might be considered a fault.... He cried more easily than any man I have ever known.[7]

The characterization is so conflicted that you know it must be true, and that it was brooded on—an assessment of his captain that did not come easily. So little appeared easy to Scott, certainly not in regard to this second expedition. Before they even got to the ice there were tensions among the crew, there were financial troubles, and their small ship was so overloaded and ill-equipped for the high seas that it almost capsized during a tremendous storm.

Upon their arrival in McMurdo Sound in early January, the men set out to construct new lodging. Scott's *Discovery* hut was still standing, about fifteen miles to the south of where they landed at Cape Evans, but its location out at Hut Point had caused the ship problems with ice, and it was never a structure intended to be fully inhabitable for winter. The new hut then would have to be big enough to house all thirty-four members of the Shore Party, and it would need superior insulation and lighting. Prefabricated in London, the hut was fifty by twenty-five feet, and was insulated with quilted seaweed. A line of crates was erected down the middle to serve as a bulkhead between the quarters of the officers and men. While half of the party set to fixing up the Evans Hut for winter, a group of twelve would use the *Discovery* hut as their outpost base for setting up a series of depots on the Barrier for the following spring. Access between the two huts would be difficult until the sound froze over, hopefully in March, so the Depot Party brought supplies to last them six weeks. In the end, they would be gone for twice that long, living off seal, penguin, and an odd collection of leftover stores. The hut leaked on them constantly, and the blubber stove had no outlet, filling the interior with acrid smoke. When the men finally returned to Cape Evans, they had not bathed in over three months.

Those Hut Point days would prove some of the happiest in my life. Just enough to eat and keep us warm, no more—no frills nor trimmings: there is many a worse and more elaborate life.... The luxuries of civilization satisfy only those wants which they themselves create.[8]

I've never lived in a hut for week after week with a dozen men, though I have lived in the backcountry before. Far from the ends of the earth, though still off-grid, in an abandoned mining town in Oregon. There I taught science for a season and came to think of that remote watershed as my second home. *No frills nor trimmings*, just a handful of people working together for a common cause, surrounded by a beautiful wilderness. As I lay down each night on the loft mattress of my one-room cabin, listening to the woodstove crackling beneath me, it was easy to dream of a worse and more elaborate life. Though, like Cherry too I suppose, I left that place before I was ready. I'd been offered a college teaching position back east, and—at the time—it seemed too good an opportunity to pass up. I've often wondered since, however, whether the real opportunity wasn't right there, in the simple and joyous life that I was leaving.

When to the beautiful tints in the sky and the delicate shading on the snow are added perhaps the deep colours of the open sea, with reflections from the ice foot and ice-cliffs in it, all brilliant blues and emerald greens, then indeed a man may realize how beautiful this world can be, and how clean.[9]

Fog, unfortunately, is what we've been gifted with today, and it has been a long morning of waiting around, hoping the weather will clear for the day's venture ashore. We are at Neko Harbor on the Danco Coast, which, Eric assures me, is one of the most beautiful locations of the entire peninsula, and a chance for us to go on more of a hike. Everything is still socked in, however, when we file into the mud room to disembark. Kendra is in her usual place with a clipboard in hand—a little hungover perhaps, though still smiling as we waddle up in our small orange inflatables.

The Depot Journey gave Scott a chance to evaluate the men under his charge, as well as the gear and animals. Shackleton's Pole Team had not taken dogs or skis, relying on pony transport instead to traverse the Barrier. While Scott chose to diversify his mode of transport—bringing both a small number of dogs and skis, in addition to three motor tractors that wound up contributing little—Scott had chosen, largely, to follow Shackleton's lead, placing his greatest trust in horsepower. Manchurian ponies had been successful at transporting heavy loads in northern China, and they performed significantly better for both Shackleton and Scott than had the *Discovery*'s poorly cared for dogs. Still, they were tragically unfit for the Antarctic. Sweating through their hides, the ponies froze easily on the march, and the combination of their great bulk and small hoofs led them to frequently break through the crust of the Barrier and sink into soft snow or fall into lidded crevasses. At each camp, Scott's men would build walls out of snow blocks to help shelter the sad, tethered beasts from the biting wind. Dogs, on the other hand, would simply bury themselves in the drift, and could therefore travel earlier and later into the season, when temperatures began to drop. As a result, Scott couldn't hope to leave for the pole before the start of November, at least three weeks later than dogs could travel. Scott knew this when he built his plans around ponies; what he never suspected was that he'd find himself involved in a race. In any case, Shackleton had made clear that, in his estimate, neither dogs nor ponies could hope to navigate the crevasse-ridden route up the Beardmore Glacier. The hope, then, was to get them as far as that (roughly four hundred miles), and to make this happen they needed to form a supply line of stores, ideally out to the eightieth parallel, where they aimed to leave their massive One Ton Depot. A three-day blizzard wreaked havoc on this plan, however, resulting in the death of two ponies.

As the expedition's only experienced horseman, the young soldier Titus Oates was placed in charge of the ponies. Unfortunately, he had nothing to do with their selection, which had been mismanaged back in Siberia, and had led Oates to describe the group upon first laying eyes on them as a "most unsuitable scrap-heap crowd of unfit animals."[10] Oates was all in favor of pushing on for the last forty miles to reach eighty degrees south, killing off the weaker animals, and depoting their meat, but Scott figured they had gotten close enough and didn't want to sacrifice animals that he might need in the spring. In the end, it was Scott's call, and they dumped their stores and headed back toward base.

Coming to shore, we can barely see anything beyond the rocky outcropping where a small band of gentoos putter about. There is a bird's-eye view available for those willing to hike up a large bluff of snow and ice. Or, rather, there would be under better conditions, and there is some discussion over whether it makes sense to continue on. Personally, I feel so restless that I would gladly hike off a cliff if it promised a little exercise.

Scott's attentions on the Depot Journey were all centered on their summer trek to the pole, but Wilson had his own strange voyage to plan for:
the midwinter trip to the emperor rookery at Cape Crozier. Of this venture—"the weirdest bird's-nesting expedition that has ever been or will
be"—Scott was rightly apprehensive, though he had promised to not stand
in his friend's way.[11] In the end, Wilson offered a rather straightforward
explanation for his selection of companions: "The two I like best of all our
party."[12] In addition to Cherry, this included a Scottish lieutenant by the
name of Henry Bowers. Described by one historian as "goblin-like," Bowers was 5'4" tall, with red hair and a pink face, though he was also a man of
immense strength.[13] Early on in the expedition he had fallen nineteen feet
into the ship's hold, and his muted reaction—he simply stood up, retrieved
his hat, and got back to work—solidified his standing among the men. According to Cherry, Bowers had "few doubts and no fears," and he had inherited a love of seafaring from his father, who died when Bowers was just
four.[14] Bowers was deeply loyal to his widowed mother and two elder sisters, writing them long letters from all corners of the globe. In one letter,
written when he was stationed in the Persian Gulf, Bowers spoke of the joy
he found in sifting through explorer accounts of the Antarctic: "If only they
will leave the South Pole itself alone for a bit they may give me a chance,"
he wrote, then adding as a footnote, "Don't laugh."[15] In truth, it was hard
not to laugh at Bowers, who had been given the nickname "Birdie" due to
his beaked nose. Yet this initial laughter only provided him the opportunity to prove how wrong people were. Bowers was originally signed on as
the ship's storekeeper, but he secured a place with the Shore Party through
his indefatigable work rate and cheerful demeanor. At twenty-seven years
of age, he bunked in "the nursery," along with Cherry and the youngest officers. "There was nothing subtle about him," as Cherry wrote. "He was
transparently simple, straightforward and unselfish."[16] He was also intensely religious, which must have appealed to Wilson on a personal level.
And if there was any doubt, Bowers was given the opportunity to prove his
bravery and coolheadedness during a mishap on their way back from laying the depots.

*"Cherry, Crean, we're floating out to sea," was the startling awakening from
Bowers, standing in his socks outside the tent at 4.30 a.m.*[17]

A party of Cherry, Bowers, and Petty Officer Thomas Crean had camped
out on the sea ice with four of the remaining ponies en route to Hut Point.

They woke in the middle of a maze of broken-up ice, heaving with the swell, and drifting dangerously out to the Ross Sea. One of the ponies was lost already, a dark streak of water showing where the ice had opened up directly under him while they slept. With Bowers leading, the party jumped across floes when they could, using one of their two sledges as a bridge between drifts when necessary, and working their way slowly to the fast ice of the Barrier. Making matters worse, several killer whales began lurking nearby, spying a potential meal. After six hours of laboring, the party had managed to get close to shore, though a thirty-foot lane of water still separated them from safety. "For my own part," Bowers later wrote in a letter to his mother, "I must say that the abandoning of the ponies was the one thing that had never entered my head."[18] Despite Bowers's best intentions, however, they would lose two more in the freezing water, unable to pull the thrashing beasts up on the ice as the killer whales encircled them. Bowers ended the life of the second pony, striking it with a pick-axe to spare it the torture of being drowned or eaten alive. By the time all parties returned to Hut Point, six of the eight ponies they had set out with had met their end, and only ten remained for next season's sledge to the pole. While the trip itself had hardly been a success, in the relative warmth and comforts of their winter quarters, the men could reflect back on their misadventures, harboring a confidence in themselves that was hardly warranted.

But now the Barrier comes back to us, with its clean, open life, and the smell of the cooker, and its soft sound sleep. So much of the trouble of this world is caused by memories, for we only remember half.[19]

At this moment, in regard to my own party, we are only seeing half, or less than that, as a dozen of us follow Eric and another naturalist uphill. Our route has taken us inland, as a high frequency of calvings off the nearest glacier make the coastline perilous. With visibility at less than twenty yards, we are urged to stick together. I am hiking alongside an outgoing couple named John and Loie. They must be in their early seventies, though they seem in great shape. It turns out they live in Colorado and that John worked as the program director of Outward Bound for a number of years. We discuss some of our favorite backpacking trips all over the West, and clearly the two of them have gone on a lot of these together. Loie mentions how glad she is to finally get to Antarctica after hearing her husband talk about it all these years.

The danger of half-remembering an event, I suppose, is that it can blind you to the harshness of the actual experience. Repeatedly, in *The Worst Journey in the World*, Cherry acknowledges our collective predisposition toward nostalgia, but rather than correcting that impulse, he delves further into its midst. As his biographer notes, Cherry's whole book is, in many ways, an attempt to redeem his losses through elevating the past.[20] He had come back to Britain a changed man, facing a rapidly changing country. The whole world, as he was to claim, "was losing its ancient faiths without having much to put in their place."[21] Having little else to offer, Cherry gives us this narrative, his half-remembered tale. But another common trouble of memory and storytelling lies in the opposite direction— that rather than arriving at only half a story, one can often find that a tale has calved or splintered into several more. You might set out with every intention of relaying a faithful account, of keeping things manageable in scope, only to find that your stories keep multiplying, and that each fractured berg feels worthy of attention.

Back in Britain, Scott had to scrounge everywhere for funds, going so far as to solicit "sponsorships" from school groups for individual dogs and ponies. More than funding a specific animal, however, those kids were sponsoring a narrative that they trusted to unfold—no doubt, one with a happier ending—but the Antarctic unfolds its own endings, despite the best intentions of schoolboys and writers.

On June 27, six days after the Winter Solstice, Wilson, Cherry, and Bowers set off for Cape Crozier—almost seventy miles away. They started out on a new moon, hoping to count on the extended moonlight later in their trip, when they'd be sledging into country far less known. Too cold for dogs or ponies, the three men pulled sledges totaling 750 pounds. Before setting out, Bowers had improvised a ridiculous hat with extensions to protect his long nose from the cold, and while Cherry did suffer from an early bout of frostbite after briefly removing his fur mitts to better pull up a steep grade, the party had reason for optimism, having traveled twenty miles in the first two days. Over the next two weeks, however, they would manage no better than three miles in a day. Temperatures dropped to negative seventy-seven degrees, colder than ever previously recorded, and this wrecked the ice surface, forming sandy crystals that slowed the sledge runners and forced them to relay their two sledges as a team. It took them forty-five minutes to chip away at the ice of their sleeping bags each night just to get inside, and over an hour the next morning to don their boots—making sure to have let them freeze, as nearly as possible, into the shape of their feet before turning in. Upon their attempt to cut the butter they carried as part of their provisions, it shattered like glass.

Given that Cherry was essentially blind without his glasses, which he could not wear while sledging, he fell repeatedly into crevasses, even when the others did their best to point them out to him. "Almost with gentleness those two men led on," Cherry wrote. "I just did what I was told."[22] On July 5, they advanced a total of only one and a half miles after eight exhausting hours of work. Wilson and Cherry were both tormented constantly by the cold—struggling with frostbite, with their inability to sleep—while Bowers proved so resilient to the low temperatures that people have gone on to reference him in official studies in medical journals.

The horror of the nineteen days it took us to travel from Cape Evans to Cape Crozier would have to be re-experienced to be appreciated; and any one would be a fool who went again: it is not possible to describe it. The weeks which followed them were comparative bliss, not because later our conditions were better—they were far worse—but because we were callous. I for one had come to that point of suffering at which I did not really care if only I could die without much pain.[23]

What had seemed, at first, a foolish undertaking for our group, starts to pan out as we climb higher up the ridge to where the fog is rapidly thinning. We level off on a plateau, and everyone fans out to take in the view. Inland, the jagged skyline of the peninsula range drifts in and out of the low-lying clouds, and the tranquil bay far below us occasionally comes into focus. The water appearing so dark it is almost black in the face of so much white. Around me, I watch the blue-coated guests ghosting in and out of the haze, and spot Eric crouching down with his camera. If anything, this patchwork of fog enhances what is already an eerie and remarkable place.

It was the darkness that did it. I don't believe minus seventy temperatures would be bad in daylight, not comparatively bad, when you could see where you were going, where you were stepping, where the sledge straps were, the cooker, the primus, the food; could see your footsteps lately trodden deep into the soft snow that you might find your way back to the rest of your load; could see the lashings of the food bags; could read a compass without striking three or four different boxes to find one dry match.... Generally

*we steered by Jupiter, and I never see him now without recalling his friend-
ship in those days.*[24]

By the time the exhausted explorers arrived on a windswept moraine at
the edge of Cape Crozier—still high above the rookery, and at the base of
Mount Terror—their real work could finally begin. Wilson planned to process the eggs onsite, before the embryos had time to freeze, and for this
they set out to build a rough igloo of banked snow and stone on the lee
side of a ridge to help shield them from the wind. The task took all day
to complete, as the hard-blown snow was nearly impossible to work with
and rocks were in short supply. The next morning, they finished off their
igloo by securing a canvas roof, tying it down with rocks and covering it
with slabs of hard snow. By that point, there were about four hours in the
middle of each day that offered a faint glimmer of light in the sky, so they
set off at the first sign of twilight to reach the rookery. Already pushing the
limits of their endurance, they had to traverse a crevasse-ridden pressure
ridge along the edge of the Barrier that was more difficult than any they
had seen. To navigate this stretch in complete darkness would be all but
impossible, and they had left their tent and sleeping gear behind. Somewhere below and beyond, they could hear the emperors' calls echoing
off the cliffs. They had taken too long and would have to try again in the
morning. On their second attempt, after repeatedly falling into crevasses
and climbing over steep hummocks that required the slow labor of cutting
steps, they got to the ice foot overlooking the sea ice, where they could look
down at the rookery a few hundred yards away.

*After indescribable effort and hardship we were witnessing a marvel of the
natural world, and we were the first and only men who had ever done so;
we had within our grasp material which might prove of the utmost importance to science; we were turning theories into facts with every observation
we made,—and we had but a moment to give.*[25]

So much of Antarctic travel has had, as its focus, some famous first—from
sighting to landing, from wintering to summiting. While the Cape Crozier
team could boast of similar feats, this was no seventh continent or trip to
the pole, and their motivations laid somewhere other than ego and fame.
What they craved was knowledge, a furthering of our understanding of the
world and our place in it. They believed—or at least Wilson did, and the
others placed their belief in him—that the evolutionary answers that were
sought lay in the almost inaccessible egg of a winter-nesting penguin, and

they had put their lives at the greatest risk to reach them. At most, they were messengers, bit-part scientists aiming to prove another's theory correct. Yet here they were at the summit of their hopes. It is impossible to know, in that moment, how heavily that view weighed on their eyes.

The sun has come fully into view for us now, and the ship and surrounding bergs glow brightly in the distance. Across the bay, we can see out as far as Mt. Francois, forming the summit of Anvers Island—the tallest point of the peninsula at over nine thousand feet. One of the things I keep being struck by down here is how rich the landscape is in color variations, even when the palette is all grays, blues, and whites. Closer in, cracks in the glacier wall on the south side of this inlet reveal a crystalline turquoise that feels lifted out of another world, the density of the ice absorbing every other color of the spectrum. Eric lowers his camera and smiles back at me. The fog may have lifted, but we all walk about in a sort of blissful daze. Eventually, I come across Loie, who is standing over her husband seated on the snow. John has taken his jacket off and is sitting on it, tying it oddly around his feet as a kind of makeshift sled. Like a wrinkled and gray-haired seven-year-old, he is staring down a big hill of hard-packed snow. Loie gives him a push, and he picks up real speed over the next fifty or so yards before the slope levels out and he flops over playfully on his side. Loie defers, both of us laughing now, as I sit down in John's track and do my best to improvise a similar contraption. I size up the route down and get ready to push off. *Is my hood on?* Loie gives me a nudge and I race down.

It is extraordinary how often angels and fools do the same thing in this life, and I have never been able to settle which we were on this journey.[26]

Of all penguins, emperors alone incubate their eggs on sea ice in winter. The female lays a single egg then passes it on, almost immediately, to the male, who will carry it in a brood pouch above his toes for over two months. If the female does not leave to feed, she will die. But time is of the essence, and if she stays away too long, the egg will be abandoned, as the starving male reaches his own breaking point.

What dim light there was for the three friends had already started to fade, and there was still a tricky route down to reach the rookery. Cherry stayed on top with the rope, as Wilson and Bowers downclimbed the ice wall and infiltrated the penguins. They worked fast, skinning three penguins for blubber and collecting five eggs. Cherry helped to pull them up in the midday twilight and they turned back toward camp. The two eggs that Cherry was entrusted with both broke in his fur mitts as they navigated over the maze of pressure ridges—the first egg emptied onto the snow, though he kept the other clutched in his mitt for the cooker. It was so dark by the end that they had to feel their way back on hands and knees over the crevasses as a storm blew in.

This I know: we on this journey were already beginning to think of death as a friend. As we groped our way back that night, sleepless, icy, and dog-tired in the dark and the wind and the drift, a crevasse seemed almost a friendly gift.[27]

With great difficulty they got the blubber stove to work, though it shot a blob of oil into Wilson's eye that left him temporarily blinded and in great pain. They were in no condition to process the three remaining eggs just then and began the nightly work of thawing their slow way into sleeping bags. They woke, if they ever got to sleep, to a howling wind that was ripping away at their canvas roof. They had banked their tent beside the stone hut loaded with gear but the following morning they were devastated to find it had somehow flown away. How they would ever manage to get back to Cape Evans without a tent was almost too terrifying to consider, but there was no way they could go out and look for it then, or even attempt to further secure the hut's billowing roof, while the blizzard raged. On July 23, which happened to be Wilson's thirty-ninth birthday—"quite the funniest birthday I have ever spent," he would write afterward—the roof finally gave out, ripping into tatters while the stones holding it into place rained down on them.[28] There was nothing else to do but burrow deep into their bags and let the snow drift over them for warmth.

Down at the bottom of the hill I dust the snow off and stand next to John.

"Do you know how to yodel?" he turns and asks me.

"Haven't a clue." I say.

"Well, mine is pretty good, and I like to give it a go every now and then when I'm in the right mood. Would you mind?"

Of course I don't. And then he lets loose—a long and beautiful sound.

The next I knew was Bowers's head across Bill's body. 'We're all right,' he yelled, and we answered in the affirmative. Despite the fact that we knew we only said so because we knew we were all wrong, this statement was helpful. Then we turned our bags over as far as possible, so that the bottom of the bag was uppermost and the flaps were more or less beneath us. And we lay and thought, and sometimes we sang.[29]

Somehow Cherry, Wilson, and Bowers managed to wait out the storm— shouting reassurances to one another through the dark and opening the flaps of their bags occasionally to press small clumps of snow in their mouths to melt. Somehow, the following day, Bowers stumbled upon the still-functional tent at the bottom of a nearby hill. "Our lives had been taken away and given back to us," Cherry wrote.[30] And though the constant shivering shattered most all of Cherry's teeth, and they were so exhausted that they each fell asleep while pulling in their traces, the three men survived the eight-day trip back to Cape Evans. Did science demand this of them? Did history? What moral can be derived? What knowledge or hope? That they endured? That they believed enduring this would prove of some lasting worth? Back at Crozier, Bowers had even wanted to have another go at the rookery, seeing as how the eggs had long since frozen in the storm, but Wilson overruled him, recognizing that they had been defeated, and that the younger men's lives were in his charge.

We did not forget the Please and Thank You, which means much in such circumstances, and all the little links with decent civilization which we could still keep going. I'll swear there was still a grace about us when we staggered in. And we kept our tempers—even with God.[31]

Two photographs. In the first, taken just outside the hut at Cape Evans, as the three men were preparing to set off on their journey, they all look slightly preposterous in their polar garb—the oversized fur gloves and finnesko boots, the outer layer that trapped in sweat, transforming their clothes into an icy armor as they sledged. Wilson stands in the center, arms akimbo, calmly assured of the voyage at hand. Being the most experienced of the group, he could entertain no illusions as to the difficulty of their task, yet his gaze looks light and untroubled, his mien betraying no ego, no overconfidence, just a sure faith in the dignity of what they will pursue. To his left stands Bowers, clearly the soldier of the group—unquestioning, unshakeable. He looks like a man who is used to taking orders, and always making sure to follow through. While both of them look straight at the camera, Cherry's eyes stray off to the side. He looks so young, child-ish really. And it is no embellishment to identify a hint of fear in his ex-pression, as though something unknown has startled him from beyond the picture's frame. In the second photograph—taken five weeks later upon their return, as they are seated at their first meal back at base—there is no longer any pose or artifice. The other men had to pry off their clothes with can openers; Cherry's garments alone weighed twenty-four pounds. Here, Bowers is at the center, lifting a large mug greedily to his face, and hunched over what, I'm imagining, must be his third or fourth helping. By all accounts he had fared best—with the cold, with the sledging and ex-haustion. The task complete, he is now recharging. Not even a full day re-moved from the journey and already he talks of attempting the feat again next winter to get more eggs. Seated to his right is Wilson—the farthest back of the three, occupying the corner of the table. Shadowed, dressed in black, his face darkened with the soot of the cooker, he looks half there, at most, even as he gazes somewhere near the camera's lens. Though it is hard to be certain, there appears to be a faint glimmer of a smile—the grin of a proper mystic. Somehow, he viewed the whole terrifying journey as a divine blessing, believing that God watched over their every step. Finally, in the foreground, there is Cherry—his face hollowed out, cadaverous. His hands are clearly swollen and misshapen from frostbite, as they gently lift his half-eaten meal from his plate. With him, there can be no false assur-ances, no firm belief in a benevolent spirit, no illusion that the toils they've suffered could ever be repaid. He looks as though, after the photograph is finally taken, he could turn back silently to his meal, or else break fully into tears.

As we began to gather our gear together to pack up for the last time, Bill said quietly, "I want to thank you two for what you have done. I couldn't have found two better companions—and what is more I never shall."

    I am proud of that.[32]

Later on, after we've returned to the ship and gotten cleaned up, I feel a hunger I haven't felt in days—thankful for that bit of exercise and for the fortunes that have somehow aligned to put me here in this place. That evening, just like all the others, we eat rich food and drink good wine, we laugh and make small talk, but when we gather afterward in the lounge for the day's recap, Kendra walks up and tells me I've been requested in the mud room.

In the last chapter of Cherry's book—titled, properly, "Never Again"—after having detailed the hardships of the following spring, the second winter, the Search Journey, and the discovered fate of the Pole Team, Cherry forces himself to arrive at some conclusion—a judgment, even, on the expedition as a whole. He does not shirk the task of identifying its tragic shortcomings. Nonetheless, the book ends stubbornly in the affirmative. He is mining back through the material of his life, searching for a silver lining, for some redemptive trace of gold.

And I tell you, if you have the desire for knowledge and the power to give it physical expression, go out and explore. . . . Some will tell you that you are mad, and nearly all will say, "What is the use?" For we are a nation of shopkeepers, and no shopkeeper will look at research which does not promise him a financial return within a year. And so you will sledge nearly alone, but those with whom you sledge will not be shopkeepers: that is worth a good deal.[33]

We have stolen a boat. Or, rather, Eric has, with the help of Kendra, and I am along for the ride. The bay is chock full of small bergs gleaming in the low sun. Eric guides us between them, up close enough to see the striated patterns, the blue-green sunken masses shining beneath. These bergs are all lopsided with melting—slump-shouldered or swaybacked—and so always liable to overturn. The protocol with guests is to keep a safe distance, but Eric is taking photographs, drifting the Zodiac into place to line up his shots. The ice shapes are all so varied—some are gnarled claws or hanging garrets, some almost look spun from a potter's wheel of ice. Until now, the Zodiac rides have always felt so cramped and filled with strange voices, but we sit mostly in silence, like countless nights in the backcountry, in no hurry to reclaim our place on the busy ship.

The evolutionary theory of recapitulation, which served as the inspiration to the Winter Journey, was soon discarded. When Cherry, upon his return to London, hand-delivered the three pirated eggs to the Natural History Museum, the specimens were, at first, refused. It was another thirty years before the eggs were properly analyzed, with the scientist's conclusion being that "they did not greatly add to our understanding of penguin embryology."[34] In 1939, now in his mid-fifties, Cherry married a young nurse who would help him through his battles with depression and multiple nervous breakdowns. Seeking alternative treatment, Cherry underwent psychoanalysis, and—later—electroshock therapy. There were bright patches for the two of them, sometimes lasting for years at a time, though Cherry always slipped back. Fearing that some of his struggles with mental illness could be passed down, the couple decided against having children.

Afterward, I help Eric and Kendra store the boat inside, and then the three of us watch the last stray colors of twilight before closing up the hatch.

CHAPTER 6

FRAM
(1910–1912)

CAPTAIN ROALD AMUNDSEN

Fram, the Norwegian word for "forward," was no doubt a fitting name for a vessel with a captain such as Roald Amundsen—proud and plainspoken, a man driven by an uncompromising desire for conquest and fame. As a university student, Amundsen barely attended lectures, and received poor grades, but after his mother's death freed him from expectations of a dependable career, the young man quickly turned to pursue his dreams of polar adventure. At twenty-five, Amundsen jumped at the chance to serve on de Gerlache's *Belgica* expedition. While despair hung over the majority of that crew throughout their time in the south, an entry in his journal, penned in the depths of winter, states confidently, "This is the life I have always wished for."[1] Soon after Amundsen returned to Norway, he fixed his gaze back on the far north, a region that had mesmerized him since childhood, when he first read of the hardships common to such exploits.

A strange ambition burned within me to endure those same sufferings. Perhaps the idealism of youth, which often takes a turn toward martyrdom, found its crusade in me in the form of Arctic exploration. I, too, would suffer in a cause—not in the blazing desert on the way to Jerusalem, but in the frozen North on the way to new knowledge in the unpierced unknown.[2]

Overnight, we shift our own attention to the north—at least, sixty miles in that direction—as we sail to the South Shetlands: a chain of eleven windswept islands, 80 to 90 percent of which are still covered by glaciers.

These islands were given their name by homesick Scottish sealers who recognized in these treeless lands some token similarity to their homeland. William Smith, back in 1819, deviated from his route south of Cape Horn, and stumbled upon the island chain—the first land confirmed south of sixty degrees latitude—and returned later that year to claim possession for Britain. It seems so simple to write it out that way, as though *arrival* was somehow synonymous with *ownership*, as if to *visit* also meant—in some quantifiable sense—to *claim*.

The next morning, I find myself seated at breakfast with the away-school family.

"This sure beats PTA meetings and shuttling between tee-ball practice," the dad says with a chuckle. "Here, take one of my cards."

"Thanks."

This guy has already given me one of his cards, though I feel awkward to tell him that. Additionally, it looks very much as though his son would benefit from some time playing team sports. The kid must be ten or eleven, with a frail build and curly light blonde hair. He is quite pale, verging on sickly, as though—for all their travel—he doesn't spend a lot of time outdoors. I try to engage with him, but he seems content to stare down at his bowl of Cheerios. From the looks of things, all the genetic strikes going against the son may actually work out in the daughter's favor. She is slim, tallish, also blonde, and with a pretty face that mostly just stared off in the distance for the duration of our meal. I'd guess she is going on fourteen (I had the sense that the two of them had been asked their respective ages about every fifteen minutes since the ship left Ushuaia, so I avoided it as a conversation starter). In any case, she is likely at that age where she is starting to have some interest in dating—at least she would, if she were ever around people that weren't three or four times her age. Neither of the kids seems overjoyed to be here this morning, and, right now, I'd place the odds of them looking back fondly on these years, as opposed to forever resenting their parents for them, at about fifty-fifty. Their mother seems sweet and full of patience; I imagine she handles most of the hard, day-to-day duties of educating the kids, and that this whole familial travel-school setup was decidedly *not* her idea. Perhaps this sort of arrangement would have been ideal for a budding explorer like Amundsen, but I get the sense that these kids are already looking forward to the end of the day, when their mom will microwave them popcorn back in their room, and they'll sit together on their separate beds, watching some movie about normal-seeming but glamorous teenagers who have to maneuver among the perilous shoals of our public school system.

Back in more quaint times, successful navigation of a Northwest Passage had long been the dream of the shipping world, and the British pursuit of such a route had led to the tragedy of John Franklin's lost expedition in 1845. Their ice-locked ships were abandoned and the entire crew of 129 men perished, with evidence suggesting they may have resorted to cannibalism. The combined efforts of subsequent search parties basically traversed a route between the oceans, but there was still no single ship that had achieved the feat. Enter Amundsen, who always had an eye for opportunity. After purchasing the small fishing boat *Gjoa* and enlisting seven men with supplies enough to see out one winter, they departed in a driving rain under cover of darkness. (Amundsen was heavily in debt, and one of his creditors had threatened to derail the journey.) Three years later, having finally achieved this aim, after multiple seasons stuck in the ice, he was feted as a hero in his homeland. The English, on the other hand, were less impressed, reneging on a monetary reward that had once been promised to the first person to navigate the passage. In any case, Amundsen had made a name for himself, though he saw this as still only a stepping-stone for greater exploits.*

"The deity of success is a woman, and she insists on being won, not courted. You've got to seize her and bear her off, instead of standing under her window with a mandolin."[3]

We all know the maxim "Never judge a book by its cover," but we need not feel a similar obligation to withhold judgment when it comes to one's choice of an epigraph. The author of the above, American novelist Rex Beach—whom I have, mercifully, never read—has been labeled by critics of the day as being cut from the "he-man school" of literature, and his novels have been decried as "formulaic" and "predictable." In this, Amundsen has chosen a kindred spirit. One does not have to look hard to find a strain of machismo posturing throughout most firsthand explorer accounts, though some of the empurpled prose of Amundsen's two-volume, nearly one-thousand-page chronicle of his trip to the South Pole deserves special mention.

* While explorers had sought out a navigable passage for centuries, eighty years of global warming have reduced Arctic sea ice to such an extent that ships can now regularly traverse the passage without difficulty.

But what does the dazzling day to the south conceal? Inviting and attrac-
tive the fair one lies before us. Yes, we hear you calling, and we shall come.
You shall have your kiss, if we pay for it with our lives.[4]

They didn't. In case you were wondering. Though this hardly serves as a
spoiler, seeing as how Amundsen tells us as much in the first paragraph
of his book, set under the shade of some tropical palm trees, "four months
since my gallant comrades and I reached the coveted spot."[5] The whole
book, in fact, reads like an overly long acceptance speech, replete with
groveling shout-outs to every Norwegian Tom, Dick, and Harry who was
met along the way.

Great praise is also due to the factories that supplied our tinned goods. By
their excellent and conscientious work they deserved well of the expedi-
tion. . . . I must also mention our paper-supply, which was in all respects
as fine and elegant as it could possibly be. . . . I do not remember if he [su-
perintendent of the dockyard] *got a cheer. If he did not, it was a mistake.*[6]

After breakfast, we steer into the tranquil harbor of Deception Island.
From a distance, the island—which is an active volcano—appears impenetrable, with steep rock walls dropping straight into the rough sea. On
its southeastern tip, however, a narrow section of the crater wall has collapsed, forming a quarter-mile passage between the basalt cliffs, flooding
into the heart of the caldera. The entrance was given the name of Neptune's Bellows by American sealer Nathaniel Palmer, who is credited with
its discovery. As a rule, sealers were extremely secretive about their findings, making it difficult to ascertain who went where first and when. In
any case, what Palmer stumbled upon is perhaps the safest anchorage in
all of Antarctica—a serene lake of seawater five miles long by three miles
wide, with a large black sand beach on the far shore. Deception Island
would serve as an essential base for commercial exploits in the far south
well into the next century. Two orcas knife playfully in and out of the water
ahead of us; the weather is rapidly clearing, and we will be spending the
whole glorious day here.

Beg leave to inform you proceeding Antarctica—Amundsen.[7]

This terse missive is likely the most infamous telegram ever sent in the history of exploration, and it reveals an elaborate deceit that had been over
a year in the making. Fresh off the success of his Northwest Passage ex-

pedition, Amundsen set to raising funds and securing a ship for an attempt at first claiming the North Pole. But when his old shipmate Frederick Cook and his rival Robert Peary each declared to have won those spoils in 1908–9, Amundsen secretly decided to reroute to the Antarctic. As was well known, Scott was already preparing his second massive expedition to the south, and Amundsen figured he stood little chance of gaining support from his backers for a rival enterprise that could upset diplomatic relations with Britain, so he confided his real destination only to his brother Leon. As luck would have it, his old plan to drift to the North Pole from west to east served as the perfect cover, as his expedition was already scheduled to round Cape Horn as part of their approach. This telegraph, then, was sent to Scott, who was still in Australia, from their last port of call—the remote Portuguese island of Madeira—thereby triggering a race of Amundsen's own devising, and forever linking their names in history.

Amundsen branded his telegram "a mark of courtesy" and defended the last-minute nature of it by declaring, "A few months sooner or later could be of no great importance."[8] The truth, however, was that for over a year now, Scott had been planning the logistics of his expedition with no idea that there would be a rival party aiming for the pole. Scott had even sought out Amundsen's counsel when he traveled to Norway the previous year, but Amundsen went to great lengths to make himself unavailable, presumably to avoid the troublesome task of lying to Scott's face. Now at his last stopover in Australia, there was little Scott could do (even if he had wanted to) to alter his plans for the prospect of a race to the pole. Sled dogs, for instance—of which Amundsen was bringing sixty-seven more of than Scott was—could be acquired only on the other side of the world. Seeking clarification on Amundsen's telegram, Scott sent a message to their mutual friend Fridtjof Nansen, receiving only the enigmatic response, "Unknown."[9]

Now that we were thus completely isolated from the outer world, the long-expected moment had arrived when I could proceed to inform all my comrades of my decision, now a year old, to make for the South. I believe all who were on board will long remember that sultry afternoon.[10]

I am sure some of the blame must be pinned on the English translator, but this is far from the only passage of Amundsen's book that winds up sounding like a dime-store romance novel—*the long-expected moment had arrived . . . will long remember that sultry afternoon.*

The story of Deception Island—at least the human one—is likewise full of greed and opportunism, along with a great deal of bloodshed. After the sealing industry collapsed on itself in the 1820s, there was a long-welcomed respite. But once the whalers established themselves in South Georgia in 1904, taking advantage of new technology and a virtually untouched population in the Southern Ocean, the carnage spilled over once again to this hidden sanctuary. Factory ships could now process whale oil with reasonable success, though this required a sheltered anchorage and a wealth of fresh water, both of which Deception offered. In truth, it is estimated that up to 40 percent of a whale's oil was lost through ship-processing, though this was never an industry committed to minimizing waste. In its heyday, as many as thirteen ships spent the season here, with hundreds of men residing in spartan and temporary shelters along the shore. A Norwegian company went so far as to establish an on-shore station in 1912, the remnants of which—rusting boilers and holding tanks—still litter the island.

When Amundsen arrived in Antarctica, he settled on the Bay of Whales for his base of operations. Shackleton had surveyed this ice harbor several years before, while on his *Nimrod* expedition, naming it after the large number of cetaceans they found in the area, though he thought the location too unstable to risk as a base. Having already visited the area several years before with Scott, Shackleton could tell that huge chunks of the Barrier's shoreline had since calved away. Amundsen, however, reasoned that this tract of the Barrier was actually grounded by small islands or shoals—as opposed to afloat, as Shackleton had assumed—and was therefore sufficiently secure. Amundsen got it about half right, which is to say that there is a small island further in, buried by the ice, but rather than protecting the Bay, this forms a junction of two separate ice systems, and the configurations of this feature are continuously changing. In fact, the Bay of Whales collapsed entirely in 1987 when an iceberg close to one hundred miles in length broke free. All the same, the advantages were worth the risk for Amundsen, who couldn't encroach on the British center of operations four hundred miles away in McMurdo Sound. Seventy years might be nothing in terms of geological time, but the prospect of the bay collapsing that winter was limited, and—unlike the British—Amundsen wasn't looking to establish a base for future exploits; all he was after was a one-time campsite. Most importantly, the Bay of Whales is the southernmost point of open ocean in the world and would give him a seventy-mile head start over Scott—albeit over uncharted terrain—in their race to the pole.

Every explorer has adventures. He gets a thrill out of them, and he takes pleasure in thinking back upon them. But he never goes about looking for them. Exploration is too serious a business.[11]

While Amundsen's claims of foresight and restraint often read like self-serving boasts, the whalers of the day saw no need to cover themselves in a righteous veneer. Clearly there were safer and less gory ways to eke out a living, so it was the adventure itself that drew them down here, with no regard for how history would later judge them. This may have been the Heroic Age of Antarctic exploration, but whatever heroism there once was in the early days of whaling had long been dispensed with. The hunt now was fully mechanized, with exploding harpoon heads and steam-powered catcher boats. No heathenish Queequegs or philosophizing Ishmaels here, just an industry hell-bent on slaughtering itself right out of business.

Fittingly, then, what looked strangely idyllic from across the bay appears more like a ghost town once we get to shore. Stacks of stones and large wooden crosses demark the abandoned cemetery, the largest in Antarctica, believed to hold thirty-five men. Sheets of corroded tin creak in the breeze, and a few ramshackle structures—the rotting wood that never belonged here anyway—still slump down in their century of obstinate decay. A series of eruptions in the 1960s led to the evacuation of a team of British scientists stationed here, leaving the remaining relics as little more than a playhouse for penguins.

After taking in the scene on the beach, a group of us hike up a slope of volcanic ash and snow to a famous viewpoint known as Neptune's Window. It is from here that Nathaniel Palmer made the dubious claim of first setting eyes on the continent, still sixty miles away. More than simply a bid for personal glory, the story is part of an intricate web of rival—and, at times, comically far-fetched—territorial claims. Britain, Argentina, and Chile all claim the South Shetland Islands for themselves, and each has gone to considerable lengths to assert their alleged sovereignty. Chilean scientists once argued that two arrowheads recovered on nearby King George Island prove that indigenous tribes from their homeland had long ago visited these shores, only for later outside research to suggest the artifacts had actually been planted. And here, on Deception Island, an Argentinean party visited in 1942, leaving signs and painted flags in an attempt to declare the island their own, only for the British—in true "did so, did not!" fashion—to come back the following year and remove them. Even Hitler decided at one point to join in the farcical territory scrum, ordering two planes to air drop thousands of steel-barbed swastikas across the sea ice of Queen Maud's Land to our east. By the 1950s, five-sixths of Antarctica had been claimed by rival nations, including many overlapping tracts of land. The establishment of the Antarctic Treaty, now ratified by fifty member nations, may have placed all such claims in abeyance, but nationalistic concerns continue to cast one of the largest shadows over the Antarctic.

The story of the rival expeditions of Amundsen and Scott would likewise be incomplete without first considering their respective nations—their culture and ambitions, their status and history. While Britain was still the largest empire on earth at the time, Norway had gained independence from Sweden only in 1905, and was in this way the epitome of the underdog. On the other hand, Norway's climate was obviously much closer to Antarctica's than England's. The men who sailed south with Amundsen were all highly skilled skiers, and many were expert dog drivers. They had, at their disposal, the expertise of Nansen—the most revered polar explorer of the day—who had long offered assistance to Amundsen, including loaning him *Fram*. And the Norwegians also had access to the wealth of knowledge regarding dress, travel, and food from their country's indigenous people, the Sami of the far north. Britain, of course, had its own lineage of polar explorers, though much of it—as shown clearly with the Franklin expedition—was riddled with tragedy and poor judgment.

A part of our equipment to which we gave special care was, of course, the ski; in all probability they would be our chief weapon in our upcoming fight. However much we might have to learn from Scott's and Shackleton's narratives, it was difficult for us to understand their statements that the use of ski on the Barrier was not a success.[12]

Much is made, by historical commentators, of the gulf in ability that separated the Norwegians from the British in regard to this piece of equipment—and certainly, while many of Scott's men became proficient skiers, they were no match for Amundsen's team. What is sometimes lost in this discussion, however, is how little skill is required to use skis in conjunction with heavy man-hauling. As the contemporary polar explorer and historian Ranulph Fiennes makes clear, "with loads, the entire business of technique and skill becomes superfluous. . . . Anybody, with a few hours' practice, can learn the simple plodding movement needed for heavy man-haul on or off skis."[13]

The size and scope of each expedition was also reflective of their comparative standings as nations. Scott's *Terra Nova* carried sixty-six men, thirty-four of them in the Shore Party, including more scientists than any prior Antarctic expedition had. Amundsen's *Fram*, on the other hand, carried all of nineteen passengers, with only nine men wintering in the Antarctic. Amundsen brought with him no scientists and no artists; even his camera broke on his way to the pole. While these differences reveal a great deal as to the available resources and infrastructure of each country, they also lay bare the singularity of purpose at the heart of Amundsen's enterprise. In short, the Norwegians came gunning for a race, but what the world stood to gain from their expedition beyond this was minimal.

The British expedition was designed entirely for scientific research. The Pole was only a side-issue, whereas in my extended plan it was the main object. On this little detour science would have to look after itself.[14]

Without question, in regard to the Antarctic, science has done just that, at levels that even the most ambitious early scientific pioneers would never have dreamed. Currently, there are 30 year-round research stations in Antarctica, with over 150 temporary scientific camps on top of that. The total population of the various bases swells to over four thousand during the summer months, with another thousand personnel doing onboard research in Antarctic waters. While numbers such as these may seem relatively small—and only a fraction of the quarter million tourists who visit annually—in many ways they represent a far bigger strain on the ecosystem.

Tourists, of course, spend the vast majority of their time on board ships, whereas scientific bases are, out of necessity, largely staked out on the limited ice-free terrain of the Antarctic, thereby presenting obstacles and direct competition for available nesting sites. Here in the South Shetlands, for instance, the most egregious example of habitat destruction is found in the 11 research stations that have been built on King George Island—a landmass of only 444 square miles, less than 10 percent of which is free of ice. These are no mom-and-pop research camps either, with the Chilean base functioning more as a village, with a four-and-a-half-mile-long airstrip, cafeterias, a bank, and a post office, as well as ranch-style family housing with satellite TV. The emphasis on *family* housing is important here, as Chile is one of the nations that has established the practice of flying pregnant women down to the South Shetlands to give birth, in hopes of strengthening their territorial claims. Other eyesores include China's nearby "Great Wall" base, which houses a full-size basketball court, and the sprawling heliport of the Argentine base, where the heavy-metal band Metallica recently performed. As the American scientist David Campbell puts it, "Parts of King George Island are rapidly becoming the urban slum of Antarctica." The worst hit, as Campbell goes on to report, has been the Fildes Peninsula, "where once there were extensive meadows of lichens and important breeding colonies of penguins."[15] This is one of the largest ice-free areas in all of Antarctica, and should have been protected as such according to terms of the Antarctic Treaty, though it now houses a half dozen international bases all its own.

I stand among strangers, peering out at a wide expanse of ocean and clouds—a view that has likely remained exactly the same since Nat Palmer first climbed up here over a century ago. A host of small petrels nestled on the cliff face take to the wing, fleeing our arrival. How in the world is there a basketball court anywhere near this majestic place? How does one look out at all of this and think of colonizing it for a distant empire? I hardly know what to think of my fellow travelers—this blue-coated tribe of the bourgeoisie—but at least they aren't here to kill or claim or build a ranch-style development.

With each base comes trash, of course, as well as sewage and other pollutants. Only three decades ago, the garbage of the U.S. base at McMurdo—the largest in all of Antarctica—was simply left out on the sea ice to await melting, forming what is still thought to be the most polluted bay of the planet. Such practices have since been curbed, along with burning, though the new policies of transporting all waste off the continent via plane and ship—while far better—still use high quantities of fossil fuels, especially when added to the already heavy transport demands of people and supplies throughout the region. Tourism may present an easy target, but it would be naïve to give science a free pass, especially when taking into account how rooted even the most important scientific pursuits in Antarctica are in the political world. The Antarctic Treaty may well declare that "no new claim, or enlargement of an existing claim to territorial sovereignty[,] . . . shall be asserted while the present Treaty is in force," but scientific bases go a long way to establishing squatters' rights—especially as demonstrating a significant research presence is required for a nation to obtain full consultative status.[16] While well intentioned, this stipulation has led to a type of scientific arms race, where countries with little or no history in the Antarctic set up shop to gain a seat at the table. In a particularly ironic twist of a related stipulation of the treaty, any nation wishing to discontinue their presence in Antarctica must remove all structures and return the land to its original state—a logistically complex and highly expensive undertaking that prompts some countries to merely hang on to their operations after drastically cutting back spending and producing little in the way of scientific contributions.

More than a mild fascination with the bureaucratic underpinnings of Antarctica, my own interests here are largely epistemological, perhaps even pedagogical in nature. As someone who makes a living from teaching creative writing, I wonder quite a lot about what facets go into crafting an individual's understanding and appreciation of the natural world. "Any good poet, in our age at least, must begin with a scientific view of the world," wrote Edward Abbey—in a desert far distant from this one—"and any scientist worth listening to must be something of a poet, must possess the ability to communicate to the rest of us his sense of love and wonder at what his work discovers."[17] I would also add, however humbly, that we can't hope to understand the Antarctic completely without also recognizing ourselves, in some essential way, as tourists, as unwelcomed and unenlightened visitors from another land.

Without question, the scientific contributions that have come out of research based in the Antarctic—which include discovering the ozone hole—are vital. And they will become even more so over the coming decades, as we struggle to understand the consequences of a rapidly changing global climate. Yet a scientific mindset alone will never fully comprehend Antarctica, nor can this lens be trusted, by itself, to succeed in offering the continent protection. The National Science Foundation's Antarctic Artists and Writers Program, along with similar programs of other nations, has been instrumental in developing a bridge between specialists and laymen, between science and art, and between Antarctica and the rest of the world. Logistical problems and expenses associated with travel to the Antarctic remain significant, but it would be admirable to see more opportunities—especially in regard to education in the humanities—open up for the general public. As the British travel writer Sara Wheeler put it in her wonderful book *Terra Incognita*, which is centered on her experiences as the NSF's first female writer-in-residence at the South Pole, "the entire human occupation of Antarctica is predicated on the belief that science is an unending process of amelioration. . . . There is a pressure to believe in the deification of science on the ice; otherwise, one would have to admit that the reason for each nation's presence in Antarctica is political, not scientific."[18]

Scientists, in the end, do not own Antarctica, and I fear we may imperil the future of this incredible place if this field of study is all that people commonly associate it with. One innovative program that Lindblad has started, in its partnership with *National Geographic*, to try to address this is a travel grant for K-12 educators, across disciplines, to join a polar expedition and develop curricula that they can take back to the classroom. While only one fellowship, it points to the beneficial role ecotourism can have—and is having—in Antarctic conservation.

If I'm starting to sound like an employee of the company, this likely has to do with the fact that I am regularly being confused for one. Eric and I happen to look quite alike—especially when we both grow out our beards—and have commonly been mistaken for brothers. Even, on occasion, for each other:

"Hey man, didn't we snort Ritalin together back in college?" (Some random guy approaching me at a house party.)

"I'm pretty sure you've got me confused with someone else."

"No, I'm positive. You left with that girl . . ."

The misidentifications of the past week have hardly been as colorful, though I'm afraid my presence may wind up hurting Eric's end-of-the-trip evaluations. It took me a while of being regularly asked how to perform this or that camera function, or to be directed to identify which species of albatross was floating nearby, before it dawned on me that many of the passengers simply can't tell us apart, and it has made me watch my step a little more in my interactions with guests.

On February 4, 1911, the Norwegians were also surprised to find themselves briefly cast in the roles of tour guides and hosts. As part of their ambitious scientific agenda, Scott had sent his first officer, Victor Campbell, and five other men, to conduct extensive surveying to the east, but when the *Terra Nova* led them to the Bay of Whales they were startled to come upon the base of their rival expedition. The encounter was civil enough, as they made a round of introductions and inspected each other's quarters. Campbell's men were impressed by the Norwegians' handling of their vast fleet of dogs, while Amundsen—never one to pass up an opportunity to slight the English—remarked dryly in his book about how, shortly after this visit, nearly all of his men caught colds.

A story that seems at least somewhat suspect, as the germs associated with the common cold find Antarctica to be an unwelcoming host. Encouragingly so, I might add, as—back on board the ship—I slip into a pair of shorts for our afternoon swim. A tradition among cruising tourists, I'm told, the beach here on Deception is the continent's favored swimming hole. There must have been some sort of memo distributed beforehand, as our shore party of about twenty is decked out in bright bathing suits and the occasional swim cap. Perhaps because I grew up by the Oregon coast, I have always enjoyed jumping into cold water, especially in the backcountry, where I rarely pass up the opportunity of an icy creek or glacial lake at the end of a day's hike. The setup here, however, is more than a little ridiculous. The ship's doctor and his assistant are stationed on the beach in case of medical emergency. Heaps of plush towels are piled on folding tables beside them, and a videographer is quickly setting up shop next to a tended bar with whiskey, gin, cocoa, and "gloog"—a hot, spiced Scandinavian wine. This is probably the most I've felt like a tourist over the entire trip, though it is too late to turn back now.

When Scott got news of Amundsen's setup at the Bay of Whales—with their seventy-mile head start and their hundred well-trained dogs—he decided to make no changes to his operation, arguing that the goals of his mission could not be sacrificed. In a letter home to his supervisor at RGS, Scott writes, "If he [Amundsen] gets to the Pole, he is bound to do it rapidly with dogs, but one guesses that success will justify him. . . . He is taking a big risk, and perhaps deserves his luck if he gets through."[19] This type of comment evidently rubbed Amundsen the wrong way, as he penned a sort of rebuke in his book years later.

Victory awaits him who has everything in order—luck people call it. Defeat is certain for him who has neglected to take the necessary precautions in time—this is called bad luck.[20]

Spoken with the smug certainty of a man who knows he has already won. And, in fact, Amundsen went to great lengths to project himself as a leader who had methodically planned out every detail of the trip with cool and unerring detachment. Both his past and present exploits, however, betrayed more than a few chinks in this lavish armor. His first proposal for conquering the North Pole, for instance, involved harnessing polar bears, and while wintering over on the *Belgica* here on the peninsula, Amundsen hatched a preposterous plan to set out for the South Pole with a companion in a small kayak, carrying a sled with six months of provisions. Amundsen planned, if they somehow made it to the other side of the continent, to paddle across the Southern Ocean all the way to Australia. I bring up these early and fortunately aborted schemes not to dismiss Amundsen, but rather to show how much was still unknown about travel in the high latitudes—what was reasonable or possible to endure and how best to achieve one's goals. It might seem easy to dismiss these as the far-fetched daydreams of youth, but even in his conquest of the South Pole, Amundsen made several rash decisions and potentially costly mistakes. The dangerous placement of his winter camp has already been mentioned, but Amundsen had also somehow forgotten to take the 1912 issue of the Nautical Almanac with him from Norway. This almanac provided figures describing the angles of the sun and other stars, as well as the phases of the moon at different latitudes. Without this, there was no way for him to confirm his arrival at the pole. He had brought the 1911 issue, and *luckily* this was all he would wind up needing, yet this oversight left him an artificial deadline that—along with his fixation on beating Scott—may have led him to jump the gun that September.

On the 12th it was –61.6 degrees F., with a breeze dead against us. This was undeniably bitter. It was easy to see that the temperature was too much for the dogs; in the morning, especially, they were a pitiful sight. They lay rolled up as tightly as possible, with their noses under their tails, and from time to time one could see a shiver run through their bodies; indeed, some of them were constantly shivering. We had to lift them up and put them into their harness. I had to admit that with this temperature it would not pay to go on.[21]

We plunge into the frigid sea one at a time, per the videographer's request. I dash into the shallow surf and the numbing cold takes my breath away. I fling myself forward into a small wave and indulge in a few harried crawl strokes—exhilarating, pointless—before standing up and retreating to towels and booze. One heavyset middle-aged woman actually stayed in for several minutes—without the shrieks and wild motions of the rest of us— calmly treading water as though she had just entered the deep end of a country club pool. The doctor and his assistant watched on with evident concern.

While our brief aquatic venture hardly seems to necessitate medical experts, a sledge journey to the farthest ends of the earth would be another matter entirely. Both Scott and Shackleton understood this—even given the latter's lifelong superstition of doctors—and a place on their Polar Teams was always reserved for a medical professional. To travel otherwise would have seemed to them irresponsible. Yet this was another circumstance where Amundsen rode his luck. Amundsen's experiences with Dr. Cook on board the *Belgica* had convinced him that a doctor—given his intimate knowledge in matters of life and death—was a rival authority to a captain's standing with his men. Cook's role in the *Belgica* expedition certainly bears Amundsen out in this assessment, and thankfully so, as Amundsen himself might not have made it through that winter alive if it was otherwise. And while you can point to instances in the journeys of both Scott and Shackleton where a doctor's authority caused them to reconsider their own plan or opinion, this always proved to be to the benefit of the party. Amundsen, however, would not stand for divided counsel, and therefore chose to travel without a doctor, imperiling the men in his charge in order to position himself as the sole authority.

Inside of fifteen minutes we are all done swimming—dried off but still shivering—and waiting to be shuttled back to the ship. As if on cue, a small group of full-grown chinstrap penguins enter from stage left, flapping about cheerfully in the calm bay, puzzled by what all the fuss was about. Witnessing an Antarctic penguin taking its first dive into the ocean, however, is hardly less farcical than our pale and elderly entourage. Reminiscent of the great factory scenes of a Charlie Chaplin film, there is a delicate blend of bullying, frenzied inevitability, and grace-saving humor to color the monochrome scene. Abandoned by their parents weeks ago, as their demands for food have become insatiable, the fledged chicks huddle together at the shoreline busily contemplating the abyss. Though water is their natural element, at this stage in their lives they know almost nothing about it. One or two at a time flop about in the shallows, testing their flippers and squawking triumphantly to their buddies on shore, but their food lies farther out. Instinctively they know this, just as they know the depths contain other bodies that must be feared. One or two leopard seals bob their heads out patiently in the channel. They have been waiting all season for this, as the buoyant and inexperienced chicks make for easy prey. Together these brave birds have withstood the elements and fought off the marauding skuas, and together as well they will take the plunge, though the mission of each penguin at this stage is to not be the first. This is where the vaudeville comes in, the Laurel and Hardy shorts, as the chicks attempt to coerce one another onto the pirate plank of a rocky perch. Eventually a body is dumped overboard, and dozens of eager followers spring free, counting on safety in numbers to navigate past the seals. In a matter of minutes, several of the new swimmers will meet their end, but the machine of portly, tuxedoed life continues.

Unlike the birds—and the tourists—Amundsen needed no prodding from others to take the plunge. An Antarctic winter is a long season to wait for one so raring to begin, but with temperatures dipping back down below negative sixty, after a brief window of milder days, Amundsen was forced now to recognize his mistake. His team of eight had set out together and in orderly fashion the week before, but after turning back in retreat on September 13, the group became increasingly disarrayed. By their last day out, still over forty miles from base, at least two of the men were showing signs of severe frostbite and a number of the failing dogs were abandoned as they struggled to keep up. Craving the comforts of base perhaps and trusting that all his men would find their way back eventually, Amundsen hitched a ride on the fastest dog sledge, arriving home at four in the afternoon. The second group would arrive several hours later, though that still left two men unaccounted for—out on the ice after dark, without fuel or food. One of the men had become crippled with a badly frostbitten heel, and the most experienced person of the expedition—Hjalmar Johansen, who had partnered with Nansen in his famous exploits in the north—had waited to assist him home. They would not arrive till midnight—seventeen hours after turning out for base, and long after Amundsen had gone to bed. Johansen had already advised Amundsen against setting out this early in the season, and the tension between the two men boiled over the following morning, when Amundsen asked brazenly what had taken them so long. This drew the ire of the veteran Johansen, who had, after all, just led an injured man back to safety. "I don't call it an expedition.

It's panic," he is reported to have said, a comment that cost Johansen his place on the Pole Team.[22] And, over time, far more than that. After being stripped of what he felt was his rightful claim to posterity, Johansen saw his life quickly unravel upon returning to Norway, in no small part because Amundsen had sent him home in disgrace, with a trumped-up charge of mutiny. Less than two years after his bust-up with Amundsen, Johansen took his own life while staying in a seedy hotel room. Many of his friends came to hold Amundsen personally responsible. In his book, Amundsen glosses over all of this, declaring codedly, "Circumstances had arisen which made me consider it necessary to divide the party into two."[23] And in addressing their false start to the pole, Amundsen is all calm and collected.

To risk men and animals out of sheer obstinacy and continue, just because we have started on our way—that would never occur to me. If we are to win this game, the pieces must be moved carefully—one false move, and everything can be lost.[24]

After a long hot shower, I meet up with Eric and Kendra in the lounge for a drink, where a group of four women are seated over a game of Scrabble. They seem to have formed a sort of a high-end clique, as this same group always sits together now in the dining hall.

First lady (looking up from her tiles): "Does 'traveling' have one 'l' or two?"

Second lady: "Either."

First lady: "Either?"

Third lady: "Maybe it depends on how long you'll be gone."

"Why didn't the Scrabble team book an all-inclusive resort in Cancun?" Kendra mutters from across the table. Eric laughs, "Because they knew you would take such good care of them."

Kendra has made no mention of her boyfriend since the night of the crew party, though an impending breakup now seems likely. Or perhaps, after a long season of attending to the whims of rich people, Kendra has simply reached a tipping point. If you work long enough in the field of hospitality—and I'm talking as someone who has logged over two years as a hotel concierge—you'll likely find yourself veering in one of two directions: either you become a twenty-four-hour-a-day fountain of indiscriminate kindness (I can think of one or two flight attendants I know who fit the bill), or else you quickly become a scoffing, two-faced hater of humanity.

That might strike some outside the industry as an extreme statement, but I for one quickly found myself in need of a change in career. And, in fact, that's just what Kendra has done, accepting a new job in the company as a second mate, after recently earning her pilot license. Starting next year, then, she'll be working for a smaller ship, leading excursions up in Alaska, steering them through the long nights, when most everyone on board is asleep. She's got to make it through this trip first, however, and compounding all the usual annoyances, Kendra has, grudgingly, allowed the busing adventure blogger to put on an informal talk this afternoon. Quite a crowd has turned out, actually, and even the Scrabble game is temporarily placed on hold.

As Amundsen and his now divided party settled back in at their base for another month of winter, they set to making small improvements to gear and made new calculations for their rations. Given that the Pole Team's size had been reduced from eight to five, the depots they had set up in the fall—the furthest over two hundred miles toward the pole—now had a surplus of supplies, providing the men with an unintentionally large margin of safety. The dog meat they were banking on for the latter stages of the trip would now also be divided between fewer mouths. So while their first attempt at the pole had been a rather embarrassing failure, they set off again on the morning of October 19 with renewed optimism.

At the start our sledges were very light, as we were only taking supplies for the trip to 80 degrees South, where all our cases were waiting for us; we could therefore sit on the sledges and flourish our whips with a jaunty air. . . . Anyone who had seen us would no doubt have thought a Polar journey looked very inviting.[25]

"One Man, Ten Weeks, 10,000 Miles," reads the opening slide—the slogan superimposed over a smiling picture of this guy boarding a Greyhound out of DC. "By making no reservations and having no daily itinerary," he tells us, "bus travel would approximate the journeys of early explorers." A bit of a head-scratcher there, if you ask me, though many in the room seem to nod back affirmatively. Nat Geo must have been likewise impressed, as they are the ones picking up the tab on this venture. He goes on to highlight some of the colorful challenges that were met along the way (running over a cow somewhere in Colombia, his inflatable neck pillow springing a leak in the Andes). The away-school dad looks on in a state of near-rapture, while his wife and kids nervously eye him from across the table, afraid they might have to start taking public transportation.

"It's all in real time," he continues excitedly. "I post every hour on Twitter! And it is all totally new. Nobody has ever done this before."

Kendra yawns. Eric leans over incredulously, "Does this guy really think he invented riding the bus?" For my own part, I can't get past the "real-time" fascination of it all, which he keeps circling back to. As a practicing/struggling writer, so much of my life just seems antithetical, even downright inimical, to "real-time"—five hours at my desk to write 100 words about something long past, 20 of which wind up being cut—that I'm struggling to wrap my head around what makes any of this, well, interesting. Even if I managed to get past the 140-character-size writing component of his trip, the boast of "adventuring" seems sad and overblown. If this is what exploration has devolved into in our current day, wouldn't it be better to simply give up the concept entirely? His conclusion is met with a wave of applause, so obviously I don't speak for everyone on this. And my intention is not to crucify this guy, who—in all our interactions—has seemed smart, funny, and obviously really excited to be in Antarctica. If I didn't dislike his current project so much, I'm sure I would have gotten along with him just fine.

While much can be said about the respective differences between the British and Norwegian polar parties—not just in regard to leadership and preparedness, but also as to things like clothing and rations—the most important distinction comes down to transportation. Scott, as I have already said, was relying on a mix of pony, dog, and motor transport to get his team to the base of the Beardmore Glacier, though that would account for hardly a fourth of the overall distance to the pole and back; for the rest of the way—roughly 1,000 miles and 10,000 feet of climbing—they would be man-hauling sledges. Shackleton's team had come close to accomplishing this feat three years before, turning back at the ends of starvation 100 miles short of the pole, and Scott felt certain that he and his men could go one better. Amundsen, for his part, was counting on dogs to take him all the way to the pole and back, killing them off periodically, as their loads became smaller and the men needed food. Amundsen placed great faith in his dogs, even though Shackleton had been confident that dogs were incapable of navigating the Beardmore Glacier up to the plateau. The British, however, were no dog experts, and Amundsen wouldn't be going up the Beardmore anyway—in fact, he mistakenly believed that his chosen route would simply rise gradually all the way to the pole. What he found instead was a glacier that was even steeper than the Beardmore, though less heavily crevassed and thus easier to navigate. Even more fortunately for Amundsen, this route rose to the plateau further inland, meaning that his party would have to travel 120 miles less while at altitude. Throughout their journey, Amundsen's team of dogs repaid his faith twofold. Unfortunately for the dogs, this did nothing to relieve them of the other role they had been cast to play in this expedition.

But the part of my work that went more quickly than usual that night was getting the Primus started, and pumping it up to high-pressure. I was hoping thereby to produce enough noise to deaden the shots that I knew would soon be heard—twenty-four of our brave companions and faithful helpers were marked out for death. It was hard—but it had to be so. We had agreed to shrink from nothing in order to reach our goal.[26]

There are approximately fifty pounds of edible food in the carcass of an Inuit sled dog. Using them as a source of nutrition became taboo—and, later, outlawed—in the decades following the Heroic Age, but dogs were still considered the most effective form of transport in mountainous regions of the Antarctic well into the 1960s. Even long after the arrival of snowmobiles, they were still kept at a number of bases as back-up transport, and to boost the morale of the people stationed there. The last dogs left Antarctica in February 1994, as a result of treaty regulations that required the removal of all nonnative species—a stipulation that, it goes without saying, we granted ourselves an exemption from. By this point in time, dogs had been playing a vital part in the history of the continent's exploration for over a century. The first dogs to visit Antarctica had been part of a British expedition in 1899; when a blizzard that season trapped seven of the men in a single tent for days, they survived by bringing in the dogs to lie on top of them like blankets for added warmth. By the end of their long Antarctic tenure, dogs would prove themselves time and again to be more adaptable, more resilient, and less destructive than were the men who had brought them here.

Scott's opposition to the use of dogs was at least threefold: (1) they had let him down in the past (a result mostly of poor handling and tainted food); (2) a quixotic view the British had long cultivated in regard to the nobility of man-hauling—"no journey ever made with dogs," Scott wrote in his journals, "can approach the height of that fine conception which is real-

ized when a party with their unaided efforts, go forth to face hardships";
and (3) moral objections—quite frankly, he thought it too cruel to proceed
with every intention of running the dogs into the ground before sacrificing
them at fixed intervals for a meal.[27] True, he had killed dogs on his first attempt at the pole, and even partook of some of their meat, but he had not
set out with that intention, and the experience was nothing he cared to re-
peat.* Amundsen, on the other hand—despite his claims of stove-pumping
empathy—was much more hardened to the fate of his dogs. And to a level
that, at various times in his book, seems downright heartless.

*No butcher's shop could have exhibited a finer sight than we showed after
flaying and cutting up ten dogs. Great masses of beautiful fresh, red meat,
with quantities of the most tempting fat, lay spread over the snow. The dogs
went round and sniffed at it. Some helped themselves to a piece; others were
digesting. We men had picked out what we thought was the youngest and
tenderest one for ourselves. . . . The meat was excellent, quite excellent, and
one cutlet after another disappeared with lightning-like rapidity. I must
admit that they would have lost nothing by being a little more tender, but
one must not expect too much of a dog.*[28]

Of the fifty-two dogs Amundsen set out with, only eleven would return
with him to base. Most of these would soon be gifted to Douglas Mawson
(who was just then venturing back to the ice), in service of the Australian
Antarctic Expedition, all but ensuring that each of these tireless servants
would soon meet a similar fate.

That night, at dinner, Eric and I sit with the Western Apparel couple from
Wichita. While we have yet to reach the entrée-sharing level of friendship,
I have become closer with the woman, Jane. As it turns out, they have a
teenage daughter who writes poetry. Understandably, they are both concerned, and Jane seems to be looking to me for some sort of assurance that
everything will turn out fine in the end. What do I tell her? What do I tell
my own mother? That an underpaid and overworked adjunctship can still
be a noble life? That even when you find some form of success it will, in all
likelihood, be couched in a greater failure? At least Amundsen had the decency to wait until his own mother passed away before he turned to chase
after his crazy dreams. At one point in the conversation I mention Abby

---

* Ironically, Scott was not as troubled by this prospect when it came to the ponies, which
he marched to the foot of the Beardmore with every intention of slaughtering them and
consuming their meat.

and Mason (the newlyweds from Chicago), and when they are unclear who it is I'm speaking of, Eric steps in to help, referring to them as "the other young couple." Great, not only do I have this guy's name permanently penned onto the inside of my boxers, but now we are officially an item. There is a sort of awkward pause where Eric realizes what he's said: "Not that . . . ," he looks at me while doing a vague back-and-forth arm gesture, his voice noticeably deepening. "Actually, Justin and I are hoping to meet some ladies after this trip." Luckily, I manage to turn my face away from the table before spewing a mouthful of red wine across the floor.

As with any old friends, Eric and I have each witnessed the other putting his foot in his mouth more than a few times, but what I've enjoyed most about this trip—at least in regard to our friendship—is seeing how Eric has come into his own. The same thing I would hope he'd find if he ever sat in on one of my classes. Though, granted, I've never had the fortune to teach in a classroom with as grand a view as this. I'll admit that I'm a bit jealous, though mostly I am just happy for him.

On December 14, the night before Amundsen's team arrived at the South Pole, they lay awake in their tent as giddy as schoolboys. They had traveled fast, faster than even they had expected, and while there must have been some lingering doubt over Scott's motor tractors, they had every reason to be confident. They had been out for fifty-seven days, having traversed over eight hundred miles, and were all in good health. Scott's team wouldn't arrive for another month, and after them, no one would return to that spot for over forty years.

Nowadays, visitors to the South Pole arrive in less than two hours, on flights leaving several times daily in summer from McMurdo base. The pole is an indiscriminate spot on a barren and featureless plateau at just over ninety-three hundred feet of elevation. The average annual temperature is −56.7 degrees, with a record low of −117. It snows only about three inches a year at the South Pole, though the relentless winds accumulate large enough snowdrifts in a year to cover a one-story house, and because there is no possibility of thawing, the ice sheet rises about eight inches annually. The only wildlife that has ever been seen at the pole is a pair of skuas (or, most certainly, several pairs) spotted three times over the past decade. Seemingly blown off course from wherever it was they had hoped to get to, in each instance the birds arrived in the middle of summer, stayed for a day or two, and then disappeared.

One must make a distinction, however, between the actual South Pole and "Pole," the common name of the U.S. Amundsen-Scott Base, which is a little like a resort town gone horribly awry. Pole has been permanently staffed since its establishment in 1956. The original station, now referred to as Old Pole, was constructed by an eighteen-man U.S. Navy crew—a project that was hurriedly put together after word that the Soviets were intending to build a station there themselves. This was the coldest setting of the Cold War, with bitter jockeying being carried out by both nations in the name of science. Lawmakers back in the United States worried that, if left unchecked, the Soviet Union would "spread the disease of communism even to the penguins."[29] The Antarctic Treaty was signed three years later, as the first multinational arms control treaty negotiated since the end of the Second World War. The treaty would cover all ocean and land south of sixty degrees, establishing Antarctica as a demilitarized zone, but the treaty would have never moved forward if the United States and the Soviet Union hadn't agreed to shelve their own prospects of territorial claims. Rather than a magnanimous gesture of goodwill and scientific inquiry, it is thought that the United States' willingness to back off establishing its own claims was made with an eye toward establishing a precedent in outer space. At the time, the Soviets seemed far more likely to win the race to the moon, and it was feared that if the United States made sweeping declarations in the Antarctic, Russia would follow suit in the solar system. Nonetheless, the American base at the South Pole represents a de facto claim at the strategic heart of the continent.[30]

The Amundsen-Scott base has been rebuilt, remodeled, demolished, and upgraded several times over, and is now capable of housing a peak population of over two hundred individuals, with numbers dropping down to about fifty each winter. The food at Pole—which includes walnut and blue cheese empanadas—is rumored to be the best on the continent, and its hydroponic greenhouse can grow enough to feed each person one to two salads a week. In 2005, the South Pole even became seasonally accessible via the McMurdo–South Pole Highway—a 995-mile compacted snow road that took four years to complete, with a budget of $350 million. Constructed by leveling snow and filling in crevasses, the highway takes an average of forty days to traverse in specially modified farm tractors. In a few more years, after the completion of an optical fiber link with the French-Italian Concordia Station, Pole will even have twenty-four-hour internet access.

It feels cruel to grudge a few dozen hard-working scientists their email and hydroponic salads, though it does seem we have sacrificed something in the way of the human imagination here, in our stubborn colonization of the last place on earth. Even with such amenities, however, the South Pole is still an extremely remote, inhospitable, and potentially fatal destination. Normally there is no travel to or from the outpost for the nine months between February and October. Every year, several visitors to Pole wind up needing a medical evacuation, often due to severe altitude sickness (given the uniquely thin polar air, being at ten thousand feet of elevation near the pole has the same effect on people as thirteen thousand at a different latitude). In the winter of 1999, a doctor at the station diagnosed herself with breast cancer, and—being unable to get out—began treating herself with chemotherapy. It is, quite literally, the end of the earth, and the people who have been there speak of a strange and singular power the place holds over them.

And Amundsen, when he arrived?

I cannot say—even although I know it would have a much greater effect— that I stood at my life's goal. That would be telling stories much too openly. I had better be honest and say right out that I believe no human being has stood so diametrically opposed to the goal of his wishes as I did on that occasion. The regions round the North Pole—oh the Devil take it—the North Pole had attracted me since the days of my childhood, and so I found myself at the South Pole. Can anything more perverse be conceived?[31]

It is a telling response, from a man whose greatest accomplishments never seemed to amount to quite what he hoped. He had won, he would return a hero, but in his latter years he would also grow embittered, turning on old allies and friends. Regularly strapped for cash, Amundsen felt his brave exploits had been underappreciated—especially by the British, who had judged him harshly for what they perceived as his underhanded dealings with Scott. Amundsen resented this and seemed to live much of his remaining life in a shadow of his own making. Others from his Pole Team held a less antagonistic view of the matter. In the reasoned words of Helmer Hanssen, who had traveled with Amundsen both to the pole and on his Northwest Passage expedition, "it is no disparagement to Amundsen and the rest of us when I say that Scott's achievement far exceeded ours. . . . We started with 52 dogs and came back with 11, and many of these wore themselves out on the journey. What shall we say of Scott and his comrades, who were their own dogs? Anyone with any experience will take off his hat to Scott's achievement. I do not believe men ever have shown such endurance at any time, nor do I believe there ever will be men to equal it."[32]

Restless and in search of new prizes, Amundsen turned to aviation in the 1920s, making several failed attempts to fly over the North Pole. In 1926, he participated in the first successful air crossing of the Arctic, in a small plane flown by Italian pilot Umberto Nobile, becoming the first person to have technically reached both poles of the earth. Amundsen was relegated to more of a passenger role in these later adventures, though the risks in early aviation were still high. In fact, this is how Amundsen would meet his end, when his plane crashed in the polar sea in 1928 while on a search mission for Nobile, whose plane had gone down on the ice days before. A lifetime bachelor, Amundsen had recently become engaged. His body was never found.

Back at the South Pole, Amundsen and his men left behind a tent, several Norwegian flags, and a few unwanted supplies, all of which lie buried now under more than fifty-six feet of ice. He also left a letter addressed to the Norwegian king, requesting that it be delivered in case he and his party failed to return. Finally, he included a brief personal note:

And a few words to Scott, who I presume will be the first to come here after us . . .[33]

CHAPTER 7

ENDURANCE
(1914–1917)

SIR ERNEST HENRY SHACKLETON

On the ice, the group huddled together near the long shadow of their stranded ship, where the man they knew simply as "the Boss" was discarding a handful of gold coins, his gold watch, gold cigarette case. From here on out, each of them would be allowed only two pounds of personal gear, so this purge was meant to serve as an example. Next, he tore out the flyleaf of a Bible gifted to him by the Queen, as well as a page from the Book of Job—*Out of whose womb came the ice?*—and dropped the remainder into the packed snow, then turned and walked away.[1] This was a grand gesture, made by a man who had always courted grandeur. "I never saw anyone enjoy success with such gusto as Shackleton," RGS librarian Hugh Robert Mill once declared. "His whole life was to him a romantic poem."[2] But success—even in its broadest measure—was a whole world away from them now, and one of the more superstitious men of the party, trusting there was need for all the good omens they could summon, circled back after the others had departed, in secret, to reclaim the holy text.

"Sometimes I think I am no good at anything but being away in the wilds just with men," Shackleton would one day write to his wife Emily.[3] The words carry the sheen of self-pity, or at least they would, if all the circumstances of his life had not borne him out in this assessment.

Ernest Shackleton grew up comfortably middle-class in a large Anglo-Irish family. Despite his great interest in books—especially poetry—he struggled in school, did not distinguish himself in sports, and gladly chucked away any prospect of further education to join the merchant navy upon turning sixteen. A deeply ambitious man, Shackleton craved glory and success on a level that seemed unobtainable in the normal, humdrum, class-riven society he was born into. As a result, he wound up turning to a land whose majestic scale and uncharted snowy interior seemed a fitting canvas to map out his own hopeful story. In a very real sense then, what drew Shackleton to the Antarctic was more philosophical than actual: "I have ideals," he came to write, in his characteristically gushing fashion, "and far away in my own white south I open my arms to the romance of it all."[4]

Upon his early and enforced return from Scott's *Discovery* expedition, this romance seemed destined to be of the short-term variety. Yet for a man of Shackleton's disposition, this perceived slight was simply added encouragement to redeem himself on the ice. Without the sort of institutional patronage that Scott could rely on, Shackleton jumped into a series of risky business ventures in an attempt to fund a private expedition, including a speculative enterprise to sell shares of a budding mining company that would pursue mineral extraction in the Antarctic. While none of his moneymaking schemes would ever amount to much, Shackleton did make some valuable business contacts, and eventually this was enough to secure him the necessary funds to outfit a small sealer known as the *Nimrod*.

Men go out into the void spaces of the world for various reasons. . . . I had been invalided home before the conclusion of the Discovery expedition, and I had a very keen desire to see more of the vast continent that lies amid the Antarctic snows and glaciers.

Thus began his first book, *The Heart of the Antarctic*, which details what would turn out to be his most successful voyage. True, his sledge team was forced to turn back at the verge of starvation when within one hundred miles of the pole, but they had traveled over twice the distance south of Scott's *Discovery* mark—the largest single advancement ever made toward either end of the earth—proving he was every bit the explorer as his rival. That story ends with Shackleton sailing off into the Ross Sea with his crew, staring out at McMurdo Sound and hoping for the chance to return and try it all again. Shackleton could not know it then, but even while he would make two more attempts to return to that land in the years ahead, this would mark the last time he ever set foot on the Antarctic continent.

═══

Far be it from me to claim grounds for comparison—and I know this is a rather abrupt entrance, though obviously I'm not the first person to find it difficult to share a stage with this explorer. All the same, and over break-fast, we are given the hard news that our ship has just lifted the season's last anchorage from Antarctic bedrock. An unfortunate change of plans, as Captain Kruess has deemed the pack ice of the Weddell Sea too thick to allow our entrance—a not uncommon event here at the tail end of the season, even in this age of rapid warming. His voice on the intercom en-courages us all to head out to the deck for a last look at the peninsula's saw-toothed peaks, as we turn north back across the Bransfield Strait, catching only a trailing glimpse of this most infamous sea.

"Don't worry, my friend," Eric says, sensing my disappointment, "there is a lot of beauty left on this trip." And though I know he's right, I can't shake the feeling that this all came too soon, that while we have been here over a week, it still feels as though I have yet to arrive, that the continent—while right here before us—has remained inaccessible, just outside our reach. Should I blame myself for this? The cruise? Perhaps, more simply, the Ant-arctic itself, which has always managed to lock itself away, even from those who have tried most devotedly to seek for it. Surely, we are all strangers here on the ice—explorers, scientists, and tourists alike. "If you returned," as Barry Lopez once said of this land, "it would be to pay your respects, for not being welcomed."[5]

═══

Shackleton, though, wasn't one to take heed or to be brushed aside. That's why—nearly a century ago—he pushed on into the pack ice of this very same sea, even after the whalers on South Georgia had advised him against it. The Weddell is said to have the clearest water of any sea, though mas-sive ice shelves and the ever-shifting pack conceal much of it, often creat-ing "flash freezes," and making this one of the most treacherous boating regions of the world. The British sailor James Weddell discovered the sea in 1823, on board the *Jane*, setting a new farthest-south mark at seventy-four degrees latitude, before fearing the worst and turning back. Now, at just over seventy-six degrees south, Shackleton found himself trapped—

roughly sixty miles short of his intended landing at Vahsel Bay. From that shore he had planned to set off into an unknown region of the interior, on a first-ever attempt at crossing the continent.

From the sentimental point of view, it is the last great Polar journey that can be made. It will be a greater journey than the journey to the Pole and back, and I feel it is up to the British nation to accomplish this.[6]

"These polar expeditions are becoming an industry," complained Winston Churchill—recently appointed the first lord of the Admiralty—when he was solicited for funding and support. "Enough life and money has been spent on this sterile quest," he continued. "The Pole has already been discovered. What is the use of another expedition?"[7] It was a fair question, especially as Britain inched closer to war. Apsley Cherry-Garrard, for his part—having just returned from the south—declared Shackleton's plan a "desperate venture," and thought it certain to end in tragedy.[8] Such objections, however, did little to steer away volunteers, even as Shackleton—always operating on a shoestring budget—could hardly afford to pay them.

Men wanted for hazardous journey. Low wages, bitter cold, long hours of complete darkness. Safe return doubtful. Honor and recognition in event of success.[9]

This legendary advertisement that Shackleton is said to have placed in a London newspaper is of doubtful authenticity. The earliest-known source of it is Carl Hopkins Elmore's book *Quit You Like Men*, which was published in 1944, three decades after the *Endurance* sailed. Elmore provided no footnote for the ad, and spells "honor" in the American style (without a *u*). Historians have scoured the records, searched through the archives of old newspapers, and even offered a small reward for anyone who could find an original copy of the advertisement, without success. It seems that even before the *Endurance* was ready to depart, the whole expedition was merging into the mythical.

Not that this should come as any surprise given its leader. In fact, even as a young sailor Shackleton was recognized as a man who sometimes "told stories that were true only in the poetic sense." Though as this same shipmate goes on to add, "his good qualities and his charm and kindness when at his best, outweighed his faults in our eyes."[10] Shackleton, of course, was not the only man on board the *Endurance* who knew how to spin a yarn, and his ragged crew made up what was, perhaps, the most memorable band of characters to ever outfit an Antarctic expedition.

Frank Worsley—"Wuzzles," as he was known on board; "Skipper," as he came to be endeared to Shackleton—was from an educated family of New Zealand settlers. Having grown up with a rugged, pioneering childhood, he was every bit the romantic dreamer as his leader. Explaining how he found his way to the Antarctic, Worsley wrote this: "One night I dreamed that Burlington Street was full of ice blocks, and that I was navigating a ship along it. . . . Next morning I hurried like mad into my togs, and down Burlington Street I went. . . . A sign on a door-post caught my eye. It bore the words 'Imperial Trans-Antarctic Expedition.' . . . I turned into the building."[11] Worsley was a dashing figure, with a broad chest and a mischievous grin, and he was already over forty when the *Endurance* set sail, though you never would have known this from his looks.

Worsley shared a name, and would wind up sharing center stage on the ice, with a young and gifted Australian photographer: Frank Hurley. Still in his twenties, Hurley had already made a name for himself in the Antarctic, having voyaged there several years before with his countryman Douglas Mawson. A teenage runaway who found work in the Sydney dockyards, Hurley bought a fifteen-shilling Kodak camera at the age of seventeen and launched his career. After hearing of Mawson's plans for the Antarctic, Hurley jumped on board a train, where the explorer was said to be traveling, showed himself into Mawson's private compartment, and charmed the older man enough to be hired on as the expedition photographer. Hurley was daring, strong, stubborn; he had lifted himself out of nothing and knew what he was capable of. As a result, Hurley did not suffer fools gladly, and could come across as vain and high-handed. His nickname with the crew was "the Prince," and Worsley hit it off with him right from the start. "He is a marvel," Worsley wrote, "with cheerful Australian profanity he perambulates alone aloft & everywhere, in the most dangerous & slippery places he can find, content & happy at all times but cursing so if he can get a good or novel picture."[12]

====

Traveling in the outdoors with a serious photographer can be a complex arrangement. Over the years, Eric and I have settled into a definite rhythm, with our days often centered around the twilights. In the summer, this may mean that you don't eat dinner before nine or ten, and in the winter time you might be hiking up some peak in the bitter cold to greet the dawn. Choosing a place to camp has little to do with comfort or mileage or access to water, and most everything to do with beauty and lighting. The whole experience becomes one big aesthetic consideration, and this appeals to me. My tendency is also to hike alone, or at least in silence, and this suits Eric just fine, except for when he has need for an occasional model—almost always from afar, silhouetted, or with my back turned, which is my sort of photo shoot.

Perhaps it has something to do with having sailed away from the continent, but all morning my thoughts have been restlessly drifting to other people and places. While I am certainly not hurrying on the rest of this trip, I am excited for what comes next for Eric and me: another month in Patagonia, most of it in and around Los Glaciares National Park, just outside a little Argentinean town by the name of El Chalten. We've got word a one-room abandoned refugio, thirty miles into the backcountry, right at the edge of the Southern Ice Field, that we hope to use as a launching off point for ventures out onto—and under—the ice. Ice caves happen to be Eric's forte as a photographer, and we've each brought crampons, ice axes, and helmets to help seek them out. Apart from aesthetic considerations, I'd wager that the single most important thing to share with a backcountry partner is a similar sense of risk and reward. While you never want to feel pressured into something, you also don't want to feel held back. Eric and I trust each other on this front and know from experience how consistently we wind up on the same page.

To cap it all off, Eric and I plan to hitchhike Ruta 40 (the so-called loneliest road in the world), over fifteen hundred mostly unpaved miles that traverse the windswept pampas, to arrive in Buenos Aires in time for our flights home. This is an absurd idea—that's why we settled on it.

=====

The Imperial Trans-Antarctic Expedition was reliant on two crews: the party, led by Shackleton, that would enter from the Weddell Sea and actually traverse the continent, and a second crew—under the command of Aeneas Mackintosh—that would travel to the Ross Sea aboard the *Aurora* and lay stores along the Barrier route that Shackleton's sledging team would eventually navigate. If the Ross Sea Party were to fail in their mission, Shackleton and his men would almost certainly perish, so a competent, dependable leader for that voyage was essential. MacIntosh had served with Shackleton on the *Nimrod* expedition, but his participation was cut short by an accident that resulted in him losing his right eye. This mission, then, was a chance for MacIntosh to redeem himself, and some historians have questioned whether this redemptive narrative—a storyline that the Boss was easily swayed by—may have blinded Shackleton to MacIntosh's other shortcomings.* In any case, as the *Endurance* sailed out from Buenos Aires, Shackleton was focused solely on managing his own rambunctious crew. What he didn't know was that he had one more set of hands on board than he had bargained for.

Perce Blackborrow had attempted to join the ranks of the *Endurance* as it docked in Buenos Aires to await the arrival of sixty-nine sledge dogs ordered from Canada. Blackborrow was all of twenty at the time, with hardly any sea experience, and no marked skills to set him apart—Shackleton turned the young man down, though he signed on his older pal William Bakewell. The two friends had other ideas, and Blackborrow stowed away in a clothing locker in the fo'c'sle. On the second day out at sea, Blackborrow was discovered, and hauled out to face the Boss. Seasick and hungry, the young man received a first-rate tongue-lashing. "If we run out of food, you will be the first to be eaten!" Shackleton is reported to have yelled at the end in a fit of rage. "They'd get a lot more meat off you, sir," Blackborrow—a rather skinny man—is said to have replied, leading the Boss to turn away and hide a grin.[13]

This comes down to us from Frank Wild, Shackleton's faithful second-in-command, as Shackleton left off all mention of the deceit in his official account. But if there was anyone on board who could be trusted to relay a surly retort like that, surely it was Wild. A short and wiry seadog with a bit of a cantankerous soul, Wild had been the one to give Shackleton the nickname "Boss," back when they voyaged together on the *Nimrod*. The moni-

* The tragedy of the Ross Sea Party—how they succeeded in laying depots that would never get used, but at the cost of the lives of three of their men—is deserving of far more than a footnote. Yet they effectively exit the stage at this juncture of Shackleton's endeavor, and will have to wait for another time.

ker was not meant to be entirely complimentary, as Wild hadn't begun as a great admirer of his boisterous leader. In fact, it was not until they shared a desperate march back from their attempt at the South Pole that the two men became close. Their last surviving pony, Socks, had vanished down a narrow crevasse as they were ascending the Beardmore Glacier, almost dragging Wild along with it. The four-man party was safe, but they had been banking on the flesh of Socks to supplement their depleted rations, as they raced for home. One night, after a particularly draining march, Shackleton had forced one of his own biscuits onto Wild. "I do not suppose that anyone else in the world can thoroughly realize how much generosity and sympathy was shown by this," Wild wrote. "I DO by GOD I shall never forget it."[14] From that day forward—to the best of my knowledge—the two men would never speak a word against one another.

That kind of intense loyalty was a trademark of Shackleton's leadership. While there were exceptions, and even bitter falling-outs along the way, Shackleton cultivated fellowship throughout his ranks. Unlike Scott, who chose to follow navy protocol in granting some separation between the officers and men, Shackleton made no such distinctions, and was also never one to hold himself apart. He liked to be among his men, laughing and sharing stories. And the selections he made as to the crew—even when it came to the scientists—were always made with an eye toward the expedition's collective spirit. In one famous example, when an accomplished and earnest young physicist from Cambridge named Reginald James interviewed for a position, instead of asking him about his scientific work, Shackleton wanted to know whether he could sing. "Oh, I don't mean any Caruso stuff," Shackleton broke in before the puzzled man could answer, "but I suppose you can shout a bit with the boys?"[15] The main living space on board the *Endurance* was christened the Ritz, which the men were expected to frequent and keep festive. Each night on the ship, the lone rotating watchman was provided access to special stores—things like cocoa and sardines—which he could share openly with any friends willing to wait up with him. These visitors they called "ghosts."

======

I like that idea: ghosts. When I was in college, it seemed like I was always up late writing papers. As was my buddy, Lunch. The apartment I rented had an automatic sprinkler system that would run between the hours of

2:00 and 3:00 each morning, and Lunch and I would often make plans to meet up on my front steps for a study break in time with the starting sprinkler. Just a half hour or so, then we'd turn in, or each sit back down at our desk to meet another deadline. There was nothing picturesque about it— just a shared yard on a quiet street—though like any ritual, however arbitrary, it brought with it a kind of peace, a serenity to the *tut-tut-tut* of the water's circling spray. "Ghosts" you might as well have called us, just sitting there on those steps in a conversation lost to history, a few shared and inconsequential thoughts while the world around us slept.

There is something special about the friendship between men, just as surely as there is something frustratingly narrow. Lunch—or Isaac as I call him now—has long since married and started a family. I was in his wedding, though I've seen him only a couple of times since. We don't write one another, and only rarely talk on the phone. Like so many of the people from my past, he seems almost an apparition to me now, like a city I've known but whose streets I can no longer navigate, like a brief way station or harbor where I stopped in for a time, before sailing on to some other place.

=====

The pressure-ridges, massive and threatening, testified to the overwhelming nature of the forces that were at work. Huge blocks of ice, weighing many tons, were lifted into the air and tossed aside as other masses rose beneath them. We were helpless intruders in a strange world.[16]

Much as the famous recruiting advertisement may have been a fabrication, Shackleton's books aren't entirely authentic themselves, as they were ghostwritten by a New Zealand journalist named Edward Saunders. This was not unusual for the time, though for a man who so clearly loved words and penned many eloquent and unique passages in his letters, this seems strange. And unfortunate, I'd add, as the finished products—while eminently competent—feel a little sterile, the separation between the voice and the page awkwardly on display. Quite simply, *South* feels dictated—as it was, in marathon sessions as their steamer sailed north to England, with Shackleton pacing restlessly as he smoked, and Saunders at his desk, dutifully carving this courageous tale into place. No, the Boss didn't write any books; he lived his life. And perhaps that would have been enough for just about anyone.

One positive aspect of this authorial arrangement is that *South* quotes liberally from the various private journals of his men. In fact, as part of the contract they had signed before sailing, all diaries were to be handed over to Shackleton at the end of the expedition. This was a little like sharing your course evaluation with your professor before receiving a grade, and without the cover of anonymity. Some element of self-censorship was, therefore, assured, though this arrangement also cultivated the atmosphere of a cut-rate, masochistic, polar writing retreat, with so many men trying to coin a memorable phrase or description. Worsley and Hurley would both go on to pen their own firsthand accounts of the voyage, but for so many of the others this was their one shot at seeing their words in print.

———

"Does that mean you are going to write about us?" a prying lady asks me over lunch with a snort of laughter. A woman who—by way of answering—I refuse to offer any description of. "He said he writes poems, dear," her husband chimes in from the other side of the table. "They're not about people!" Normally, a comment like that might elicit a cutting response, but after my last two mornings up at the library, which have produced little more than overwrought descriptions of the scenery, I'm almost inclined to agree with him. A landscape such as this unfolds always in greatness, but how do we find our place in that?

———

For Frank Hurley, the expedition was about far more than coming up with the right words, and the misfortune of their ice-locked ship provided him with a uniquely powerful object of study for his photography. Using a large-format glass-plate still camera, Hurley documented the ship in its long death throes, at all hours and from all angles. In what is probably one of the two most famous photographs he ever took—shot at night near the end of winter—Hurley set up a series of photo flares to hauntingly light up the ship's spars and rigging, as the *Endurance* was lifted upward by the pressure ridges of the frozen sea. In this image, the ship appears so clearly symbolic of the human endeavor—misplaced and overmatched by the elements, yet still shining in some way, even if only by artificial light.

For over nine months the men stayed on board, long enough to see out the harsh polar winter, and holding out hope that their ship might still break free and bear them home. The *Endurance*, however, was not made with this in mind; in fact, not unlike our own ship, it was built as a tourist vessel to shuttle small groups of the wealthy around the Arctic in summertime. But the Weddell is a tortuous, churning sea that could destroy virtually any ship once it becomes beset in the ice.

Shipwrecks in Antarctic waters are hardly a historic relic. The Argentine cruise ship *Bahia Paraiso* met its end here on the peninsula in 1989, when it struck a reef off Anvers Island near America's Palmer Base. An estimated 160,000 gallons of diesel spilled into the surrounding waters, devastating the local wildlife. The ship was never recovered, though all hands survived safely at Palmer Base, where the resident scientists served as unwilling hosts for the 234 passengers, until other arrangements could be made. And in 2007, right here in the Bransfield Strait, the first tour vessel to ever operate in the Antarctic—the original Lindblad *Explorer*—came to grief. The company had long since sold the ship off to a Canadian competitor, though a Lindblad cruise—captained by none other than Oliver Kruess— was the first to respond to its distress call. The vessel had crashed into submerged ice and began taking on water through its cracked hull. Over 150 passengers and crew were rushed to lifeboats in the early dawn, where they would wait for hours in the open sea—unusually calm weather conditions may have been all that saved them from further tragedy.

In late October, the crew of the *Endurance* partook of one last meal on board—"taken in silent gravity, whilst the crushing is in progress and an ominous sound of splintering timbers arises from below"—before retreating to the relative safety of the ice.[17] As the story goes, eight emperor penguins appeared out of nowhere to sing a mournful dirge for the ship. Tom McLeod, the same superstitious sailor who would go on to reclaim the discarded Bible the following morning, whispered to a companion, "Do you hear that? We'll none of us get back to our homes again."[18] While few of the men were as willing to say it, the thought must have hung over everyone as they took to the ice. Well, almost everyone.

"Ship and stores have gone—so now we'll go home," Shackleton is reported to have said the following morning to the gathered men.[19] This was
a shockingly matter-of-fact declaration. They were now at 69.5 S, 51.3 W,
having drifted over 500 miles to the north since the *Endurance* had become trapped. Nobody had ever been there before. They were 346 miles
from Paulet Island, the nearest point where there was anything even re-
sembling food and shelter. A small hut had been built there by a Swedish
expedition in 1902 and filled with stores left by an Argentine relief ship.
Shackleton knew all about this, for he had purchased the supplies himself on behalf of the Argentine government. All that was left was to somehow get there, or anywhere else where they could set foot on solid ground,
but even then, there was no assurance that they would ever be found and
saved. They were a party of 28 men, sixty-some dogs, and three small
wooden lifeboats surrounded by nearly one million square miles of ice.

After a quickly aborted effort to haul their tremendous loads through the
labyrinth of the splintered pack, they settled in on an aged floe, a little over
a mile from the wreck of their ship. This became known as Ocean Camp.
Over the next two months they made frequent trips back to the *Endurance*
to salvage stores and reclaim abandoned items—including, oddly, most of
the volumes of an Encyclopedia Britannica that proved invaluable in settling arguments that would crop up amongst the men. As the Cambridge
man Reginald James wryly noted, "Lack of knowledge of a subject rather
stimulates argument in the Antarctic."[20] Most importantly, at least to one
man, they also recovered a store of glass-plate negatives. "During the day
I hacked through the thick walls of the refrigerator to retrieve the negatives stored therein," Hurley wrote in his journal. "They were located beneath four feet of mush ice and by stripping to the waist and diving under
I hauled them out."[21] Now that the decision had been made to wait out the
thawing of the sea ice, there was less need for restricting personal gear.
Besides, Shackleton was well aware of the worth of those photographs, assuming they ever made it back home. The Boss allowed Hurley to choose
150 of his best negatives, along with his cinematic film, to haul back to
camp, smashing the remaining 400 plates there on the ice so as to put
an end to the matter. Of his equipment, Hurley would keep only a pocket
camera and three rolls of film.

Finally, on November 21, at roughly 5:00 P.M., their doomed ship sank beneath the ice. "She's going, boys!" Shackleton shouted from their makeshift lookout tower, and everyone hurried out of the tents to watch.[22] The whole thing took less than ten minutes, and almost as soon as the *Endurance* was gone, the ice closed back up over it, as though it had never been.

She went down bows first, her stern raised in the air. She then gave one quick dive and the ice closed over her forever. It gave one a sickening sensation to see it, for, mastless and useless as she was, she seemed to be a link with the outer world.[23]

═══

Here's another sort of shipwreck, though I use the term loosely.

Once—*once upon a time*, let's say—I had a bench. It wasn't a bench I owned or had any real claim to, apart from the fact that I liked to visit it occasionally, driving over an hour to go and sit there. It was old and rickety, like many of the best things, and it sat just down from a small hotel that I never once stayed at, along a stretch of rocky shoreline on the Oregon coast. At high tide, sneaker waves would pummel against the rocky crevices and overhanging caves from underneath, spraying water upward in huge arcing displays like elaborate fireworks. After my first year away at college, I came back to find my bench gone. Or, rather, replaced: by two new benches with their sturdy legs bolted into the hard ground. I guess it was the fact that there were two of them that I found upsetting. That I could be resting there, happily alone, and some stranger might sit down and start talking to me. That evening, I went to town and bought a hand axe. I had a friend with me—a good friend, loyal even in the face of such shenanigans—and the two of us returned well after midnight to chop one of those benches loose, hacking off each of its wooden arms for keepsakes, and tossing the remaining hunk of lumber over the slick rocks and down into the towering spray. This was meant as a sort of compromise, a truce. And for years I held on to that bench arm, nailing it up on one of the otherwise empty walls in the rotating, rented rooms of my early twenties, using it as an extra shelf for a handful of my favorite books. Then it got thrown out, mistakenly, and not by me.

I guess that bench—the first one, though also maybe the second—was a link to another world for me, a past self that, really, I was fine to have moved on from, though I still miss him every now and then. That obstinate kid who was always stirring up trouble, always quick to take offense, and always trying to craft his small life into some sort of heroic tale, or at least a subject worthy enough for another one of his floundering poems. In fact, I think I may have arranged this whole trip—meeting up with Eric, taking my leave from teaching—to get back in touch with that kid, with that mindset that looked to the world as something always to be overcome, or defied, or otherwise turned into an imperfect piece of art. I guess I thought there might be something else I needed from him, before I could sail on fully into the next stage of my life.

——

At the end of the hard year of 1915, fighting raged all across Europe. Poison gas had been introduced into the trench warfare of the western front. Einstein's theory of relativity was formulated. A Georgia man by the name of William J. Simmons revived the Ku Klux Klan. And, down in Antarctica, the twenty-eight shipwrecked men of the *Endurance*—shielded from nothing else but the news—set off again for Paulet Island. They had thrown together a tolerably comfortable home at Ocean Camp, salvaging lumber from the busted hull of their ship to set up tent platforms to help them stay dry. They built a galley with a windbreak of spars driven into the ice and pieces of torn sail lashed into place. Hurley had even fashioned an improved stove from an oil drum and a cast-iron ash chute. But the summer was passing them by, and Shackleton was worried that they weren't getting anywhere fast enough.

Since abandoning ship, they had drifted only eighty miles, most of it due north, though they were also angling slightly to the east, away from land. Some of the men were deeply skeptical of this new plan, while others were simply anxious to do something—*anything*—that might assist with their own salvation. Again, they would have to leave behind most of what little they had, so they observed Christmas on December 22, scrounging together a suitable feast of the last, best pickings from the ship's stores, including anchovies in oil and jugged hare. All hands were encouraged to eat as much as they could, and the next day they started out in a long, ragged, backbreaking caravan. Dogs pulled the supplies in relays, while the men were yoked to the boats that had been mounted on sledges, having to stop every twenty yards for a rest. At the end of the first day—after eight exhausting hours of toil—they had managed to cover only one and a quarter miles. After two more days of similar results, the crew's carpenter, Henry "Chippy" McNish, refused to go on. Shackleton was summoned from the front, where he was prospecting for their route, and the two men had a horrible row. Shackleton threatened to have McNish shot, while the carpenter felt certain that the Boss was already leading them to the grave. They broke for a short meal, then the men were called back to the traces. McNish took his place alongside the others, and they marched on.

But McNish was right: this was a fool's errand, if not quite a death march. After a week of appalling struggle, they had gained all of eight miles. At this rate, it would take them a year to reach Paulet Island.

Turned in but could not sleep. Thought the whole matter over & decided to retreat to more secure ice: it is the only safe thing to do. . . . I do not like retreating but prudence demands this course: Everyone working well except the carpenter: I shall never forget him in this time of strain & stress.[24]

This passage is taken from Shackleton's journals, as once again he chose to leave out all mention of the altercation in his book. The party would now have to wait where they were until the ice broke up and they could take to the boats. The handful of puppies and the carpenter's cat had been put down over a month ago, when they had first attempted to set out across the ice, but now Shackleton ordered the killing of the dog teams, as they could no longer afford to feed them—a cruel, if unavoidable, inauguration to the place that would become known as Patience Camp.

⸻

Some of the names of the dogs were Rugby, Upton, Bristol, Songster, and Slobbers. Most, if not all of them, would have been marked for death even if the ship had successfully landed on the continent. At this point, they simply served no purpose. "This duty fell upon me and was the worst job I ever had," Wild wrote. "I have known many men I would rather shoot than the worst of the dogs."[25]

So much of the early human tale in the Antarctic seems predicated on killing—the animals they had brought with them, and the ones already there that they encountered. While it is impossible to make an accurate count, this expedition alone would wind up killing thousands of penguins for food and oil, along with hundreds of seals. But the dogs were something else. "How dreary the frozen captivity of our life, but for the dogs," Hurley had written many months before, and each of the men had come to feel much the same.[26] All had picked out favorites; all had helped to build the elaborate line of "dog-loos" that sheltered the animals through the harsh winter. More than any other expedition, these men had cherished the dogs. They had little choice in the matter—what else did they have? Now, one by one, Wild took the dogs out of their traces and led them behind a row of large ice hummocks. I don't know how he managed it, sitting each animal down in the snow—*so obedient, so hopeful*—then lifting his revolver to its head. What else can I do, by way of an offering, than to list here a few more of their names: Bob, Swanker, Millhill; Sadie, Bosun, Rufus; Noel, Snowball, Shakespeare.

=====

It is astonishing—in a story long defined by heroism and bravery—how little up until this point had actually been done. Since their ship had been beset in the ice over a year ago, the men had marched less than ten total miles. The meals hardly changed, the weather was mostly awful. There was little to do but sit around in one's sleeping bag and try not to smoke away all of the tobacco. But perhaps this was for the best. One can only speculate what would have become of their shore party had they reached the continent. If Amundsen's triumph of the pole had shown that the most efficient form of polar travel involved highly trained dogs in conjunction with skiing, then Shackleton's expedition was not well placed to replicate this. Their sole experienced dog driver had dropped out at the last minute over a financial squabble, and only one of the men of his party was an experienced skier. Besides this, Shackleton was over forty now, and his health had long been a cause of concern. He drank and smoked too much, and before the *Endurance* sailed he was noticeably putting on weight. Shackleton's collapse on the *Discovery* expedition's southern trek was largely chalked up to scurvy, though both Wilson and Scott worried that Shackleton suffered from some other undiagnosed ailment—undiagnosed because Shackleton had always refused to submit to a thorough examination. A similar collapse on Shackleton's second attempt at the pole seems to have borne them out in this, though he had recovered fully and was back to his old self in a matter of days. Still, one wonders whether he could have sustained the sort of extended grueling effort that sledging across the continent would have entailed. The Boss had a wealth of experience and a superhuman determination to succeed, but there were limitations even to this.

For three long months they stayed on that floe. What could they possibly still find to say to one another? Past exploits with women—even when spectacularly exaggerated—could go only so far, though from the diaries it does appear that subject came up a fair amount. Wild was known to have his share of stories, and one of the sailors spoke of a cocktail called the Bosom Caresser, which he swore was a guaranteed aphrodisiac.* But more frequently than they discussed women, the crew talked about the wind, incessantly. They even came up with a medical condition, *amenomania,* to describe the condition of being morbidly anxious about the wind's prevailing direction. This made perfect sense, as wind and current would largely determine what chance they had of being saved. The end of the Weddell Sea was rapidly approaching—a prospect they had long craved, though had reason now to fear. Over the last month, the current had gathered such force that they could feel their battered floe rising with the swells beneath them. They drifted on to the north, shooting well past Paulet Island now, but also edging dangerously to the east. It looked like their best and only real chance rested on Elephant Island and its much smaller companion island named Clarence. These isolated rock outcroppings marked the furthest end of the South Shetland group, at the northeastern terminus of the Bransfield Strait. If they missed those then they would be swept into the abyss of the South Atlantic.

They had lived so long with the ice that it had become routine, a comfort to them, though now it was melting away before their eyes, and they were approaching the point of no return.

═══

So much of heroism comes down simply to knowing when to act, to recognizing when the propped-open window of opportunity will soon come slamming down. It is estimated that there will be as many as 150 million "climate refugees" by the year 2050, with sea levels expected to rise by well

---

* Recipes of the drink vary somewhat, but basically it is a mixture of cognac, Grand Marnier, grenadine syrup, fortified wine, and egg yolk. (Personally, I'd wager that if you can find someone willing to share such a vile drink with you to begin with, then you are probably already on solid ground.)

over a foot in the intervening time. Over the last decade alone, the rate at which Antarctica is melting has almost tripled. In the event that the Antarctic Ice Cap ever melts completely, all coastal cities will be submerged, and over half of the world's population will be displaced.

How fragile and precarious had been our resting place! Yet usage had dulled our sense of danger. The floe had become our home, and during the early months of the drift we had almost ceased to realize that it was but a sheet of ice floating on unfathomed seas.[27]

Many of the glacier studies being done now in the Antarctic are focused on evaluating the growing instability of the West Antarctic Ice Sheet. It is thought that if the Amundsen Sea Sector, which appears increasingly vulnerable, were to discharge, then the entire ice sheet would be compromised, and we would reach the point of an unstoppable retreat. Many scientists fear that West Antarctica may have already reached this tipping point.

We, as a culture, have long glorified stories of courage and determination. Yet the biggest failure of our society now seems to be our inability—our utter lack of courage—in recognizing the full implications of what we've done, and of what we are still unwilling to do. It can be enough to drive one to despair. Yet Shackleton judged a man—above all else—by the degree of optimism he projected, even when faced with the longest of odds. What the Boss valued was not so much blind faith in oneself as it was a belief in action—the trust that at some point in time, and on some level, our deeds really can make a difference. And if we can seize our moment, if we can summon up the necessary courage to strike off to some new and more solid ground, then there is hope.

Man can sustain life with very scant means. The trappings of civilization are soon cast aside in the face of stern realities, and given the barest opportunity[,] . . . man can live and even find his laughter ringing true.[28]

———

On April 9, 1916, the men took to their boats. They would be at sea for six days. After the first, the castaways set up camp on a large floe, but it split down the middle in the dead of night, and one of the men spilled over into the water while tucked dangerously in his sleeping bag. Luckily, Shackleton had been awake, pacing the length of the camp nearby, and he managed to heave the man up onto the ice just before it slammed violently closed. There would be no more landings, not until they reached solid ground.

Over the next five days they battled gale-force winds, steady rain, and repeated snow squalls. All of the boats were taking on water, and several of the men complained of no longer being able to feel their feet. The men bailed for their lives, many openly wept. "I doubted if all the men would survive that night," Shackleton confessed near the end, when the boats became separated in the dark.[29] Yet somehow they persevered.

This was the first landing ever made on Elephant Island, and a thought came to me that the honor should belong to the youngest member of the Expedition, so I told Blackborrow to jump over. He seemed to be in a state almost of coma, and in order to avoid delay I helped him, perhaps a little roughly, over the side of the boat. He promptly sat down in the surf and did not move. Then I suddenly realized what I had forgotten, that both his feet were frostbitten badly.[30]

Blackborrow was the stowaway. Good natured, quiet, a favorite of all hands. Back on board the *Endurance*, Shackleton had taken a liking to the young man, helping him attend to his schooling. Now, he sat helplessly in the surf. Several of the men jumped over, dragging him further up the beach. They were dying of thirst, of hunger, of exhaustion. Shackleton had not slept for one hundred hours.

Some of the men were reeling about the beach as if they had found an unlimited supply of alcoholic liquor on the desolate shore. They were laughing uproariously, picking up stones and letting handfuls of pebbles trickle between their fingers like misers gloating over hoarded gold.[31]

Some of the men. Those that fit snugly into their leader's heroic tale. Though the diaries of others paint a far grimmer, less embellished picture. "In the *Wills*, only two men were fit to do anything," one of the men recorded. "Some fellows moreover were half crazy: one got an axe and did not stop till he had killed about ten seals."[32] "At least half of the party were insane," Wild added, "helpless and hopeless."[33] Perhaps Wild already had an inkling that these men would soon become his charges—looking after them an unenviable task that would, for the most part, be conducted off stage. Regardless, they had done it—after 497 days they were back on solid ground—but it was only the barest of footholds, and even then, they knew that no one would come save them here.

———

"Had we but half their physical courage none could stand against us," Apsley Cherry-Garrard has written, though it wasn't Shackleton and his men he was referring to—it was the penguins, the only current occupants of Elephant Island.[34] Most of them, judging by the looks of things, are of the chinstrap variety, though there is also a small colony of nesting macaroni penguins waddling about on shore. The total ridiculousness of this species almost makes the others look like solemn dignitaries. A macaroni's distinguishing mark—apart from a proportionally ginormous beak that it can mount near-vertical rock slopes with—is a yellow cowlick-like crest arising from a patch on the center of the forehead. Named after a particular fashion style of eighteenth-century England that was known for its flamboyant ornamentation, macaronis might be the most populous penguin of the whole world, though their numbers have been in decline since the 1970s, and their conservation status has been listed as vulnerable.

Vulnerable, to put it mildly, would be the condition of any shipwrecked men on this bitter shoreline, as its jutting rock faces and pounding surf hardly seem fit even for the wildlife. Foggy with powerful winds, the conditions are too poor for us to risk a landing, though we take a Zodiac ride over to Point Wild, where twenty-two men lived for five months under two overturned boats. "The site where they camped was actually just over the other side of that isthmus," Tom Richie hollers over the sound of the waves, lifting a hand briefly from the tiller to point across the shore. "That's where the boulder beach was built up, though now it has eroded almost entirely away."

Elephant Island is really just a half-sunk mountain massif, with an ice sheet stretching across its broad elephant-shaped back. The land is stunning, with its cascading glaciers and its sheer three-thousand-foot peaks, but also ruthless. I turn my eyes back to the open horizon to the east—it is from this spot that Frank Hurley's other most famous photograph was taken, of the beach party gathered along the now submerged shoreline, waving out to a small boat drifting on the choppy sea. The men are waving goodbye to their most seaworthy lifeboat, the *James Caird*.[35] All of twenty feet long, the *James Caird* rose only a little more than two feet out of the water—not much higher, as one polar writer has pointed out, than your average bath tub.[36]

Viewing the photograph, it seems clear that these men have been standing like this for some time, their arms growing heavy as they try to offer an air of hopefulness to the departing party. They all know that their lives depend on that small boat; they all know how unlikely this venture is to succeed. Hurley has climbed a small rise to look down slightly on the backs of these men. He seems both a part of this group, and also separated by the cold vantage of his camera lens. While the moment captured is one of stubborn optimism, the burden of what comes after for these men hovers around the edges of the frame.

Dear Sir,

In the event of my not surviving the boat journey to South Georgia you [Frank Wild] will do your best for the rescue of the party. You are in full command from the time the boat leaves this island, and all hands are under your orders. On your return to England you are to communicate with the Committee. I wish you, Lees & Hurley to write the book. . . . I have every confidence in you and always have had, may God prosper your work and your life. You can convey my love to my people and say I tried my best.[37]

Shackleton scrawled this out hurriedly before departing with a crew of five men. McNish had made what improvements he could to the small boat: strengthening the keel, building a deck of wood and canvas, caulking the seams with a mixture of artist's paint and seal blood. The carpenter would be coming along—his ingenuity with such improvisations might come in handy, and Shackleton was worried to force him on Wild given his past insubordination. The sea voyage might be the riskier venture, but Shackleton was also anxious regarding the morale of the group left behind. Several of the men had already broken down in body and mind and their looking after would not be easy. Worsley's great skills as a navigator would be indispensable, and he had also proven himself as one of the most stalwart members of the expedition. This left three spots for the crew. Shackleton didn't want to deprive Wild of all the best men, knowing that if the sea voyage failed, the others would have to attempt some other desperate escape. Still, Shackleton needed at least one more experienced hand, someone whom he could count on to keep heart no matter what difficulties lay ahead. He chose Thomas Crean.

One of the memories that comes to me from those days is Crean singing at
the tiller. He always sang while he was steering, and nobody ever discov-
ered what the song was. It was devoid of tune and as monotonous as the
chanting of a Buddhist monk at his prayers; yet somehow it was cheerful.[38]

Tom Crean was a strong and benevolent petty officer from a remote part
of County Kerry, Ireland. While nowhere near as famous as the much-
valorized leaders with whom he served, Crean was one of the finest polar travelers to ever live. By this point in his career, he had already traveled with Scott on board both the *Discovery* and the *Terra Nova*. On the
latter expedition, Crean survived the pony depot disaster alongside Apsley Cherry-Garrard and Birdie Bowers, then—near the end of that expedition—he wound up saving the lives of two companions as they struggled back from the polar plateau. For this feat he earned the Albert Medal,
Britain's highest award for bravery in a civilian situation. Crean, then, was
a rare bird—a creature to give pause and take special note of—even if he
seemed patently unaware of this himself.

———

Early the next morning, as we're cruising east into the South Orkney Island chain, our ship is blessed with a rare sighting of its own: a blue whale
mother and her calf. By this point in our voyage, we have probably already
seen close to a dozen whales, and the usual protocol involves Stephanie—
the resident whale expert—getting on the intercom to offer a little commentary, as the barnacle-crusted sea monster snorts out a few jarring
rounds of steam from its blowhole, and—if we're lucky—lifts its long tail
into the air in one slow and fluid gesture before diving back into the un-
derworld. This sighting, however, is much more unusual, and Stephanie
has other things in mind—in particular, she wants a skin sample. Since
this is all going down early in the morning, I'm in my usual spot in the library and am getting a bird's-eye view of a Zodiac setting off in pursuit—
with Tom Richie at the tiller, and Stephanie bracing a large compound
crossbow across her knee.

Among the most mysterious and untamed animals, whales are all for-
malists when it comes to poetry—their subphrases patterned by rhyme,
in what may be a mechanism to help them memorize their songs. And
just like the ancient bards, their aesthetic preferences largely tilt toward

the epic, with the longest recorded humpback song lasting over twenty straight hours. Even more impressively—along with a single bird from the Amazon—whales are the only nonhuman species known to alter their songs from year to year. Today, these herculean songsters are seen only infrequently in the Southern Ocean, as populations of humpbacks, fins, and blue whales have all been decimated to the verge of extinction. At the peak of the whaling industry, it is estimated that as many as 175,000 whales were processed on the island of South Georgia alone.

———

The distance between Elephant Island and South Georgia is roughly eight hundred miles—more than ten times the distance that Shackleton's men had just traveled from the edge of the pack ice. To reach this lonely outpost of whalers, the *James Caird* would have to cross the most formidable ocean on the planet, and at the onset of winter. They could expect winds of eighty miles an hour, along with heaving waves. Worsley would be navigating them toward a small island, with no points of land in between, using only a sextant and chronometer. If he steered them even a mile off course, their boat would be swept into three thousand miles of open water.

———

"The seas were bumpy, and I was at least fifty yards away, but I figured what the heck, and made the shot of my life." This is what Stephanie tells us afterward, still clearly feeling a rush of adrenaline as she recounts the event. Like many of the naturalists on board, Stephanie has her own research projects that extend far beyond the scope of a tourist cruise. Fortunately, this job gives her access to remote areas that even scientists based in the Antarctic rarely travel to. With one skin sample, she hopes to gain a clear sense of where these two whales descended from, along with what sort of pollutants they have accumulated in their blubber. Beyond that, she says, "the sighting alone gives me real hope that blue whale populations are in recovery." Stephanie opens the floor for questions, though mostly people seem to want to hear about her crossbow. Part of the fascination is obviously wrapped up with her being the only female naturalist on board, with one of the guests cracking a joke about needing the weapon "to keep the boys in line." She smiles at this, but you can see clearly that she has heard this all before, and that this bit of humor has long since grown old.

Whales were chiefly hunted for their prodigious amounts of oil, yet baleen—or whalebone—was also the preferred material for making the "stays" of women's corsets. At first, this may seem ironic, that the by-product of such a bloody and manly undertaking would become a trademark in women's fashion. But the corset was hardly a model of delicacy. Rather, it was an article meant to hold and train, to force a woman's body into a desired shape.

"Oh, baby, that's right! Show it to me! Give me that tail fin, honey!" One of the official photographers on board likes to talk dirty to the wildlife, encouraging this seal or that whale to move around in some way, as if it were an exotic dancer, or as if he were presiding over a bawdy photo shoot. Though it is intended, no doubt, as a playful jest, by the second or third time you hear him doing this, it starts to feel jarringly in poor taste. "Yes, yes, like that baby! Give it to me!"

Male adolescent whales are commonly driven away from their families as a mechanism for preventing inbreeding. These abandoned juveniles then gather in what are referred to as "bachelor pods." Scientists characterize these groups as being made up of males that are "sexually mature but socially immature"—a fairly accurate description of some corresponding human cohorts.[39]

====

The boy's club of Antarctic science took most of a century to break up, with the first female scientists having to wait until almost 1970 to be "allowed" access to the continent. Of course, up until 1997, U.S. scientific projects in the Antarctic were all overseen by the navy, and this brought with it a great deal of baggage—a lot of smoke and mirrors about shared bathrooms and the need to protect women from sex-starved men. As a result, American bases lagged far behind those of some other nations when it came to providing opportunities for women. Given this, it seems sadly fitting that the first female scientific officer to head a U.S. Antarctic station—a krill expert named Mary McWhinnie—was accompanied by a nun when she wintered over in 1974. Granted, Sister Mary Cahoon also happened to be a gifted biologist, but her vows of celibacy were likely seen as an additional selling point. Nowadays, it is estimated that over 40 percent of the people stationed at McMurdo are women. And, along with engaging in scientific pursuits, women have also worked to dismantle the patriarchate legacy of polar exploration. In 1993, for instance, the first all-women expedition skied to the South Pole, and in 2001, two schoolteachers—an American named Ann Bancroft and a Norwegian named Liv Arneson—became the first women to achieve the task that had so spectacularly eluded the crew of the *Endurance*: traversing the entire continent on foot.

———

Back in the cramped confines of the *James Caird*, the six-man crew had settled into a grueling, if temporarily sustainable, routine. Crean had been given the domestic task of running the "kitchen"—lighting the primus stove while doubled over and jamming it between his and another man's legs to keep it from spilling over. There wasn't enough room to sit upright, and since the boat was always taking on water, everyone's feet and legs were swollen with frostbite. On the eleventh day, Worsley estimated that they had finally reached the halfway mark. As their boat was only six feet wide, all they could manage for sleeping arrangements was a line of moldering reindeer-hair bags crammed into the bows. Turning in after each watch was like crawling into one's grave, as they packed themselves in on top of food cases and nearly a ton of sharp rocks that served as ballast.

Worsley headed the watch opposite of Shackleton and Crean, and he writes fondly of overhearing Crean's pillow talk as the two Irishmen would turn in: "Boss I can't eat those reindeer hairs. I'll have an inside on me like a billygoats neck. Let's give 'em to the Skipper & McCarthy. They never know what they're eatin'."[40]

Unfortunately, it is at this point in the unfolding narrative where Shackleton's book starts to feel rather one-dimensional, a little too consistent in its tone, as though looking for every opportunity to spin a yarn about superhuman perseverance. Or maybe I'm just starting to tire of my subject matter—these bachelor chronicles of the unknown, this long line of melancholic masculine affairs.

We were a tiny speck in the vast vista of the sea—the ocean that is open to all and merciful to none, that threatens even when it seems to yield, and that is pitiless always to weakness.[41]

Over a thousand miles away, in London, Shackleton's wife, Emily, was struggling to make ends meet and raise their three children—living oftentimes off the charity of Shackleton's benefactors. How many times had he promised her that he'd never again return to the Antarctic? That one of his countless business ventures was sure to pan out? Though in a way, this separation was easier. To not have to deal with his pent-up energy, his mistresses, his disappointments. "I must have failed him somehow," she wrote in a moving letter to a friend. "Perhaps I was too sure. . . . I am conscious of my own limitations. He sat so lightly to the things of this world—and was big, where I am often small. I looked after the small things and they rather stifle the soul."[42]

In Ursula K. Le Guin's short story "Sur," a small group of fictional South American women venture to Antarctica, claiming the South Pole in 1909—a year after Shackleton had established his farthest-south mark, and two years before Amundsen and Scott had raced to the pole. Le Guin's shrewd story challenges many of the guiding motives and heroic ideals of the customary male explorer, while also turning a critical eye on the patriarchal society of the day. "I deeply respect the scientific accomplishments of Captain Scott's expedition," her narrator claims, "but having had no training in any science, nor any opportunity for such training, my ignorance obliged me to forego any thought of adding to the body of scientific knowledge concerning Antarctica." Instead, the women venture south merely to go and see: "A simple ambition, I think, and essentially a modest one."[43] Of the team's organization and structure of leadership, she says only this: "The nine of us worked things out amongst us from beginning to end without any orders being given by anybody."[44]

Finally, when the three-woman Pole Team returns to base they are shocked by the impending birth of a child by one of the women who had stayed behind. Initially, at the discovery of the pregnancy, the narrator is upset at her companion for having withheld her condition, only to learn that the young woman had done nothing of the sort: "Only those who had concealed from her what she most needed to know were to blame. Brought up by servants, with four years' schooling in a convent, and married at sixteen, the poor girl was still so ignorant at twenty years of age that she thought it was 'the cold weather' that made her miss her periods." The delivery goes smoothly—after all, the narrator adds, "several of us had borne children and had helped with deliveries"—and ultimately the mother decides to name her child Rosa del Sur, the Compass Rose.[45]

If there is such a thing as reincarnation, please let me be reborn as a fur seal pup. I came to this conclusion within the first five minutes of our arrival at Coronation Island—the largest of the South Orkney archipelago, and the one lonely outpost of the Scotia Sea. There must be close to one hundred pups here, playing around on the beach and in the shallows. They look like little family dogs whose bottom halves have somehow all gotten stuck inside sleeping bags. They rear up on their tiny flippers and, with the dodge and weave of featherweight boxers, make playful feints at one another, and at us as we come to shore. Not even the river otter appears to have as much fun as these rug rats.

Of course, if you start out as a fur seal pup, you eventually wind up becoming a full-grown adult, which seems entirely less appealing. Pugnacious and highly territorial, bull fur seals establish large harems on beaches where the females come to give birth. This is no ecstatic courtship, as the females have little choice in the matter—they have to be there—and view the males with more or less open disdain as they engage in their bloody battles.

But whereas the male fur seal is at least gifted an adorable childhood, the elephant seal is basically always repugnant. Like huge wallowing grubs, these beasts are the very epitome of sloth. Their voices are, as one writer put it, "like massive, prolonged belches," and for any child of the eighties, their obvious pop-culture kinship lies with Jabba the Hutt.[46] These are true seals—meaning that they lack the forelimbs of their flashier cousins. And while the fur seal is known for its luxuriant coat that protects it from the bitter cold, elephant seal insulation is provided, instead, by a thick layer of subcutaneous fat. To put this in perspective, cow's milk is made up of 4 percent fat, while an elephant seal's milk is about 45 percent. Because of this, their pups grow as much as twenty pounds a day, and a full-grown bull can weigh as much as nine thousand pounds, making them the largest seals in the world. When they head to shore in late August—a few weeks before the females arrive—they start a steel-cage grudge match of bashing and biting that seems to have been taken right out of the script of a B-rate horror flick. As a species, seals have an extremely high amount of blood in relation to their body size (about twice the ratio of a human). This allows them to stay underwater for long spells, but it also means—unsurprisingly—that they bleed a whole lot. Successful male elephant seals are known as "beachmasters," and they can defend the territory of over one hundred females, siring as many pups. Not that the male has any paternal affection for his offspring, as the child won't be born for another year, and almost certainly on another male's turf. What's more, a bull elephant seal also takes no interest in the welfare of his harem's pups, and regularly kills or maims them as he wallows on top of them or rushes around to protect his territory. Finally, the act of copulation is by no means an act of delicacy, as the male is roughly four times the size of the female and seemingly envelops her with his great blubbery embrace.

South Georgia—where our ship will be landing in another day or two—is the epicenter of all this, hosting the densest mass of marine mammals on earth during the breeding season, with as many as six thousand elephant seals alone crowding the beaches each October. Luckily, we tourists don't see any of this, as the elephant seals have returned to ocean feeding by the time the summer cruise ships arrive, and the only species still breeding by then are the legions of lovable penguins—though even they have lessons of biology to behold and cringe at. For example, an easy way to identify a female penguin is to look for the footprints left on her back.

On May 8—fourteen days after departing from Elephant Island—the *James Caird* came in sight of the dark cliffs of South Georgia. They had done it. They had almost capsized in a deathly wave, they had had to chisel away the ice coating the outside of their boat as it began to sink like a stone, but somehow they had made it. Only they weren't there just yet, and a storm of hurricane-force winds arose, preventing all possibility of landing. They were on the uninhabited south side of the island, but there was no hope of steering themselves around to the whale stations up north—they would have to land wherever they could, then strike out across the island on foot. Their last cask of water had turned out to be brackish and their mouths had become so swollen with thirst that they could hardly swallow or speak as they attempted to ride out the storm. The weight of the ballast made their craft almost impossible to steer, and Shackleton thought it certain that they would be dashed against the rocks.

The chance of surviving the night, with the driving gale and the implacable sea forcing us on to the lee shore, seemed small. I think most of us had a feeling that the end was very near.[47]

"The thoughts of the others I did not know—" Worsley would later write. "Mine were regret for having brought my diary and annoyance that no one would ever know we had got so far."[48]

═══

When the three heroines of Le Guin's story arrive at the South Pole, they choose not to leave any record of their accomplishment: "We discussed leaving some kind of mark or monument, a snow cairn, a tent pole and flag; but there seemed no particular reason to do so. Anything we could do, anything we were, was insignificant, in that awful place."[49] And upon the expedition's return to civilization, they decide to likewise keep their voyage a secret, questioning the very idea of legacy: "Achievement is smaller than men think. What is large is the sky, the earth, the sea, the soul."[50]

═══

That afternoon, after we return to the ship, there is an announcement that there will be another guest lecture before dinner. I'm still reeling from the memory of the adventure blogger's talk, but Kendra—who is clearly plugged in to all of this—tells me that I'll definitely want to be there. When I arrive at the lounge, I'm surprised to see John—the yodeling improvised-sledder from a couple of days ago—standing at the front of the room. On the screen behind him there is an old photograph of a group of young men in polar garb standing in front of a backdrop of massive snowy peaks. It takes me a minute, but then I can pick out his face with certainty—very handsome, maybe a little cocky, though with a warm Paul Newman–esque smile that comes through clearly even in this grainy photograph.

John Evans, as we would all learn, was a member of a historic 1966 expedition that became the first to summit 16,067-foot-tall Mount Vinson—Antarctica's highest peak and, at the time, the only unclimbed continental high point. John served as the chief scientist for the ten-man team—a title that, as he is quick to point out, was a bit of a stretch. In fact, he was only a PhD student, and, at times, he wasn't even that.

"I did everything for the wrong reasons," as he put it, "but it always seemed to turn out okay."[51] The University of Michigan, where he was studying geology, had the best Antarctic research program in the country, and a brief research stint at McMurdo had thrown a crank in his scholarly pursuits. "It was so much fun I quit school and got a job there." A few years on, and he was back at Michigan, where he met Loie and decided that it was finally time to follow through on getting that degree.

Back in 1957, a U.S. aerial survey identified Mount Vinson as Antarctica's highest peak, but it wasn't until the mid-sixties that the upper brass of the U.S. services decided to act on this. "There was a political side to it," John tells us. "They thought it would be a shame if the Russians, or Italians, or somebody beat us to it." With John already being a highly regarded climber in the States, his familiarity with the Antarctic made him an obvious choice to head the expedition. "My advisor wasn't too happy to hear about all of this, but it was too good to pass up." *National Geographic* agreed to underwrite the expedition, but then at the last minute asked for a research component to give the expedition more of a scientific bent. "It was up to me—I couldn't believe it. So, I woke up my advisor at the crack of dawn and the two of us hammered out a proposal."

As John is telling us all of this, he clicks through a series of photographs—of the men goofing around with penguins, man-hauling an overloaded sledge, and gaining an exposed ridge with huge exterior frame packs. It was almost fifty years ago now, though if you swapped out their bright-colored outdoor gear for turtleneck sweaters and knitted Burberry hats, they could be men from another time entirely, alongside the likes of Scott and Shackleton. I glance over at Loie, who is sitting at a nearby table—she looks downright glowing.

———

Worsley and Crean were coming with me, and after consultation we decided to leave the sleeping bags behind us and make the journey in very light marching order. We would take three days' provisions for each man in the form of sledging ration and biscuit. . . . No man had ever penetrated a mile from the coast of South Georgia at any point, and the whalers I knew regarded the country as inaccessible.[52]

The last heroic feat of Shackleton's voyage has been retold in many books and films—how they hiked thirty-two miles in thirty-six hours across a treacherous interior of ragged peaks and glaciers, how they had to cut steps in the ice with a carpenter's adze, and how, at the very end, after they had heard the heartening blast of a steam whistle calling the whalers to work, they still had to rope up and descend a waterfall. Perhaps no Antarctic narrative has been so repeatedly valorized. So how about a different story?

====

Mount Vinson, as John tells us, turned out to be a pretty straightforward climb, and over the next few days all ten of the men from their party would summit. "Well, after that we could have just closed up shop, but our plane wasn't coming back to get us for another couple of weeks, so we started going up some of the other peaks, and the one that really got our attention was Tyree."

As Antarctica's second-largest peak, Mt. Tyree is less than one hundred feet shorter than Mount Vinson, though it is a far more difficult climb. It took the ten-man team over a week to settle on an approach—an extremely steep slope of solid ice that they would have to descend from the summit of nearby Mount Gardner to access the knife-edged col of Tyree. "Not impossible," as John had reported back to the others after an earlier reconnaissance, "but a darn poor choice." In the end, that was all they had, and after traversing the route, John and one other man, Barry Corbet, set up a small camp to tackle the summit. "We alternated leads," John tells us. "One of us would anchor to a piton or to a rope sling thrown over a rock, while the other led upward. It took us five and a half hours to get up that face. But then, suddenly, we came over a steep snow cornice—and we had it! We stood on the top. Mount Tyree, the rugged old so-and-so, was licked!"

"Ever since the whole Seven Summits thing started," John adds, "over a thousand people have climbed Mount Vinson—they've got guided tours that head up there and everything. But to this day, Tyree has only been climbed five times, by a total of ten people." The "Seven Summits" mountaineering challenge involves climbing each of the continent's highest peaks. Though, as climber and writer Jon Krakauer pointed out in his book about Everest, *Into Thin Air*, it would be a far more technical challenge to tackle each of the continents' second-highest peaks.

At the conclusion of their expedition, John hurried back to Minneapolis, where he had promised to attend a winter formal dance with Loie through her sorority. "John seems real nice," one of Loie's friends evidently told her afterward. "But he sure has a red face."

In 2006, John and three other members of the original climbing party were invited to climb Mount Vinson again, forty years after their first ascent. They were almost at the summit when the trip leader turned them around. "We were just too slow," John says with a smile. "We were within an hour of the top, and we could have easily done it, but we were just too slow."

The room fills with applause. People get up and start talking to each other, though I notice Tom Richie still seated at a table, staring up at the screen where a picture of John and the rest of his team is on display. Speechless. And from a guy who must have thought he'd heard everything about the Antarctic.

———

"Don't you know me?" I said.
*   "I know your voice," he replied doubtfully. . . .*
*   "My name is Shackleton," I said.*
*   Immediately, he put out his hand and said, "Come in. Come in."*
*   "Tell me, when was the war over?" I asked.*
*   "The war is not over," he answered. "Millions are being killed. Europe is mad. The world is mad."*[53]

It is a memorable end to a remarkable journey, though like much of the recorded dialogue of the book, it feels too stilted, too rehearsed. As though—throughout all the struggle and uncertainty—they were all auditioning for some grandiose play, always worried that they'd fall short of what was expected of their heroic part. And the immediate question regarding the war feels a little too pandering, too aware of its own eventual audience back home. In this instance, however, the tale far outweighs the telling, and when—after taking their first bath in over a year and a half—they were treated to a full banquet and recounted the incredible stages of their journey, one of the old Norwegian whalers came up and rested his hand on Shackleton's shoulder, declaring simply, "These are men."[54]

These are men. Certainly, this was meant as the greatest of compliments, and just as certainly it was received as such. But Shackleton wasn't some laconic, gun-toting cowboy from the movies. He was known for being openly affectionate toward his crew—"snuggled close together all night," Worsley had written about an evening he had shared with the Boss as they stood watch together on the *James Caird*.[55] And from his letters to friends, we see that he wrote openly, even unguardedly, about his emotions, his fears—"A man rarely writes out his heart but I would to you . . . ," he begins in a letter to Edward Wilson shortly after their *Discovery* days.[56] Shackleton's personality was a rich blend of sensitivity and aggression, always spouting out bits of poetry, always favoring sincerity over irony. Perhaps all of this was well understood by that old Norwegian whaler, perhaps what he meant to praise was more than just the cardboard cutout of masculinity. Though sadly it often seems like we have lost sight of this in our own times.

———

Years later, when Shackleton was getting ready to publish *South*, he added another passage near the end of the text:

When I look back at those days I have no doubt that Providence guided us, not only across those snow fields, but across the storm-white sea. . . . I know that during that long and racking march of thirty-six hours over the un-named mountains and glaciers of South Georgia it seemed to me often that we were four, not three. I said nothing to my companions on the point, but afterwards Worsley said to me, "Boss, I had a curious feeling on the march that there was another person with us." Crean confessed to the same idea. One feels "the dearth of human words, the roughness of mortal speech" in trying to describe things intangible, but a record of our journeys would be incomplete without a reference to a subject very near to our hearts.[57]

Given its late insertion into the book, the veracity of this passage has been questioned by some historians, conjecturing that it may have been a last-minute fabrication meant to add an air of spirituality as the story comes to a close. Shackleton, after all, had always had the instincts of a showman. He had also always had a love of poets, and it is Keats he is quoting there at the end, though the poet we most associate with this passage is actually T. S. Eliot—

> Who is the third who walks always beside you?
> When I count, there are only you and I together
> But when I look ahead up the white road
> There is always another walking beside you.[58]

Eliot credits Shackleton for these lines in the inscrutable notes at the back of *The Waste Land*. One wonders whom Eliot had decided to kick to the curb in his rendition, given that he shrinks the party size from three to two. Eliot was a rather class-conscious individual, so it was probably the petty officer—well, I'm sure Tom Crean didn't lose any sleep over the matter.

Regardless, what is now generally referred to as the "Third Man Factor"— the idea of an unseen presence or ghost that provides comfort during a traumatic event—has earned a place in the popular culture of outdoor survival lore, with many well-known climbers, including Reinhold Messner and Peter Hilary, having come forth with their own similar accounts. And so the legacy surrounding the last great voyage of the Heroic Age continues to grow and puzzle us.

═

"We gave them three hearty cheers," Frank Wild wrote back on Elephant Island, "and watched the boat getting smaller and smaller in the distance. Then seeing some of the party in tears I immediately set them all to work. My own heart was full. I heard one of the few pessimists remark, 'that's the last of them' and I almost knocked him down with a rock."[59] For some reason, I find myself more drawn to the story of the twenty-two men who were forced to wait out a winter under two overturned boats. Perhaps this is because their story is less well known. Perhaps it is simply because their brand of heroism seems more approachable to me.

"Lash up and stow!" Wild would yell to rouse the men each morning. "The Boss may come today."[60] What Wild himself thought the chances of this were is hard to say, but he was determined to keep a tenor of hope alive for his men. Wild was the son of a schoolmaster, who liked to claim—disingenuously—that he was a direct descendent of James Cook. His intelligence and foresight were rated highly by the men, perhaps even more so than those of the Boss. Shackleton, as they all knew, was a dreamer—a romantic idealist of the tallest order—but Wild was a straight shooter. If he claimed there was still a chance, then there was. It was as simple as that.

Lash up and stow, the bellowing refrain entering their dreams, *the Boss may come today*. The repeated phrase must have gotten on their nerves, losing all meaning, but then what hadn't? "About 30 Gentoo Penguins came ashore & I am pleased the weather was too bad to slay them," wrote Hurley at one point. "We are heartily sick of being compelled to kill every bird that comes ashore."[61]

At night, one of the men would read out a single recipe from a small penny cookery book that had somehow managed to find its way with them to this deserted place. This would then be discussed with great seriousness, with improvements and alterations proposed as they lay down in their bags. I wonder whether, years later, any of the men followed through with those recipes? If the guy who took the book home to England didn't just work his way through the entire damn thing, preparing, all for himself, each and every meal? Leonard Hussey, the expedition's meteorologist, also played the banjo, and Shackleton had allowed him to pack his instrument along through their various tribulations because he thought it would come in handy for raising the spirits of the men. I'm sure it did, and that each of the men was thankful for the music, but how could any of them ever listen to the folksy twang of a banjo again in life without welling up instantly with tears?

Running out of tobacco, the men tried a dozen different ways to invent some adequate, smokable substitute. One such scheme, carried out by the scientists with laboratory zeal, involved collecting everyone's pipe and boiling them in a pot with the sennegrass that insulated their fur boots. They also invented a vile homebrew that consisted of methylated spirits used to preserve specimens, along with a little sugar and a bit of ginger (a small tin of which had been brought along by mistake). They named this drink Gut Rot 1916 and toasted one another as though they were gathered at some great banquet put on in their honor.

On a more serious note, by early June, the toes on Blackborrow's left foot had become gangrenous and the two surgeons were forced to amputate, without proper instruments and inside a grimy makeshift hut. All they had for anesthetic was a small amount of chloroform, which necessitated keeping the hut hot enough that it could vaporize. The surgery was successful, but as winter loomed near, it became apparent that Blackborrow's foot was not healing properly; in fact, it was swelling from a bone infection, though the young man had gained the admiration of all for staying positive throughout the ordeal. By then, it must have been hard for any of them to believe that the sea voyage to South Georgia hadn't ended in failure, and that their friends hadn't all perished somewhere in the South Atlantic. Otherwise, why were they still there?

The truth was that Shackleton had already made three attempts at rescuing them, only to be turned back each time by ice. The castaways were running out of food, and with winter almost upon them, they had to start thinking about attempting to save themselves. On August 30, they were out gathering limpets along the rocky shore—one of their only remaining sources of food. For lunch, the cook was preparing a stew made of old seal's backbone. That's when they saw the ship. Hurley hurried to light a bonfire, and two of the men carried Blackborrow outside so that he could have the chance of seeing for himself. The tug lowered a small boat, and as it rowed closer the men could make out clearly the figures of Shackleton and Crean.

===

In cases of gangrene, it is necessary, before one amputates, to wait for what is called "the line of demarcation" to be formed, in order to make sure where the live tissue begins. When it comes to storytelling, however, there is no corresponding border between fact and fiction.

In Hurley's photographic record of the expedition, his image "The Rescue" closes the courageous tale. In this picture, a ragged line of men stand out on the edge of the beach waving wildly at a lifeboat seemingly coming to shore. Only this is all wrong, and from the original film negative it is clear that Hurley has doctored the image of the *James Caird* setting off for South Georgia over four months before. Historian Caroline Alexander takes issue with this, and rightly so, I'd argue: "Hurley's predilection for 'fiddling' with his images was usually harmless, but in this case, he committed a grave indiscretion, for the original irretrievable image was the greater. In it, he captured both sides of this impossible story, the razor's edge of its endeavor—success and failure in the balance, the momentous departure and that patient bravery of those left behind."[62] Hurley had sacrificed nuance and uncertainty for a straightforward tug at the heartstrings. Like the Boss, he too had always had the instincts of a showman. Yet the entire voyage had been, in many ways, an exercise in mythmaking—from an ice-locked ship to the shadowy figure of one-eyed Aeneas. Can we really blame them, then, for buying in too fully to their own story?

=====

That evening, just before dinner, I steal a little more time up in the library to work on some writing. Tomorrow will be a sea day, as we leave the Antarctic fully behind and journey out to South Georgia.

Once, not so long ago now, it was the act of leaving that most held me. And absence, with its lonely dignity, its austere gray repose. But people can live by such a myth for only so long before they sense that chapter coming fully to a close.

=====

On Frank Hurley's first night in London upon his return to civilization, the city was bombed. "Emerged from a war with nature, we were destined to take our place in a war of nations," he wrote. "Life is one long call to conflict, anyway."[63] And on the opening page of *South*, Shackleton includes the following dedication: "To my comrades who fell in the white war-fare of the south and on the red fields of France and Flanders."[64] Linking imagery of war and conflict with Antarctic exploration was nothing new; in fact, it was a widely used trope, and—in some ways—a sad commentary on the limits of the imagination. But while offering such comparisons in peacetime may simply be written off as an excess of the genre, it seems far more problematic here. Even before the *Endurance* had arrived in Antarctic waters, the expedition had been linked with the war. The British order for general mobilization was released three days before they set sail, and Shackleton had offered to place the expedition at the disposal of the Admiralty, only to receive a one-word telegram in response: "Proceed."[65] Now, having missed several years of a war that was far bloodier and less decisive than any of them could have imagined, there was a need to justify their absence from it, if only for themselves. But what did the largely self-generated struggles of a group of explorers at the bottom of the world have in common with those of a conscripted man holed up in a trench, facing the prospect of death by poison gas? For a great number of the men who voyaged on the *Endurance*, they were about to find out. Timothy McCarthy was the first to die, less than a year after completing the open boat voyage to South

Georgia with Shackleton. His ship was torpedoed just west of the British Isles and all hands were lost—he was twenty-eight at the time.

For his part, Shackleton was now forty-two, legally exempt from service, though still longing for a role to play—a means for positioning himself again somewhere near a heroic center. But as a middle-aged explorer with a distrust of authority and a questionable bill of health, his services were not in demand, and he struggled to get any sort of meaningful commission. Eventually he was sent on a propaganda mission to South America, with a vague assignment to raise morale and promote the British war effort. Having felt himself largely at odds with the world during times of peace, Shackleton was finding it no easier now that there was war. And it wasn't that he was failing or falling short; for a man of Shackleton's disposition, it was something far worse—he was superfluous.

It is interesting to compare Shackleton's *South* with Apsley Cherry-Garrard's *The Worst Journey in the World*. The two books were published within a couple of years of one another, both centered on the same far-away land and recounting events only a few years apart. Yet theirs was a period in history of insurmountable change, with so many of the old ideals of their country coming under attack. While the gap between the two voyages was less than a year, they existed in different times—the *Terra Nova* returned shortly before the Great War, while the *Endurance* was the first to leave after it had begun. Both books were clearly tales of suffering and overcoming great challenges, but the war had produced a surfeit of all that, and what they truly had to offer their readers was something else entirely. To me, both are deeply personal books, concerned more than all else with crafting their own mythology.[66] For Cherry, his years in the Antarctic represented the last real innocence of his life—a sense of elevated purpose and sacrifice that would be forever changed by the loss of his friends and the ruthlessness of the Great War. But Shackleton was too much of an optimist for that—and, unlike Cherry, he had to be the hero of his own story. For Shackleton, the Antarctic was a grand stage to act out the timeless struggles of the human heart—it was about what persisted, what endured. One book was a meditation on what had been saved, the other on what had been lost. In this, they appeal to different sorts of readers, even to this day.

=====

By the time the war ended, Shackleton was fully adrift. After the publication of *South* in 1919, he spent six months appearing twice daily at the Philharmonic Hall, recounting the travails of the *Endurance* to an auditorium of half empty seats. He was drinking heavily and was also heavily in debt. For weeks at a time he would avoid Emily and their kids, staying instead with his American mistress. Shackleton had never been perfect, far from it in fact, but he also refused to let his life be defined by his failures. In the end, more than expertise or sound judgment, this was the real strength of Shackleton's leadership: he gave his men hope. Not simply for rescue or survival, but hope that they too could transcend their own limitations, as well as the strict boundaries that society had set for them. Shackleton never held himself apart. He was one of them, repeatedly kicked to the curb by life, yet also always reciting stray bits of poetry that must have seemed far beyond the scope of their lives. In the end, he taught his men to believe in their own potential for greatness, and they loved him for it.

"A born poet," Frank Hurley would end up writing of the Boss, "through all his oppressions he could see glory and beauty in the stern forces which reduced us to destitution."[67] But was that all it took? Could you be identified by such a title without consideration of what you had managed to produce? Could you somehow stake a claim for yourself, despite your best laid plans coming to waste?

===

Almost out of the blue, it seemed, one of Shackleton's old school friends offered him a way out. John Quiller Rowett—who had made a fortune off the trade of wines and spirits—agreed to underwrite one last expedition. By cable Shackleton called his old shipmates, and they came: Worsley, Wild, Macklin, McIlroy, Hussey with his banjo, McLeod, Kerr, and even Green (the cook). Some of them he still owed wages to, but they came all the same. It was a poorly equipped expedition, with no clear plan. Their ship, the *Quest*, would require repairs at every port of call.

Before his departure, Shackleton had written in a letter to a friend, "We . . . go into the ice into the life that is mine and I do pray that we will make good. It will be my last time."[68] In reality, though, the end was even closer than he thought. In Rio, Shackleton suffered a heart attack, but refused to turn back, or even be examined. When they pulled into the Grytviken harbor at South Georgia on January 4, the explorers were given a hero's welcome, though early the next morning Shackleton summoned Macklin—the doctor who had amputated Blackborrow's frostbitten toes back on Elephant Island. A little before three in the morning, Shackleton—at the age of forty-seven—suffered a massive heart attack. In the hour before his death, Macklin had sat with the Boss and the two friends had talked—just that, as Shackleton was still unwilling to submit to an examination. Macklin didn't force it but stressed to him that he needed to take things easy for a while. "You are always wanting me to give up something," the Boss barked back at him. "What do you want me to give up now?"[69] These were Shackleton's last words.

———

I arrive late to dinner and can't find anywhere to sit. Finally, I join an elderly Japanese couple whom I have never talked to, and whom I strangely can't remember seeing anywhere off the ship. Not on a shore walk or even on a Zodiac ride. Maybe they just spend their days up in their room between meals, wishing they had sailed to the Bahamas. The woman doesn't speak much English and I am struggling to keep conversation going with her husband. He mentions that he is really looking forward to arriving in the Falklands, which surprises me. We will be spending our last two days there—with an afternoon to kill in the town of Port Stanley—and I just assumed that everyone, like me, would rather be spending that time somewhere off in the wilds. I ask him about this, and he tells me that he will actually be inspecting a hospital there. Evidently that is his job, and this was a big part of the reason for them coming on this cruise.

"What kind of medicine do you practice?" I ask, trying to sound interested.

"I am a heart surgeon," he answers, and then adds somewhat offhandedly, "I invented the coronary bypass."

Who knew there were still so many heroes left in the world? Who else was naïve enough to think they could simply be picked out in a crowd?

———

Leonard Hussey, the banjo-playing meteorologist, volunteered to leave the expedition and escort the Boss's body back home. Upon arriving at his first port of call, he was intercepted by a message from Emily, requesting that her husband be buried in South Georgia instead. Despite the great distances that had formed between them over the years, she still knew Shackleton better than anyone, and understood, ultimately, where he belonged: the small whaling cemetery of Grytviken, where our party will be paying a visit in a couple more days. His tombstone should be easy to spot, as it is the only one facing south instead of east.

After the funeral, the *Quest* sailed on under Wild's command. It could hardly be considered a successful voyage. By this time, Wild was drinking regularly, and without the Boss, there seemed little to hold them all together. But before they sailed on to England, Wild did lead them back to Elephant Island.

====

What is left after our private mythologies fail us? Or we, them? When our dreams of discovery or art no longer seem to sustain us? Tomorrow, I won't even get out of bed. Eric has informed me that the crew is expecting rough seas on our passage through the south Atlantic. I'm no sailor, and I've got nothing to prove. After dinner, I swing back by the library to pick up a copy of Scott's last expedition journals—a rather grim bedside companion—and turn in.

====

Almost out of necessity it would seem, all postscripts are bound for sadness.

After the letdown of the *Quest*, Frank Wild settled in South Africa, where years of drought and floods ruined his cotton farm and drove him further to drink. A journalist discovered Wild, years later, working as a ruined bartender in a Zulu village at the head of a mine. Some of his old polar friends tried to help him out by securing a pension, but the assistance came too late, and he died there in 1939.

Frank Worsley continued to seek out adventure at every turn of his life. He served with distinction in World War I, receiving a Distinguished Service Order when the ship he was in charge of sank a German submarine. He also volunteered in World War II and was given command of a merchant ship, though he was removed from his post upon being discovered to be almost seventy years old. He would die of lung cancer a year later, in 1943.

Perhaps of all the men who had sailed on board the *Endurance*, Frank Hurley seemed least suited for an anticlimax. After years of working as a highly esteemed war photographer, he continued to make expeditions to remote locations in pursuit of his art. During World War II, he was sent to Palestine, where he met a beautiful young opera singer whom he married only ten days later. They would go on to have four children together. At the end of his long life, Hurley published several books on Australian and Tasmanian wildflowers. He had gone from photographing the harsh and limitless expanses of the Antarctic to taking quaint pictures of daisies and bluebells. But it was never his subject matter that Hurley had cared most about—it was what he could transform it into through his art. In this, he had always remained a faithful servant.

As for Tom Crean, he returned home to County Kerry on the southwest tip of Ireland, living out a disciplined, happy, and somewhat ordinary life. By the time Shackleton came calling about the *Quest*, Crean had opened up a small pub, married a country girl, and was quietly raising a family. There would be no more voyaging for him. After his return to Ireland, Crean is said to have tucked away all his medals and to have rarely spoken of his adventures on the ice. Always the humblest of explorers, it made sense that he would continue on as a humble citizen. In his later years, Crean enjoyed working in the garden with his wife, Ellen, and he acquired two dogs that he named after the sled pups that were put down upon abandoning the *Endurance*. The name of his pub was the South Pole Inn.

====

Yet what I had intended as a chronicle of those voyages that set out has really been a record only of those that returned, and there is one more party that has been left back on the ice.

CHAPTER 8

TERRA NOVA
(1910–1912)
POLE JOURNEY

CAPTAIN ROBERT
FALCON SCOTT

Tuesday, January 16. . . . The worst has happened, or nearly the worst. We marched well in the morning and covered 7½ miles. Noon sight showed us in Lat. 89 degrees 42 minutes S., and we started off in high spirits in the afternoon. . . . About the second hour of the march Bowers' sharp eyes detected what he thought was a cairn; he was uneasy about it, but argued that it must be a sastrugus. Half an hour later he detected a black speck ahead.[1]

By this time, Scott's Pole Team had been on the march for two and a half months. They had been man-hauling their own sledge since starting up the Beardmore Glacier on December 10, had parted from their last support team on January 4, and had passed Shackleton's farthest-south mark a week ago, with Scott commemorating the event in his journal with the trusting words, "All is new ahead."[2] They were at that time roughly nine hundred miles away from safety, and over twenty-five hundred miles away from the closest permanent human habitation—while each of the five men must have harbored doubts as to whether they would ever make it back, to stumble upon any sign of mankind here would bring no comfort.

We marched on, found that it was a black flag tied to a sledge bearer; near by the remains of a camp; sledge tracks and ski tracks going and coming and the clear trace of dogs' paws—many dogs. This told us the whole story.

The Norwegians have forestalled us and are first at the Pole.... It will be a wearisome return. Certainly we are descending in altitude—certainly also the Norwegians found an easy way up.[3]

Scott knew how formidable Amundsen was as a rival, and he knew that dogs could start earlier in the season than ponies, but he also knew how much his team had endured to get there, and his first instinct was to short-change the victors, to assume that they must have profited from an easier route. As much as anything, perhaps, Scott believed in his own capacity for suffering, and that is the snow-swept ground he was unwilling to forfeit.

Wednesday, January 17.—Camp 69. T. −22 at start. Night −21. The Pole. Yes, but under very different circumstances from those expected. We have had a horrible day—add to our disappointment a head wind 4 to 5, with a temperature of −22, and companions labouring on with cold feet and hands. We started at 7.30, none of us having slept much after the shock of our discovery.... To-night little Bowers is laying himself out to get sights in terrible difficult circumstances; the wind is blowing hard, T. −21, and there is that curious damp, cold feeling in the air which chills one to the bone in no time.[4]

Bowers had previously been the member of a support party that had de-poted their skis roughly two hundred miles north of the pole. His inclusion as an extra man on the team was a last-minute decision by Scott, one that—in hindsight—has received much criticism. The historian Roland Huntford, who consistently offers a disparaging portrayal of Scott's leadership and decision-making, argues that Bowers was necessary because Scott himself was too out of practice to serve effectively as a navigator. Huntford, though, is reaching—reading too much between the lines and always looking for an opportunity to slight Scott, when multiple journals from the expeditions show Scott fully capable of taking sightings and performing the necessary calculations.* But without Bowers, Scott would have to shoulder this draining responsibility all on his own, and Bowers's boundless energy and incomparable resistance to the cold were already firmly established. This is not to say that there weren't strong arguments against Scott's decision to increase the party's size to five, though it does make clear that his selection of Bowers was beyond reproach.

* For a fuller discussion of Huntford's questionable views on Scott and the wider controversy surrounding historians' appraisal of the rival Pole Teams, see appendix 1.

*Great God! This is an awful place and terrible enough for us to have la-
boured to it without the reward of priority. Well, it is something to have got
here. . . . Now for the run home and a desperate struggle. I wonder if we can
do it.*[5]

This entry, along with many others from Scott's journal, was lightly edited
for publication, with the original entry actually reading, "and a desperate
struggle *to get the news through first.*"[6] In a time of exclusive newspaper
contracts, there was more at stake here than you might think. Not that
there would be any contesting of Amundsen's victory at the pole, but both
explorers were well aware of the money involved in breaking that news to
the world. Scott, then, is grasping at straws here, hoping to alleviate some
of the financial burden of the expedition by getting the news out first.
What is more revealing from the original entry, however, is how confident
Scott is at this moment. With the edited version you get the sense that he is
aware of the fix they are in, that he is fearful of the onset of winter, and that
he is beginning to have doubts over the collective strength of his party—yet
the original makes apparent that his actual concerns lay elsewhere.

*Thursday morning, January 18.—Decided after summing up all observa-
tions that we were 3.5 miles away from the Pole—one mile beyond it and 3
to the right. More or less in this direction Bowers saw a cairn or tent. . . . We
built a cairn, put up our poor slighted Union Jack, and photographed ourselves—mighty cold work all of it.*[7]

In the iconic shot we have of them, it is hard not to find fault with Scott's
confidence in his party. Clearly, it seems, the cold has begun to sink in
deeper now, and the dragging weight of their own bodies—even after all
the pounds they'd lost—is more than they can bear. Scott stands at the
center—his face blackened with soot, and his eyes seemingly closed, as if
already lost in thoughts of how history will judge him. At Scott's left is PO
Evans, and it is difficult to make out the expression on his face—he is the
workhorse, the biggest man of the group at nearly two hundred pounds,
though his eyes look glazed over and far away. To Scott's right—somehow
holding himself a little apart, even in this photo—is Titus Oates. He stands
with an uneven slouch, as though already showing signs of a limp. In the
snow of the foreground, Wilson and Bowers are seated obligingly—their
friendship and faith in one another firmly established through the struggles of the Winter Journey. If you were to bank on any of them pulling

through, surely it would be these two, but the whole party looks defeated, and by much more than Amundsen. Yet at this stage their journey is only half complete.

I fancy the Norwegians arrived at the Pole on the 15th Dec. and left on the 17th. . . . Well, we have turned our back now on the goal of our ambition and must face our 800 miles of solid dragging—and good-bye to most of the day-dreams.[8]

The letter Amundsen had left for Scott reads as follows: "As you are probably the first to reach this area after us, I will ask you kindly to forward this letter to King Haakon VII. If you can use any of the articles left in the tent please do not hesitate to do so. With kind regards. I wish you a safe return."[9] Amundsen had turned the last place on earth into a letterbox. Scott—the grudging messenger—may have felt slighted by this, but given the extreme circumstances, the gesture made sense. As Amundsen was to write in his own journal, "The way home was a long one, and so many things might happen to make it impossible for us to give an account of our expedition."[10] Scott pocketed the letter and his team turned to the north.

Saturday, January 20.—Lunch camp, 9810. We have come along very well this morning, although the surface was terrible bad—9.3 miles in 5 hours 20 m. This has brought us to our Southern Depot, and we pick up 4 days' food. We carry on 7 days from to-night with 55 miles to go to the Half Degree Depot made on January 10. The same sort of weather and a little more wind, sail drawing well.[11]

Scott's decision to bring five men to the pole was, in many ways, a shocking one. The whole journey had been designed and proportioned for teams of four—from their tents to their rations to their fuel. As Cherry-Garrard would later write, "Scott had nothing to gain and a good deal to lose by taking an extra man to the Pole. That he did so means, I think, that he considered his position a very good one."[12] And why not—if you felt assured of success—share that glory with as many men as you could? But what if this meant sending the last support team back shorthanded? What if it meant a much finer margin as to rations for that last 150-mile stretch to and from the pole? Of course, it was hard to think through everything—to weigh all matters accordingly—and Scott admitted as much in his journal, the day after the parties had separated, when he noted, with surprise, that cooking and melting snow for five wound up taking an extra half hour for the day.

"Half an hour off your sleep, or half an hour off your march?" Cherry wonders, and either way—for men already pushed to their utmost—this shortage was sure to exact a toll.[13]

I shall be very glad when Bowers gets his ski; I'm afraid he must find these long marches very trying with short legs, but he is an undefeated little sportsman.... It is blowing pretty hard to-night, but with a good march we have earned one good hoosh and are very comfortable in the tent. It is everything now to keep up a good marching pace.[14]

The issue of Bowers's skis is another that has been pointed to as evidence of Scott's ineptitude. While hauling heavy loads greatly reduces the advantage of skiing, and thus Bowers managed to keep the same pace as his sledge-mates, trudging through deep snow for close to four hundred miles was an added hardship that would likely have been prohibitive to most anyone other than him. Hardships were often seen as opportunities by Bowers, and no doubt he greeted this one with a similar fortitude. In a sadly prophetic letter written to his mother over a year before, while the *Terra Nova* was sailing south, Bowers laid out the underpinnings of his philosophy—"One night on deck when things were at their blackest, it seemed to me that Christ came to me and showed me why we are here, and what the purpose of life really is. It is to make a great decision—to choose between the material and the spiritual, and if we choose the spiritual we must work out our choice, and then it will run like a silver thread through the material. It is very difficult to express in words what I saw so plainly[,] ... but I can never forget that I did realize, in a flash, that nothing that happens to our bodies really matters."[15]

Tuesday, January 23.—Lowest Minimum last night –30, Temp. at start –28. Lunch height 10,100. Temp., with wind 6 to 7, –19. Little wind and heavy marching at start. Then wind increased and we did 8.7 miles by lunch, when it was practically blowing a blizzard.... We came along at a great rate and should have got within an easy march of our depot had not Wilson suddenly discovered that Evans' nose was frostbitten—it was white and hard. We thought it best to camp at 6.45. Got the tent up with some difficulty, and now pretty cosy after good hoosh.[16]

Like all of us, Scott had his favorites—those he believed in and felt most loyal to. Some of these men were certainly chosen for the pole, while others (such as Cherry) had been ordered back with earlier support teams. The idea was to allow for Scott to make assessments of the men along the way, as opposed to making these decisions at the outset. Amundsen's plan was much simpler—one team to the pole and back, with the dogs to shoulder the necessary weight—but Scott had tried that before, and he had come to regret (rightly or wrongly) his choice of relying both on dogs and on Shackleton to fill out his team. This new plan, then, would give him more opportunity to consider the relative strength and health of his men, and perhaps give everyone an added motivation to push hard for a final place on the Pole Team.

Edgar Evans, known as Taff, was a rugged and exuberant Welshman who had already served under Scott on the *Discovery*. Scott's dedication to the man was shown clearly from the outset of this expedition, when Taff had gotten spectacularly drunk on board before a noonday service by the bishop of Christchurch—so drunk, in fact, that he wound up spilling overboard during the service. This episode almost cost Evans his place with the expedition, though Scott reluctantly stood by the seaman. For this, Evans had largely repaid Scott—not only through his great strength as a sledger, but also through his ingenuity in designing improvements to gear. He crafted a stiffer ski boot with a sole of sealskin and wood, improvised a new tent liner, and made improvements to their crampons. Yet even before they had reached the pole, Evans's health was becoming a cause of concern.

There is no doubt Evans is a good deal run down—his fingers are badly blistered and his nose is rather seriously congested with frequent frost bites. He is very much annoyed with himself, which is not a good sign.[17]

Given Evans's talents for refashioning gear, it was only logical that Scott had entrusted him with the task of cutting down the sledges at the top of the plateau. Scott had decided that they would make better headway if they trimmed two feet off the bulky twelve-foot sledges now that they had less to pull, an alteration that lost them a half day of travel and—more significantly—resulted in Evans cutting his hand. This was back on December 31, several days before the last support team was sent back, though the accident is not mentioned in either of the journals of Scott or Wilson until a week later (after the parties had separated). "Evans has a nasty cut on his hand (sledge-making)," Scott writes. "I hope it won't give trouble."[18] What is unclear is whether Evans had revealed the cut earlier, and how soon they began to see it as a complication.* Flesh injuries at that elevation and in freezing temperatures are slow to heal and easily aggravated, especially when paired with a lack of vitamin C in one's diet. As the doctor, Wilson began dressing it regularly, commenting in his journals on the large amounts of pus he'd find, and it is from this point on that Evans's overall health begins to deteriorate.

Wednesday, January 24.—Lunch Temp. −8. Things beginning to look a little serious. A strong wind at the start has developed into a full blizzard at lunch, and we have had to get into our sleeping-bags. . . . We are only 7 miles from our depot, but I made sure we should be there to-night. This is the second full gale since we left the Pole. I don't like the look of it. Is the weather breaking up? If so, God help us, with the tremendous summit journey and scant food. Wilson and Bowers are my standby. I don't like the easy way in which Oates and Evans get frostbitten.[19]

While Evans has clearly become the biggest concern at this stage of the journey, this is not the first time Oates has been called out in Scott's journal. Several days before their arrival at the pole, for instance, Scott writes, "Oates seems to be feeling the cold and fatigue more than the rest of us."[20] This was not a surprising revelation, as Scott had already noted Oates's propensity for getting frostbite on the Depot Journey the previous fall. What is more surprising, perhaps, is that Oates was chosen for the Pole Team at all.

Known as Titus to all on board, Lawrence Oates was also nicknamed "the Soldier," as he was the only member of the expedition from the army. Cherry characterized him as a "cheerful and lovable old pessimist" (though he was all of thirty when they set sail).[21] Like Cherry, Oates had contributed £1,000 to ensure his place with the expedition, and the two got along quite well as the only independently wealthy gentlemen on board. Oates's contributions to the expedition, however, far exceeded his donation of funds, as he was placed in charge of the ponies from the outset. Oates couldn't have taken the job more seriously, even going so far as to sleep in the stables some nights when one of them was sick. But the ponies were long since dead, and there are serious questions as to what role he was to

* Given the perpetual concern of frostbite, it was rare for sledgers to not have their large reindeer fur gloves on. As long as it wasn't Evans's turn to serve as cook, it would have been quite easy for him to conceal his injury from the others.

play in continuing on to the south. In truth, it may have been a sentimental decision, with Scott wanting both the navy and army present when Britain claimed the pole.

Thursday, January 25.—Temp. Lunch –11. Temp. night –16. Thank God we found our Half Degree Depot. After lying in our bags yesterday afternoon and all night, we debated breakfast; decided to have it later and go without lunch. At the time the gale seemed as bad as ever, but during breakfast the sun showed and there was light enough to see the old track.[22]

With a Pole Team of five men, the length of time they could be out with full rations on this last leg of the trip was significantly reduced. This was the first meal they had missed, though obviously they were teetering right at the edge, and the added strain of cutting things this close was surely weighing on them. To rely on food depots in a land where weather regularly makes travel impossible for days at a time is precarious and anxiety-filled work, and while Amundsen's Pole Team relied on the same system, they had the added safety of traveling with dogs that could be sacrificed at a moment's notice.

Only 89 miles (geogr.) to the next depot, but it's time we cleared off this plateau. We are not without ailments: Oates suffers from a very cold foot; Evans' fingers and nose are in a bad state, and to-night Wilson is suffering tortures from his eyes.[23]

"May I be there!" reads one of Wilson's entries of the previous summer. "About this time next year may I be there or thereabouts! With so many young bloods in the heyday of youth and strength beyond my own I feel there will be a most difficult task in making choice towards the end."[24] Scott's allegiance to Wilson, however, was beyond question: "I should like to have Bill to hold my hand when we get to the Pole," he had written, long before they had set out, and Cherry even went so far as to question whether Scott would have returned to the Antarctic at all if Wilson had not agreed to join him.[25] By this time, Wilson was an old hand when it came to sledge journeys, though he still suffered regularly from snow blindness. More often than not these bouts came from Wilson's insistence on sketching, though here it was the strain of tracking as they traveled into the sun. Like all of them, Wilson had dreamed of making it to the pole, though his hopes for the expedition far exceeded this task alone, as his muted reaction at being forestalled by Amundsen reveals: "He has beaten us in so far as he had made a race of it. We have done what we came for all the same."[26]

On the next day, after the pain of Wilson's eyes had kept him up all night in the tent, Amundsen's team—nearly eight hundred miles to the north and ten thousand feet below—arrived safely back at their base.

Saturday, January 27.—R. 10. Temp. –16 (lunch), –14.3 (evening). Minimum –19. Height 9900. Barometer low? Called the hands half an hour late, but we got away in good time. The forenoon march was over the belt of storm-tossed sastrugi; it looked like a rough sea. . . . We are slowly getting more hungry, and it would be an advantage to have a little more food, especially for lunch. If we get to the next depot in a few marches (it is now less than 60 miles and we have a full week's food) we ought to be able to open out a little, but we can't look for a real feed till we get to the pony food depot.[27]

The rations that Scott had settled on for the polar trek were arrived at after the trials of the Winter Journey, where Wilson, Bowers, and Cherry all stuck to slightly different diets throughout the five-week excursion. Yet these calculations were made at sea level, and the Pole Team was finding them insufficient here at altitude. The full range of complications associated with traveling at altitude was not known at the time. Shackleton's men reported back on persistent headaches, nosebleeds, and shortness of breath while on the plateau, but the fact that our bodies' need for food and water actually increases at such altitude was beyond the realm of available science.

Monday, January 29.—R. 12. Lunch Temp. –23. Supper Temp. –25. Height 10,000. Excellent march of 19½ miles, 10.5 before lunch. Wind helping greatly, considerable drift; tracks for the most part very plain. Some time before lunch we picked up the return track of the supporting party, so that there are now three distinct sledge impressions. We are only 24 miles from our depot—an easy day and a half. Given a fine day to-morrow we ought to get it without difficulty.[28]

The last two parties had separated back on January 3—"A last note from a hopeful position," Scott had sent back to his wife—and of the men who were turning back shorthanded to base, he wrote, "I was glad to find their sledge is a mere nothing to them, and thus, no doubt, they will make a quick journey back."[29] On this, too, he was mistaken.

Already handicapped by the loss of a sledge meter from earlier in the trip, which increased substantially the difficulties of navigating the route home, a fourth member to the team would surely have helped to keep up with the distances required to maintain full rations. Bowers, as has already been detailed, was well worth adding to the Pole Team, though why Evans or Oates weren't ordered to take his place is hard to fathom. While Evans had just cut up his hand, Oates may have been struggling with a flare-up of an old wound he had gotten while serving as a subaltern during the Boer War. He had recovered fully, and had completed tours of duty in Ireland, Egypt, and India since then, but at the top of the Beardmore—according to his friend, Dr. Atkinson—Oates confided that he was having doubts as to whether he was fit to go on. The decision, though, was made, with Oates choosing to remain silent. Sledges had been hauled great distances with three men before, but as Scott had learned from his first attempt at reaching the pole, a team of three is only one injury away from a rather desperate situation.

Tuesday, January 30.—R. 13. 9860. Lunch Temp. −25, Supper Temp. −24.5. Thank the Lord another fine march—19 miles. We have passed the last cairn before the depot, the track is clear ahead, the weather fair, the wind helpful, the gradient down—with any luck we should pick up our depot in the middle of the morning march. This is the bright side; the reverse of the medal is serious. Wilson has strained a tendon in his leg; it has given pain all day and is swollen to-night. Of course, he is full of pluck over it, but I don't like the idea of such an accident here. To add to the trouble Evans has dislodged two finger-nails to-night; his hands are really bad, and to my surprise he shows signs of losing heart over it. He hasn't been cheerful since the accident.[30]

As the biggest man by some margin in the party, Evans may have been feeling the insufficiency of the ration more than the others, and his repeated frostbites and the injury to his hand were also clearly taking their toll. Wilson, for his part, has suffered a fall while on ski—"a nasty bruise" is how he characterizes it that night in his journal, though he will recover fully inside of another few days, and it is what Wilson writes down just after this, simply in passing, that stands out much more alarmingly: "We are now only 22 miles from our depot and 400 miles about to go before meeting the dogs."[31] At this juncture, they were less than two hundred miles north of the pole, and four hundred more miles would get them only to eighty-two degrees latitude, somewhere around the Mid-Barrier Depot, and a little over two-thirds of the distance back to base. This is a point they will get to—or, at least, most of them will—though they won't find any dogs there to greet them.

Wilson, of course, knew his distances—knew them well enough to refigure the mileage after every march, like all of them. So this was no slipup, no error in calculations, but rather the first sign that the Pole Team was expecting more assistance from the dogs than they would come to get.

Thursday, February 1.—R. 15. 9778. Lunch Temp. –20, Supper Temp. –19.8. Heavy collar work most of the day. Wind light. Did 8 miles, 4¾ hours. . . . Working on past 8 P.M. we just fetched a lunch cairn on December 29, when we were only a week out from the depot. It ought to be easy to get in with a margin, having 8 days' food in hand (full feeding). We have opened out on the 1/7th increase, and it makes a lot of difference. Wilson's leg much better. Evans' fingers now very bad, two nails coming off, blisters burst.[32]

On the previous day's march, Bowers had finally picked up his skis—an impressive feat to march without them for a month, especially when paired with all the other tasks that he took on, such as sights for positioning and maintaining the meteorological log. Though perhaps all this was too much, even for someone of Bowers's indefatigable nature. January 29 marks his last full journal entry, followed by fragments until "February 3rd (I suppose)."[33] Then nothing. "We ought to have more sleep," Scott writes on the night of February 2, as well as remarking that even with the extra food all are getting hungrier.[34] Bowers had pushed himself this hard before, or even harder, during the Winter Journey, but that was only five weeks in duration, whereas here, on their return from the pole, they had already been out nearly three times as long.

Sunday, February 4.—R. 18. 8620 feet. Temp.: Lunch –22; Supper –23. Pulled on foot in the morning over good hard surface and covered 9.7 miles. Just before lunch unexpectedly fell into crevasses, Evans and I together—a second fall for Evans. . . . The temperature is 20 degrees lower than when we were here before; the party is not improving in condition, especially Evans, who is becoming rather dull and incapable. Thank the Lord we have good food at each meal, but we get hungrier in spite of it.[35]

Concerns over Evans's wound and recurring frostbite have been noted in
Scott's entries for weeks, but the change of language here in characterizing
Evans is unnerving, especially as it coincides with multiple falls through
the ice. Scott declares him "a good deal crocked up" in his next entry from
February 5, and in judgments over the next few days that were edited out of
the published journals, Scott describes his actions as *stupid* and *clumsy*.[36]
It is still more than a week, however, before Wilson—the only person there
with medical training—will use similar words in his journal to describe Evans's increasingly erratic behavior.

Over the next two days they struggled with crevasses and sastrugi as they
made their way down off the plateau. The Beardmore Glacier is roughly
fourteen miles wide and gains more than a mile in elevation as it climbs
from the Barrier, making it one of the largest glaciers in the world. Of
course, this vantage point of description is misleading, as the glacier actually descends, moving downhill at a rate of about three feet per day. This
dynamic makes for unsettled and ever-shifting terrain that renders navigation extremely difficult. A heavy blizzard had made for slow going on the
outward march here over a month ago, but it had also covered up many of
the troubling features they were faced with now.

*Wednesday, February 7.—Mount Darwin [or Upper Glacier] Depot, R. 21.
Height 7100. Lunch Temp. –9; Supper Temp. [a blank here]. A wretched
day with satisfactory ending. First panic, certainty that biscuit-box was
short. Great doubt as to how this has come about, as we certainly haven't
over-issued allowances. Bowers is dreadfully disturbed about it. The shortage is a full day's allowance.*[37]

The cause of this shortage is never explained in the journals, and with such
an elaborate depot system—one that required each passing team to measure out and proportion their share—the fault could have lain anywhere.
Scott's recurring anxiety over food is certainly justified, as recent studies
have argued that their standard full summit rations were over two thousand calories short of the daily intake necessary for such physical demands
at altitude. When a 2006 reenactment of Scott's travels was attempted, the
team had to abort at the pole as all members had suffered severe weight
loss. While Scott's journals are always circling back to matters of food,
much less is said about water, though this too was in short supply. Ac-
counting for both their tea and the liquid in their pemmican stew, Scott's
team was getting only about two and a half quarts of water per day. At high

altitudes, even sedentary individuals require a daily intake of two to four quarts of water, and with the heavy exertions of sledging, the Pole Team was losing moisture at a frenzied rate. The metabolic cost of consuming snow to obtain moisture is largely self-defeating, so to drink water they must melt snow, which can only be done when they are camped, and only as long as they have sufficient fuel. Scott's margins here were narrow, just as they were with everything else: "Our fuel only just does it," he wrote back in December, "but that is all we want."[38]

We have come through our 7 weeks' ice camp journey and most of us are fit, but I think another week might have had a very bad effect on PO Evans, who is going steadily downhill.[39]

Despite Scott's continued concern over Evans, there is also a sense in this entry that the worst was over, that having left the harsh conditions of the plateau things were bound to improve. A resupply of food and a warm weather spell seemed to bear him out in this, though neither could be counted on to last.

Thursday, February 8.—R. 22. Height 6260. Start Temp. –11; Lunch Temp. –5; Supper, zero. 9.2 miles. Started from the depot rather late owing to weighing biscuit, &c., and rearranging matters. Had a beastly morning. Wind very strong and cold. . . . We decided to steer for the moraine under Mt. Buckley and, pulling with crampons, we crossed some very irregular steep slopes with big crevasses and slid down towards the rocks. The moraine was obviously so interesting that when we had advanced some miles and got out of the wind, I decided to camp and spend the rest of the day geologizing.[40]

This investigative layover—which took up the bulk of two days—has been questioned ever since. Was Scott lulled into a false sense of security? Was he hoping that a short break from marching would improve Evans' health? Some have even wondered whether this short detour for science wasn't simply a consolation prize—a sad attempt to salvage meaning for their journey now that Amundsen had beaten them to the pole. But if we look at the journals from the outbound trip, we see that such a stopover was already alluded to for the return. "We must get to know more of the geology before leaving the glacier finally," Scott writes, back on December 18, as they traversed these same miles. And Wilson laments on several occasions that their decision to ascend in the middle of the glacier gave them no chance to study the rocks and moraine that extends through this very stretch.[41] Most likely, Wilson would have pushed for some sort of stopover regardless, and whatever other variables Scott was weighing at this juncture, they didn't cause him to reconsider.

We found ourselves under perpendicular cliffs of Beacon sandstone, weathering rapidly and carrying veritable coal seams. From the last Wilson, with his sharp eyes, has picked several plant impressions, the last a piece of coal with beautifully traced leaves in layers, also some excellently preserved impressions of thick stems, showing cellular structure. . . . Altogether we have had a most interesting afternoon, and the relief of being out of the wind and in a warmer temperature is inexpressible. I hope and trust we shall all buck up again now that the conditions are more favorable.[42]

The entry doesn't call out Evans by name, though it seems safe to assume he was still at the forefront of Scott's mind. Wilson, on the other hand, seems fully engrossed with their discoveries—"I was very late turning in, examining the moraine after supper," and, "Had a regular field day and got some splendid things in the short time."[43] All told, they loaded up thirty-five pounds worth of specimens before continuing on.

Sunday, February 11.—R. 25. Lunch Temp. –6.5; Supper –3.5. The worst day we have had during the trip and greatly owing to our own fault. We started on a wretched surface with light S.W. wind, sail set, and pulling on ski— horrible light, which made everything look fantastic. As we went on light got worse, and suddenly we found ourselves in pressure. Then came the fatal decision to steer east. We went on for 6 hours, hoping to do a good distance, which in fact I suppose we did, but for the last hour or two we pressed on into a regular trap. . . . We won through at 10 P.M. and I write after 12 hours on the march. I think we are on or about the right track now, but we are still a good number of miles from the depot, so we reduced rations tonight. We had three pemmican meals left and decided to make them into four. To-morrow's lunch must serve for two if we do not make big progress.[44]

But the next day's march went even worse, placing them in a critical condition: unsure of their location and nearly out of food. The return parties had all found this stretch difficult to navigate, though certainly the time spent geologizing made their position more perilous. Repeatedly, they attempted to cut corners, or pushed on through steeply terraced ice-slopes when backtracking was the surer option. Then the weather turned for the worst, the terrain hidden by a thick fog just when the need for picking up their outbound track became most necessary. Wilson's entry on the twelfth consists of only one sentence, ending with the following: "plunged into an icefall and wandered about in it absolutely lost for hours and hours."[45] Their food was all but gone, and they went to sleep that night fearing they had missed their depot.

"We mustn't get into a hole like this again," Scott writes with great relief, after they stumbled upon the Mid-Glacier Depot on the morning of the thirteenth.[46] In truth, the revelation feels foolishly slow in coming, given the numerous close calls they had already experienced. Wilson and Bowers were both suffering again from snow blindness, and Scott ends his entry on this day by noting that Evans has become too weak to assist with camp work.

Friday, February 16.—12.5 m. Lunch Temp. +6.1; Supper Temp. +7. A rather trying position. Evans has nearly broken down in brain, we think. He is absolutely changed from his normal self-reliant self. This morning and this afternoon he stopped the march on some trivial excuse. We are on short rations but not very short, food spins out till to-morrow night. We cannot be more than 10 or 12 miles from the depot, but the weather is all against us.[47]

After eight straight days without a mention of Evans in his journal, Wilson finally seemed to register the severity of his condition: "after 3¼ hours Evans collapsed—sick and giddy and unable to walk even by the sledge on ski."[48] The journals alone can't paint a full picture, especially as Evans himself did not keep one. We have no way of knowing how concerned Wilson was about his tentmate before this point, though his notes on Evans's health had thus far all been centered on his physical condition—the wound to his hand and his repeated frostbites. Perhaps Wilson chose to focus on these surface ailments because that was all he could hope to treat him for, knowing that any prospect of rest and recovery was still over four hundred miles away.

Saturday, February 17.—A very terrible day. Evans looked a little better after a good sleep, and declared, as he always did, that he was quite well. He started in his place on the traces, but half an hour later worked his ski shoes adrift, and had to leave the sledge. . . . We had to push on, and the remainder of us were forced to pull very hard, sweating heavily. Abreast the Monument Rock we stopped, and seeing Evans a long way astern, I camped for lunch. There was no alarm at first, and we prepared tea and our own meal, consuming the latter. After lunch, and Evans still not appearing, we looked out, to see him still afar off. By this time we were alarmed, and all four started back on ski. I was first to reach the poor man and shocked at his appearance; he was on his knees with clothing disarranged, hands uncovered and frostbitten, and a wild look in his eyes. Asked what was the matter, he replied with a slow speech that he didn't know, but thought he must have fainted. We got him on his feet, but after two or three steps he sank down again. He showed every sign of complete collapse. Wilson, Bowers, and I went back for the sledge, whilst Oates remained with him. When we returned he was practically unconscious, and when we got him into the tent quite comatose. He died quietly at 12.30 A.M. On discussing the symptoms we think he began to get weaker just before we reached the Pole, and that his downward path was accelerated first by the shock of his frostbitten fingers, and later by falls during rough travelling on the glacier, further by his loss of all confidence in himself. Wilson thinks it certain he must have injured his brain by a fall. It is a terrible thing to lose a companion in this way, but calm reflection shows that there could not have been a better ending to the terrible anxieties of the past week. Discussion of the situation at lunch yesterday shows us what a desperate pass we were in with a sick man on our hands at such a distance from home.

At 1 A.M. we packed up and came down over the pressure ridges, finding our depot easily.[49]

The exact cause of Evans's death can only be speculated on, and certainly there were a host of alarming circumstances—insufficient diet, dehydration, complications with the cut on his hand, and bouts of frostbite, perhaps even a sustained form of altitude sickness. From what we can piece together from the journals, however, there does appear to have been some sort of mental collapse, quite possibly associated with a concussion from a fall on the ice. What is clear is that he had been suffering for some time, and largely without complaint—he was pulling a sledge, after all, on the day he died.

After five hours of sleep at the Lower Glacier Depot, the four men pushed on to Shambles Camp, a sadly fitting location to return to now. Back in December, after being held up by a three-day blizzard that had exhausted their supply of pony feed, Wilson had given his horse Nobby all five of his biscuits as they pushed the remaining animals on for one last march. "It was beastly work," Wilson wrote afterward, "and the horses constantly collapsed and lay down and sank down, and eventually we could only get them on for 5 or 6 yards at a time—they were clean done. Then we camped. Shot them all."[50]

They were off the glacier now, back on the familiar Barrier where they had cause to think their fortunes would improve. In spite of Evans's deteriorating condition, they had maintained a rate of travel that was comparable to those of the other return parties, as well as their outbound pace, averaging close to fifteen miles a day. Now their rations would have to be divided only by four, and the store of pony meat would bolster this further. While Scott was rightly concerned with the condition of the Barrier surface, there was also a peace of mind in knowing that some of the most treacherous land features—the icefalls and heavy pressure areas—were behind them. When the last support team had gotten to this spot, after the difficulties of traversing the lower Beardmore, Thomas Crean unleashed a huge and joyous yell, "enough to frighten the ponies out of their graves," wrote his companion, the ship's chief stoker William Lashly, though in this same entry Lashly remarks on how the third member of their party, Lt. Evans,* had begun to show signs of scurvy.[51] Their trip home would prove a desperate struggle, with Crean and Lashly having to strap Lt. Evans to the sledge by the end. On this very day, thirty-five miles short of Hut Point, Lt. Evans collapsed completely, and Tom Crean—"in a miniature polar epic all of his own"—left his companions in their tent, along with all their gear, to trudge over eighteen straight hours back to base.[52] Three biscuits and two sticks of chocolate were all he carried. A blizzard that would certainly have killed him, and thereby his stranded companions, broke only a half hour after he came in.

Friday, February 24.—Lunch. Beautiful day—too beautiful—an hour after starting loose ice crystals spoiling surface. Saw depot and reached it middle forenoon. Found store in order except shortage oil—shall have to be very saving with fuel—otherwise have ten full days' provision from to-night and shall have less than 70 miles to go.[53]

Over the past week their average marching distance has slipped to under ten miles a day, as they struggled with loose sandy snow that caused fric-

*The *Terra Nova* expedition had two men named Evans—Petty Officer Taft Evans, and the ship's second-in-command, Lieutenant Teddy Evans.

tion to their sledge. Scott has begun to express regular concern over the lateness of the season, and his prose has become more fragmented, leaving out simple words. While the subject of PO Evans's death is not returned to explicitly in these entries, Scott's tone has grown more urgent and somber. Now, with this unexpected shortage of fuel, they have another troubling cause for anxiety.

Scott's predilection for working with only the finest of margins in regard to fuel quantity has come back to haunt him, though the cause for the short-age is more complicated than just cutting corners. Going back to the *Dis-covery* expedition, Scott had experienced a problem with leakage of stored fuel, attributing it to the cork stoppers that were commonly employed. Scott aimed to remedy this by using leather washers with screwed metal caps this time around, though whatever tests were performed to appraise this change were critically inadequate. Amundsen also carried oil in this type of container, though he had wisely chosen to have the lids soldered to provide greater protection from leakage. Stress on the seams of the cans was unavoidable given the roughness of travel, the exposure to harsh and variable temperatures, and the very system of the depots that required each team to open and close the cans for their resupply.* The oil was seep-ing out. Lashly had recorded this fact in his own journals as the last sup-port team rushed back to Hut Point, but by then there was little that could be done about it, beyond leaving as much of it behind as they could while still getting back themselves.

Monday, February 27.—Desperately cold last night: –33 when we got up, with –37 minimum. Some suffering from cold feet, but all got good rest. We must open out on food soon. But we have done 7 miles this morning and hope for some 5 this afternoon. . . . We are naturally always discussing pos-sibility of meeting dogs, where and when, &c. It is a critical position. We may find ourselves in safety at next depot, but there is a horrid element of doubt.[54]

The day's entry records a new lowest temperature for the trip, over ten de-grees colder than the worst they experienced on the plateau, and it comes at a time when they were already slipping toward the edge. They had just crossed the eighty-second parallel, and if we consider Scott's journal in

*For this very reason, soldering the canisters would not have worked with Scott's depot system.

isolation, this is the first mention of meeting the dogs this far south. This makes the passage read like wishful thinking, yet Wilson brought this same prospect up calmly and directly almost a month earlier, back when there was much less cause for concern, and Lashly refers to this as well, as the last support team draws nearer to Hut Point, hoping that they themselves might get relief from the dog teams as they headed out to meet Scott. Were Scott's orders unclear? Assuming, even, that they were fully understood, were they still possible to carry out? History would come to have much to say on these matters, though what is certain, at that moment, as the four men were struggling on to the north, was that they were anxiously watching the horizon in hopes that the expected dog teams would appear.

"Turned in at –37," ends Wilson's brief entry from this day, and here his diary ends.[55] In truth, he had written little more than fragments since they had watched Evans die in their tent ten days before. All his life Wilson has kept a diary, writing full daily entries even through the worst of the Winter Journey, so its abrupt conclusion here speaks volumes. As surely as there had become a shortness of food and fuel, there had also emerged an alarming shortness of time, all the more so for someone who had taken on the added task of looking after others. The shock of Evans's death had clearly affected them all, but it may have been hardest on Wilson, who likely questioned whether there was—in his capacity as doctor—more he could have done to help the man. "This is the most fascinating ideal I think I ever imagined," he had written back on the plateau, "to become entirely careless of your own soul or body in looking after the welfare of others."[56] If Wilson had somehow felt that he'd fallen short of that ideal in the event of Evans's death, he had three more companions at his side that he was determined to do all he could for now.

Friday, March 2.—Lunch. Misfortunes rarely come singly. We marched to the [Middle Barrier] depot fairly easily yesterday afternoon, and since that have suffered three distinct blows which have placed us in a bad position. First we found a shortage of oil; with most rigid economy it can scarce carry us to the next depot on this surface [71 miles away]. Second, Titus Oates disclosed his feet, the toes showing very bad indeed, evidently bitten by the late temperatures. The third blow came in the night, when the wind, which we had hailed with some joy, brought dark overcast weather. It fell below –40 in the night, and this morning it took 1½ hours to get our foot gear on.[57]

The basic structure of Scott's journal has changed. Instead of each day being recorded with a double entry from the day's march and at night, we get simply *Lunch* followed by a rundown of the preceding twenty-four hours. Here, Scott recorded the first concern over Oates since they'd left the summit. On the previous day, with a low temperature reading of –41.5, they had managed to travel ten miles—this would prove to be the last time they'd reach double digits.

Two years earlier, almost to the day, Shackleton had returned to Hut Point, his four-man team exhausted and bordering on starvation. Scott's men were in a similarly perilous condition, yet they still had nearly three hundred miles to go. And the temperatures they were facing were significantly worse than those met by Shackleton. In the previous September, during Amundsen's false start to the pole, he was forced to retreat after only four days of travel, when faced with temperatures in the negative fifties, as the dogs laid down in their harnesses and several men suffered from debilitating frostbite. The three-man team of the Winter Journey saw temperatures regularly slip into the negative seventies, but the Crozier trip was less than 140 total miles in distance, and the men were out for only five weeks. To compare only the temperatures distorts their position entirely, as Scott's team had been out four months now, were suffering from an insufficient diet, had spent seven weeks at altitude, and had watched on, helplessly, as one of their companions died.

Saturday, March 3.—Lunch. We picked up the track again yesterday, finding ourselves to the eastward. Did close on 10 miles and things looked a trifle better; but this morning the outlook is blacker than ever. Started well and with good breeze; for an hour made good headway; then the surface grew awful beyond words. The wind drew forward; every circumstance was against us. After 4½ hours things so bad that we camped, having covered 4½ miles. . . . God help us, we can't keep up this pulling, that is certain. Amongst ourselves we are unendingly cheerful, but what each man feels in his heart I can only guess. Putting on foot gear in the morning is getting slower and slower, therefore every day more dangerous.[58]

Given the fact that their daily mileage had plummeted, and the length of time that they had been without fresh foods, many historians argue that the men must also have been struggling with advanced scurvy. Wilson was well aware of the symptoms and progression of scurvy, and it is

highly unlikely that any occurrence of the disease was not promptly diagnosed. Wilson, however, had stopped keeping his diary, and in Scott's
mind there was a stigma to the disease. We know this because he placed
the blame on turning back from his first expedition to the south largely
on Shackleton's bout of scurvy, referring to his condition as a type of constitutional weakness. So it is conceivable that Scott would leave such details out of his log. One of the earliest symptoms of scurvy is a reduced
range of motion, showing itself first as stiffness in the back of the legs—a
burdensome condition in most circumstances, though a life-threatening
one for people on a polar march. They were traveling lightly, at least in
comparison with some of the earlier marches, though they were still carrying the thirty-five pounds of geological specimens that had been gathered on the glacier. Much more important than issues of weight, however,
were the conditions of the surface—as the temperatures plummeted, the
sledge's glide became hampered by the rough ice crystals that form on
the Barrier.

*Monday, March 5.—Lunch. Regret to say going from bad to worse. . . . We
went to bed on a cup of cocoa and pemmican solid with the chill off. The
result is telling on all, but mainly on Oates, whose feet are in a wretched
condition. One swelled up tremendously last night and he is very lame this
morning. . . . We are two pony marches and 4 miles about from our depot.
Our fuel dreadfully low and the poor Soldier nearly done. It is pathetic
enough because we can do nothing for him; more hot food might do a little,
but only a little, I fear. We none of us expected these terribly low temperatures, and of the rest of us Wilson is feeling them most; mainly, I fear, from
his self-sacrificing devotion in doctoring Oates' feet. We cannot help each
other, each has enough to do to take care of himself.*[59]

Solid with the chill off, it hardly sounds palatable, and the reserves of
strength and warmth that the body uses up to process such fare must be
immense, especially at that moment, as the four men had no body fat left
to insulate them from the cold. How much water were they allowing themselves? Close to nothing, it would seem, and even that can only last out so
long. By the end, everything they ate would be fully frozen.

Would they have been better off if Scott had taken only four to the pole?
Which four? It is not an idle question. If Scott had simply not added Bowers, it is hard to see how their situation would have improved; Scott's jour-

nals are full of praise for that man—for his imperviousness toward the cold, his great skills at tracking, all the additional labors he has taken on, and his uplifting influence on the others. Besides, by this time, Oates was unable to pull, and with the wretched surface and their weakening state they were lucky to make five miles in a day, and that was pulling with three men. Yes, they would have more to eat, and a little more fuel, though hardly enough of the latter given their rate of travel. Wilson and Scott had pulled a sledge alone over a similar distance, after Shackleton had become too weak to share the burden during their first attempt at the pole, but that was in warmer temperatures, with a better surface, and having spent a month less time out in the field. As for Evans, it bears repeating that their decline in sledging distances began not when Evans's health was rapidly deteriorating, but rather after he was gone. Oates then? Maybe Oates, though it was only over the preceding few days that—after great tribulations—his health had begun to falter. And as Scott's outbound entries make clear, when speaking strictly on the basis of strength of pulling, he rated Oates as highly as Bowers. What we can't know is the role Oates's old war injury was playing. The injury was to his left femur and the surrounding tissue, which may have affected the strength and circulation of his entire leg, and the frostbite that was crippling him had taken root in his left foot.

Thursday, March 8.—Lunch. Worse and worse in morning; poor Oates' left foot can never last out, and time over foot gear something awful. Have to wait in night foot gear for nearly an hour before I start changing, and then am generally first to be ready. Wilson's feet giving troubles now, but this mainly because he gives so much help to others. We did 4½ miles this morning and are now 8½ miles from the depot—a ridiculously small distance to feel in difficulties, yet on this surface we know we cannot equal half our old marches, and that for that effort we expend nearly double the energy. The great question is, What shall we find at the depot? If the dogs have visited it we may get along a good distance, but if there is another short allowance of fuel, God help us indeed.[60]

If there was one component where all would assume the British expedition far exceeded that of the Norwegians it certainly was manpower. After all, Scott's Shore Party of thirty-four men was almost four times the size of Amundsen's. Yet as the last support team finally made it back safely to Cape Evans, there was almost no one available to head south with the dogs. Victor Campbell (Scott's first officer) had led a group of six men on an exploratory scientific venture to the north that—unbeknownst to Scott—had been forced to winter over in treacherous conditions. Of the other officers, Scott, Bowers, and Oates were obviously still out on the ice, and Atkinson—as the only doctor presently at camp—felt he should stay with the scurvy-stricken Lt. Evans. Compounding problems, the ship had arrived and many of the scientific staff and petty officers (most crucially Cecil Meares, who was in charge of the dogs) would soon be heading back to New Zealand. In the end, Atkinson asked Cherry to make the trip out on the Barrier with the young Russian dog-driver Dimitri.

Cherry, of course, had more than proven himself as a capable member of the expedition, but he had no experience driving dogs, nor navigating, and his nearsightedness was a severe impediment. Nonetheless, he set off on February 26 with orders to lay the remaining rations of food for the Pole Team at the One Ton Depot, and, assuming Scott hadn't arrived, to judge for himself what to do. Clearly, any idea of traveling all the way out to eighty-two degrees south had been dispensed with, though by whom and for what reasons is unclear. Was Atkinson worried that he was asking too much of Cherry? Or was he concerned that they were asking too much of the dogs, given how hard they had already been driven? By that point, it had become quite difficult to know where to place the blame.*

Saturday, March 10.—Things steadily downhill. Oates' foot worse. He has rare pluck and must know that he can never get through. He asked Wilson if he had a chance this morning, and of course Bill had to say he didn't know. In point of fact he has none. Apart from him, if he went under now, I doubt whether we could get through. With great care we might have a dog's chance, but no more. The weather conditions are awful, and our gear gets steadily more icy and difficult to manage. At the same time of course poor Titus is the greatest handicap. He keeps us waiting in the morning until we have partly lost the warming effect of our good breakfast, when the only wise policy is to be up and away at once; again at lunch. Poor chap! It is too pathetic to watch him; one cannot but try to cheer him up.

Yesterday we marched up the depot, Mt. Hooper. Cold comfort. Shortage on our allowance all round. I don't know that anyone is to blame. The dogs which would have been our salvation have evidently failed. Meares had a bad trip home I suppose.[61]

*For a detailed look at the breakdown of command back at Cape Evans and the controversy surrounding Scott's orders for the dogs, see appendix 2.

But the dogs hadn't failed. Even as hard as they had been driven, they had pulled through consummately. Yet on that day, roughly seventy-five miles away from Scott, Cherry turned the dogs back toward home. He had been at One Ton for six days, pinned down in a tent during a blizzard for four of them. The dog food that they had brought with them had dwindled by that time to barely enough to get the teams back to base. Cherry could have pushed on further to the south, killing dogs as necessary, in hopes of encountering his friends, but his instructions from Atkinson were to not risk the dogs. Besides, Cherry was in over his head. Dimitri, who hardly spoke English and was one of the only members of the expedition who was younger than Cherry, had been complaining greatly of the cold and of headaches, and his entire right side had strangely begun to atrophy. Dimitri, of course, was leading the dogs, and given Cherry's shortsightedness was essentially functioning as the eyes of the unit. If something happened to him, Cherry knew, it would be a desperate struggle to lead them back to base on his own. "Lately I have felt that it has almost been too much," Cherry wrote ominously in his journal, as they turned back to Hut Point.[62] Within the first days of leaving One Ton, Dimitri's right side became largely incapacitated, and Cherry was left to navigate by the gleam of the sun, and the howling of the wind in his ear. Within a week of returning to base, Cherry would break down entirely.

Sunday, March 11.—Titus Oates is very near the end, one feels. What we or he will do, God only knows. We discussed the matter after breakfast; he is a brave fine fellow and understands the situation, but he practically asked for advice. Nothing could be said but to urge him to march as long as he could. One satisfactory result to the discussion; I practically ordered Wilson to hand over the means of ending our troubles to us, so that any one of us may know how to do so. Wilson had no choice between doing so and our ransacking the medicine case. We have 30 opium tabloids apiece and he is left with a tube of morphine. So far the tragical side of our story.

The sky completely overcast when we started this morning. We could see nothing, lost the tracks, and doubtless have been swaying a good deal since—3.1 miles for the forenoon—terribly heavy dragging—expected it. Know that 6 miles is about the limit of our endurance now, if we get no help from wind or surfaces. We have 7 days' food and should be about 55 miles from One Ton Camp to-night, 6 × 7 = 42, leaving us 13 miles short of our distance, even if things get no worse.[63]

The communal pronoun "our" seems doubtful here. Was Bowers going to ransack Wilson's medicine case? Was Oates? With only the one journal, and such short entries, there is a great deal that is left unsaid. *6 x 7, 55 miles, 7 days' food*—agonizingly Scott works over the math, though the numbers simply don't add up. The math for Oates was even grimmer, and he asks Wilson to see that his journal is passed on to his mother, confiding to him that she is the only woman he has ever loved.

Wednesday, March 14.—No doubt about the going downhill, but everything going wrong for us. Yesterday we woke to a strong northerly wind with temp. –37. Couldn't face it, so remained in camp till 2, then did 5¼ miles. Wanted to march later, but party feeling the cold badly. . . .

We must *go on, but now the making of every camp must be more difficult and dangerous. It must be near the end, but a pretty merciful end. Poor Oates got it again in the foot. I shudder to think what it will be like to-morrow. It is only with greatest pains rest of us keep off frostbites. No idea there could be temperatures like this at this time of year with such winds. Truly awful outside the tent. Must fight it out to the last biscuit, but can't reduce rations.*[64]

They had just crossed the eightieth parallel. If Scott had kept to his original plan as to depots, if Oates had gotten his wish to push on a few more marches last fall—killing the weakest ponies once they arrived—this would have been the site of the One Ton Depot. But what difference would this have made? A resupply of food and fuel would, no doubt, make a significant impact, but at the rate they were traveling, it would take them over a month to get back to Hut Point, and deteriorating weather conditions would only have extended the trip, past April 23 to be sure—the last day of the sun at such latitudes. If the advanced stages of scurvy weren't already crippling them, surely they would have begun to by then. But what if this repositioning had meant they would have met Cherry and the dogs? Here Scott was right: the dogs might have been their salvation, yet on this very day Cherry led them safely back to Hut Point. So as long as the dogs weren't taken past the One Ton Depot (no matter where it was located), the dates wouldn't match up, and the Pole Team would be left out on the ice.

March 17 would mark Oates's thirty-second birthday. Scott doesn't mention this in his diary, though others record it back at base. Perhaps they had forgotten, and Oates chose not to remind them, or perhaps Scott simply found this detail too sad to write down.

Friday, March 16 or Saturday 17.—Lost track of dates, but think the last correct. Tragedy all along the line. At lunch, the day before yesterday, poor Titus Oates said he couldn't go on; he proposed we should leave him in his sleeping bag. That we could not do, and we induced him to come on, on the afternoon march. In spite of its awful nature for him he struggled on and we made a few miles. At night he was worse and we knew the end had come.

Should this be found I want these facts recorded. Oates' last thoughts were of his Mother, but immediately before he took pride in thinking that his regiment would be pleased with the bold way in which he met his death. We can testify to his bravery. He has borne intense suffering for weeks without complaint, and to the very last was able and willing to discuss outside subjects. He did not—would not—give up hope till the very end. He was a brave soul. This was the end. He slept through the night before last, hoping not to wake; but he woke in the morning—yesterday. It was blowing a blizzard. He said, "I am just going outside and may be some time." He went out in the blizzard and we have not seen him since.

I take this opportunity of saying that we have stuck to our sick companions to the last. In case of Edgar Evans, when absolutely out of food and he lay insensible, the safety of the remainder seemed to demand his abandonment, but Providence mercifully removed him at this critical moment. He died a natural death, and we did not leave him till two hours after his death. We knew that poor Oates was walking to his death, but though we tried to dissuade him, we knew it was the act of a brave man and an English gentleman. We all hope to meet the end with a similar spirit, and assuredly the end is not far.

I can only write at lunch and then only occasionally. The cold is intense, –40 at midday. My companions are unendingly cheerful, but we are all on the verge of serious frostbites, and though we constantly talk of fetching through I don't think any one of us believes it in his heart.

We are cold on the march now, and at all times except meals. Yesterday we had to lay up for a blizzard and to-day we move dreadfully slowly. We are at No 14 pony camp, only two pony marches from One Ton Depot. We leave here our theodolite, a camera, and Oates' sleeping-bags. Diaries, &c., and geological specimens carried at Wilson's special request, will be found with us or on our sledge.

Sunday, March 18.—To-day, lunch, we are 21 miles from the depot. Ill for-
tune presses, but better may come. We have had more wind and drift from
ahead yesterday; had to stop marching; wind N.W., force 4, temp. –35. No
human being could face it, and we are worn out nearly.

My right foot has gone, nearly all the toes—two days ago I was proud
possessor of best feet. . . . Bowers takes first place in condition, but there
is not much to choose after all. The others are still confident of getting
through—or pretend to be—I don't know! We have the last half *fill of oil*
in our primus and a very small quantity of spirit—this alone between us
and thirst. The wind is fair for the moment, and that is perhaps a fact to
help. The mileage would have seemed ridiculously small on our outward
journey.

Monday, March 19.—Lunch. We camped with difficulty last night, and
were dreadfully cold till after our supper of cold pemmican and biscuit and
a half a pannikin of cocoa cooked over the spirit. Then, contrary to expec-
tation, we got warm and all slept well. To-day we started in the usual drag-
ging manner. Sledge dreadfully heavy. We are 15½ miles from the depot
and ought to get there in three days. What progress! We have two days' food
but barely a day's fuel. All our feet are getting bad—Wilson's best, my right
foot worst, left all right. There is no chance to nurse one's feet till we get hot
food into us. Amputation is the least I can hope for now, but will the trouble
spread? That is the serious question. The weather doesn't give us a chance—
the wind from N. to N.W. and –40 temp. to-day.

[No entry for March 20]

Wednesday, March 21.—Got within 11 miles of depot Monday night; had
to lay up all yesterday in severe blizzard. To-day forlorn hope, Wilson and
Bowers going to depot for fuel.

Thursday, March 22 and 23.—Blizzard bad as ever—Wilson and Bowers
unable to start—to-morrow last chance—no fuel and only one or two of
food left—must be near the end. Have decided it shall be natural—we shall
march for the depot with or without our effects and die in our tracks.

[No entries between this and March 29]

Thursday, March 29.—Since the 21st we have had a continuous gale from W.S.W. and S.W. We had fuel to make two cups of tea apiece and bare food for two days on the 20th. Every day we have been ready to start for our depot 11 miles away, but outside the door of the tent it remains a scene of whirling drift. I do not think we can hope for any better things now. We shall stick it out to the end, but we are getting weaker, of course, and the end cannot be far.

It seems a pity, but I do not think I can write more.

R. Scott

Last entry.
For God's sake look after our people.[65]

—

Sunday, February 21—We have arrived. The tall clumps of tussock grass carpeting the hillsides of shore signal clearly that we have crossed over to another world. The sunlight ripples off the dark bay. We crowd to the decks, where the sounds of birds circling overhead mix with the ocean scent of salt and the cold rush of wind on our faces.

History, as it is commonly said, is written by the victors, and if it were as simple as that Amundsen's account would suffice, but history is also written—oftentimes more compellingly—by the survivors. And so, eight months later, they found the bodies. This was not what they had expected. All winter the men back at base had known with certainty that the Pole Team had perished, yet they imagined them swallowed up by a crevasse on the Beardmore, not lying together in their tent so close to safety. Wilson and Bowers had closed their sleeping bags over their heads, just as they would have for a normal night's sleep. Scott's body sat upright, facing the entrance—his skin yellow and mottled by frostbite. While the rest of the men stood solemnly outside, Dr. Atkinson searched the tent for Scott's diary. They heard a harsh crack from within—this was Scott's arm breaking. "I am almost afraid to go to sleep now," Cherry writes in his journal entry for the day.[66]

One way or another, history will come to assign blame. And for Cherry, this took on an unavoidably personal dimension. Two of his closest friends were dead, their bodies found eleven miles away from the depot where he had turned back. Cherry could look, we all can look, to those elements beyond their control—extreme weather, the limitations of available science—but in this tragedy there was also, inevitably, a significant element of human error. Whose? Certainly, Scott must shoulder a great deal of the blame, and—being dead—he was an easy scapegoat. To blame Scott entirely, however, disgraces his memory and those of his closest friends, and this Cherry was unwilling to do. But if it could not all be pinned on Scott, then it was the survivors who must bear responsibility. For Cherry, this meant a lifetime of self-recrimination, of sometimes debilitating bouts of depression and grief.

Among Scott's papers were a handful of letters penned in his final days:

My Dear Mrs. Bowers,
I am afraid this will reach you after one of the heaviest blows of your life.
    I write when we are very near the end of our journey, and I am finishing it in company with two gallant, noble gentlemen. One of these is your son. He had come to be one of my closest and soundest friends, and I appreciate his wonderful upright nature, his ability and energy. As the troubles have thickened his dauntless spirit ever shone brighter and he has remained cheerful, hopeful, and indomitable to the end.
    The ways of Providence are inscrutable, but there must be some reason why such a young, vigorous and promising life is taken.
    My whole heart goes out in pity for you.... [67]

The end of the Heroic Age of Antarctic exploration is sometimes marked here, in 1912, after Amundsen won the race to the pole and Scott's team perished on their return. Other historians claim that the era continued on for another three years, until the *Endurance* was crushed by the ice, and the entire crew somehow came back alive, to find all of Europe engaged in war. Some even insist that the true end of the age wasn't until Shackleton spoke his last words on board the *Quest*, when his band of aging explorers were docked at South Georgia in 1922. What is beyond question, however, is that this era has long since passed, that with the deaths of these flawed but ambitious men, a great legacy was brought to a close. Yet beauty, discoveries, and even heroism are still present in our own time, and we have to seek them here.

My Dear Mrs. Wilson,
If this letter reaches you Bill and I will have gone out together. We are very near it now and I should like you to know how splendid he was at the end—

everlastingly cheerful and ready to sacrifice himself for others, never a
word of blame to me for leading him into this mess. He is not suffering,
luckily, at least only minor discomforts.

His eyes have a comfortable blue look of hope and his mind is peace-
ful with the satisfaction of his faith in regarding himself as part of the
great scheme of the Almighty. I can do no more to comfort you than to tell
you that he died as he lived, a brave, true man—the best of comrades and
staunchest of friends.

My whole heart goes out to you in pity. . . . [68]

"Welcome to South Georgia," Kendra calls out, as a group of us step down, unsteadily, into one of the familiar Zodiacs, where Stefan stands at the helm, ready to guide us to shore. Penguins porpoise all around us, and Stefan cuts the engine as we close in on a flock of small birds feeding at the water. "Wilson's storm petrels," he tells us in an excited hush. "They can't rest on the wing to eat, so their feet patter on the surface as though they are dancing." These tiny birds—all of eighteen centimeters in length— breed only in the southern oceans, though they travel as far as the Gulf of Alaska each year, having one of the longest migrations of any animal. The name petrel comes from "Peter," referring to the biblical story of St. Peter attempting to walk on water. And they do dance upon the surface— like hummingbirds fluttering among the blooms—as they dip their dark heads swiftly to peck morsels from the water at their feet. They feed mostly on crustaceans and small fish, though they are also dedicated scavengers, trained to find sustenance in what little remains, following in the wake of the great ships to feast off their refuse.

The bodies of Scott, Wilson, and Bowers were never moved. The search party simply took the bamboo pole away and the tent collapsed. Given the slow churning of the Barrier ice, however, their remains—buried beneath a century of snow—may already have broken off in a tabular berg, to drift north in the open sea, and continue their own strange migration.

In his final days, Wilson wrote to Oates's mother, as well as two short let- ters to his wife, Oriana: "Life has been a struggle for some weeks now on this return journey from the Pole—so much so that I have not been able to keep my diary going. To-day may be the last effort. . . . Don't be unhappy— all is for the best. We are playing a good part in a great scheme arranged by God himself."[69]

Upon the *Terra Nova*'s return to England, the geological specimens that were recovered from the Pole Team—the thirty-five pounds of rocks that Wilson insisted they carry until the end—were delivered to a professor of botany at the University of Cambridge. Among the impressions that Wilson had gathered, Dr. Seward identified the long-sought *Glossopteris* plant, whose presence had already been confirmed in India, South America, southern Africa, and Australia. Its discovery deep in the interior of Antarctica was the last piece needed to confirm the theory that the southern continents once formed an immense supercontinent. "The discovery of *Glossopteris* on the Buckley Island moraine," wrote Dr. Seward, "supplies what is needed to bring hypothesis within the range of established fact."[70]

Also included among Scott's diaries was a final letter written to his wife, Kathleen:

Since writing the above we got within 11 miles of our depot, with one hot meal and two days' cold food. We should have got through but have been held for four days by a frightful storm. I think the best chance has gone. . . . You know I cherish no sentimental rubbish about re-marriage. When the right man comes to help you in life you ought to be your happy self again—I wasn't a very good husband, but I hope I shall be a good memory.

We step out into the shallow surf where Eric stands to greet us and offer an available hand. A crowd of guests has gathered around a colony of nesting king penguins—literally tens of thousands of squawking, majestic birds. A little ways down the shore, I see the two away-school kids playing on a small beach. Their parents seem to have drifted off some place, leaving them unattended.

Make the boy interested in natural history if you can; it is better than games; they encourage it at some schools. I know you will keep him in the open air. Above all, he must guard and you must guard him against indolence. Make him a strenuous man. I had to force myself into being strenuous, as you know—had always an inclination to be idle.*

The two kids have found a ropelike piece of giant sea kelp that they are playing tug-of-war with, kicking up sand and spinning each other around

*Peter Markham Scott would grow up to become a renowned ornithologist and environmentalist.

on the beach. Then the girl slips, losing her grip on the slimy thing. Her brother waves it around triumphantly, chasing her down shore.

What lots and lots I could tell you of this journey. How much better has it been than lounging in too great comfort at home. What tales you would have for the boy. But what a price to pay![71]

Having run his sister off, the boy pauses for a moment, as though finally registering just where he is. He stares down at the otherworldly strand of kelp he holds in his hands, then lifts his eyes to look out at all that surrounds him. In wonder. In joy.

ON HISTORIAN ROLAND HUNTFORD
AND CONTROVERSIES SURROUNDING
SCOTT AND AMUNDSEN

I am not a historian. My chief interests, and therefore my biases, are all literary in nature. I hold an MFA in poetry, and BAs in English and philosophy. Beyond the eleventh grade, the only history class I ever took was an honors-level course titled "Vikings of the North Sea," while I was studying abroad in Scotland. To gain admittance, I had to lie about my major; I nearly failed.

Nonetheless, to write a book such as this, one has to delve a fair bit into the world of historians. Antarctic exploration—especially concerning the Heroic Age—is a popular field of study. And in this domain, perhaps the most well-known historian, and certainly the most controversial one, is Roland Huntford. His joint biography *Scott and Amundsen*, retitled in its American edition as *The Last Place on Earth*, was published with much clamor in 1979, and reissued twenty years later as part of the Modern Library's eight-book Exploration Series. In this latest edition, Huntford's biography is prefaced with praise-filled introductions by Jon Krakauer and Paul Theroux—endorsements that show the general level of esteem that Huntford's text is held in to this day. Among his book's most eye-catching claims are the "revelations" that Scott's mentor, Sir Clements Markham, was a closeted homosexual, and that Scott's wife, Kathleen, consummated an affair with Nansen in a Berlin hotel while Scott was marching to his death. Huntford presents both of these allegations as verifiable truths, though each has—*at the most*—only circumstantial evidence to back it up.

Of course, neither of these salacious claims have any bearing on the central events surrounding the tragedy of Scott's Pole Party, but they make for good melodrama. And, in fact, Huntford's controversial book was soon turned into a seven-part miniseries (with a young and dashing Hugh Grant cast in the role of Apsley Cherry-Garrard, no less!).

This is not to say that Huntford has received anything close to universal praise, as many reviewers, both past and present, have taken issue with Huntford's "mis-use of evidence and subjectivity," lamenting his "paranoid dislike of Scott."[1] Yet even while shortcomings in Huntford's scholarship have long been known, and many of his most glaringly far-fetched accusations have been questioned, if not outright disproven, Huntford's portrayal of the rival Pole Teams has, in many ways, become the popular truth. *The Last Place on Earth*, along with Huntford's later companion book, *Race for the South Pole*, has burrowed into our collective historical understanding, and has had an outsized influence on the work of polar historians ever since. I say this regretfully, as I find Huntford's condemnation of Scott to be so overblown and pervasive that even his valid critiques of Scott's leadership feel crippled with subjectivity. Virtually every point of difference between the two expeditions is seen as a further sign of Scott's ineptitude, and, much too frequently, Huntford peddles ad hominem attacks and conspiracy theories. He aims to discredit "the myth" of Scott, though he winds up painting a picture that feels even more distorted, not to mention gratuitously mean-spirited.

As Wayland Young points out in his 1980 *Encounter* article in critique of Huntford's scholarship, "On the Debunking of Captain Scott," the index entries at the back of *The Last Place on Earth* shed a great deal of light on the issue of authorial bias. There, Scott is allowed one solitary virtue—"Literary Gifts"—alongside Amundsen's trove of personal (often questionable) assets—"Love of Animals, Sense of Destiny, Intellect, Capacity for Leadership, Loyalty, Magnetism, Modesty, Physical Fitness, Sense of Rectitude, Sensitivity, Sexual Reticence, Singlemindedness, and Stoicism." On the reverse side, Amundsen is spared virtually all blemishes, while Scott is hit with a deluge of unsavory traits—"Absentmindedness, Unsuitability for Command, Refusal to Accept Criticism, Bouts of Depression, Emotionalism, Impatience, Belief in Improvisation, Sense of Inadequacy, Insecurity, Lack of Insight, Irrationality, Isolation, Jealousy, Defective Judgment, Failure in Leadership, Readiness to Panic, Recklessness, Instinct to Evade Responsibility, Sentimentality, and Vacillation."[2] Incidentally, the dual-biography structure of the book was reportedly pushed on Huntford by his editor, after Huntford's proposed biography on Amundsen was rejected out of concern that it held little interest to the wider public. Fittingly then, even as Huntford takes great joy in ripping apart the legend of Scott, the sections of the book that are dedicated to him all read as though Huntford is rather impatient to get back to his proper subject.

There are moments in Huntford's books where the disparity between the depictions of the two men is downright comical, as when he addresses the issue of humor itself. Seizing on a remark from Cherry-Garrard's *The Worst Journey in the World* that Scott had "little sense of humor," Huntford culls together a series of painfully unfunny remarks from Amundsen's diaries that Huntford pawns off as shining examples of wit to prove that *his* man did not suffer from a similar deficiency.

Furthermore, while Huntford is quick to call out Cherry-Garrard for any remarks in his published account that don't coincide with his own view of events—citing the fact that the author is writing them down ten years after the time in question—Huntford doesn't so much as bat an eyelash when relaying an experience Amundsen doles out in his own autobiography, about a routine medical check-up that took place thirty years before, never doubting the veracity of such a self-indulgent tale:

> The doctor was elderly and, to my great pleasure and surprise, a keen student of the human body. Naturally I was entirely without clothes during the examination. The old doctor inspected me with minute care, and suddenly burst out into rhapsodic praise over my appearance. Apparently eight years' uninterrupted training had not been without effect. He said, "Young man, what on earth have you been doing to acquire such muscles?" I explained that I was fond of physical exercise, which I practiced assiduously. The old gentleman was so enthused by his discovery, which he regarded as something quite unusual, that he called some officers from the next room to look at the wonder.[3]

Bear in mind that this is from the explorer upon whom Huntford bestowed the virtue of "Modesty" in his accompanying index.

If all of Huntford's mischaracterizations and hero-worshipping could be as easily dismissed with a laugh, I would stop here, but there are other, more problematic distortions as well. Such as Huntford's weirdly persistent emasculating depictions of Scott: "At the eleventh hour, Kathleen had doubts about marriage, partly because she saw that Scott was a mother worshipper, and therefore might not be quite the man she wanted."[4] Or his insistence on discrediting not just the scientific results, but also the basic scientific impulses of the *Terra Nova* expedition, claiming that Scott used science as an excuse to participate, while Amundsen "did not stoop to use science as an agent of prestige."[5]

Ever since his experiences on the *Belgica*, Amundsen had harbored a great distrust of academics and scientists (along with his distrust of doctors), feeling inadequate in the face of their specialized knowledge, and worrying that they would undermine his authority as a leader. While this seems a rather naïve and philistine position for a leader to take, it seems downright absurd that his biographer would share a similar mindset. Nonetheless, this is what we find in passage after passage of Huntford's book—as when he writes dismissively of the Winter Journey as having "a scientific sheen," when clearly its scientific goals were the very backbone of the endeavor.[6] Or when Huntford speaks of the geologizing that Scott's team undertook at the Buckley moraine on their way back from the pole, declaring it "a pathetic little gesture to salvage something from defeat" and adding that "half the weight in seal meat would have saved them. A pint of paraffin or a tin of pemmican would have been worth more to them than the most valuable stone in the world."[7] This makes it sound as though the Buckley moraine also functioned as a supply outlet, as though Scott and his companions stood there ponderously with their reindeer fur gloves on their hips, asking themselves: *Hmm, should we pick up some seal meat and fuel while we're here, or just these rocks?*

On a more literary bent, there is also the bizarre matter of correspondence, where Huntford criticizes Scott for writing letters home before disembarking for the pole: "Amundsen, so far as we know, wrote no letters at all. Scott seems to be looking over his shoulder at an unseen audience, concerned more with his reputation than his actions."[8] Since when is not having anyone to write to considered a virtue? Scott had a young wife and child at home; he wrote tender letters to his mother and his niece; he had friends, associates, supervisors; he wrote to Cherry-Garrard's uncle to let him know how proud he should be of his nephew. While it has been rumored that Amundsen fathered a child to an Inuit woman during his voyage of the Northwest Passage, Amundsen lived his entire life as a bachelor. His parents were both long gone, and in the years after his return from the Antarctic Amundsen would have a bitter falling-out with his only brother, Leon. On the eve of his departure to the pole, Amundsen had also lied to almost everyone, straining allegiances at home, and he had every reason to believe that he had forever alienated his mentor, Fridtjof Nansen. Quite literally, Amundsen was alone at the bottom of the world, and while I don't intend this as a disparagement of the man, he doesn't win points for it either.

Unfortunately, the distortions don't simply stop at the doorsteps of Scott and Amundsen, as they spill over into Huntford's characterizations of almost everyone that either of them came into contact with. Hjalmar Johansen, for instance, is thrown unceremoniously under the bus by Huntford, for his disagreements with—and so-called insubordination toward— Amundsen, while those who remain most loyal to Scott, such as Edward Wilson, are belittled and discredited. On the other hand, anyone who runs afoul of Scott is unreservedly lionized, despite whatever natural shortcomings they otherwise display. You can see this in Huntford's characterizations of Shackleton, Meares, and Lt. Evans, though it is perhaps shown most clearly in his depiction of Titus Oates.

In both his journals and in the letters that Oates sent home to his mother from Antarctica, it is evident that Oates had issues with Scott, as well as with many of the other men on the expedition. "I dislike Scott intensely," he writes at one point, and the two butted heads repeatedly in regard to the care and transport of the ponies, long before they set off across the plateau together to claim the pole.[9] Of course, disparaging one's sledge-companions in the privacy of one's journal is as time-honored an English tradition in polar travel as are hoosh mugs and frostbite. In perhaps my favorite instance of this venerable pastime, Frank Wild—while accompanying Shackleton on his *Nimrod* expedition's Farthest-South Journey—writes out the following, somewhere on the Beardmore Glacier, having just partaken of an extra dinner ration in celebration of Christmas: "For the first time for many days, I feel replete and therefore I will not make any nasty remarks about anyone, although I should very much like to."[10]

Just like Wild, Oates recognized his own propensity for using his diaries and letters home to vent his frustrations with others—"Please remember," he writes in a late note to his mother, "that when a man is having a hard time he says hard things about other people which he would regret afterwards."[11] While Huntford relishes in sharing other passages of Oates's letters, he makes no mention of this more conciliatory note. Yet what is most striking, and misleading, in Huntford's characterization of Oates is how he brands him as regretfully trudging toward the pole—"He went forward, driven only by a sense of duty, half-hearted and uninspired," and, "He had never wanted to go to the Pole; he had been ordered there against his wishes."[12] In Huntford's herculean efforts to blame Scott *for ev-*

erything, he paints a portrait of Oates (almost entirely lacking in supporting evidence) of a man stripped of free will and blinded by duty, having no choice but to march to his death. Of course, several of Oates's letters state directly that he wishes to go to the pole, and after being chosen he writes unequivocally, "I am of course delighted."[13]

And Huntford doesn't cherry-pick and misrepresent quotes only from Scott's expedition, but from Amundsen's own party as well, such as a statement by Helmer Hanssen, who chose to break ranks in a sense, after traveling with Amundsen to the pole, by offering some mitigated praise of Scott. Of course, one would never know this if one relied solely on Huntford's book, which supplies its own skewed translation, and a criminal use of ellipses, as it obfuscates and even contradicts Hanssen's intended meaning: "As Helmer Hanssen put it: 'What shall one say of Scott and his companions who were their own sledge dogs? . . . I don't think anyone will ever copy him.'"*[14]

Again, I am no historian, but I have graded more than my adjunct-share of composition research papers over the years, and on the grounds of maintaining objectivity, being conscientious and thorough with one's sources, and avoiding unnecessary editorializing, I'd give Huntford a D+, a C– if he were lucky. And it is not enough to simply ignore Huntford, given the outsized influence his writing has had on contemporary perspectives surrounding these two explorers. Even as late as 2000, for instance, the movie adaptation of *The Last Place on Earth* was still being shown at scientific stations in Antarctica as an important part of South Polar history. As Dr. Susan Solomon has noted, "once such seeds were sown, Scott's mistakes grew to assume legendary proportions, radically transforming the figures of all of the men of Scott's fatal expedition from heroism and tragedy to folly and even farce."[15] Much recent scholarship has moved beyond Huntford's problematic depiction of the rival expeditions, but it seems that the wider cultural understanding of the events—while dismissing some of Huntford's most egregious claims—still buys in to the wider depiction of Scott as the effeminate bungler and sentimental know-nothing.

My intention for this book was never to craft an apologia for Scott, though it makes sense—given that my interests are largely literary in na-

---

*A more extended, and more faithful, statement by Hanssen was already quoted in chapter 7, though for ease of reference here is the quoted passage: "We started with fifty-two dogs and came back with eleven, and many of these wore themselves out on the journey. What shall we say of Scott and his comrades, who were their own dogs? Anyone with any experience will take off his hat to Scott's achievement. I do not believe men have ever shown such endurance at any time, nor do I believe there ever will be men to equal it."

ture—that Scott's expedition would receive the more sympathetic portrayal, as he was a far better writer than was Amundsen. And the *Terra Nova* expedition also produced—by way of Apsley Cherry-Garrard—what is arguably the best book ever written about Antarctica. (This is certainly my view, and it is one that is widely shared. Huntford, on the other hand, branded Cherry-Garrard's book as "immature but persuasive.")[16] Additionally, Wilson's dedication as an artist greatly appeals to me. In matters of photography, while Herbert Ponting produced many wonderful images of Scott's expedition, it should be clear from the contents of this book that I am more drawn to the work (and character) of Frank Hurley. Amundsen, of course, brought no artists or photographers with him to the pole, and neither his subsequent books nor any of the collected writings from the other members of his party are noteworthy as literary texts.

As for the comparison of leadership among the big three of the Heroic Age—Scott, Shackleton, and Amundsen—I find myself in agreement with Ranulph Fiennes, who argues in his book *Race to the Pole* that "all three made deadly errors, had grave character flaws, and, at some point in their careers, caused other men to die."[17] While many have disagreed, claiming that Shackleton never lost a man under his charge, I find that his carelessness in overseeing the Ross Sea Party—the inadequacy of funding and supplies, and his poor selection of the men placed in charge—renders him at least partly responsible for the three deaths that occurred. Shackleton concedes as much himself, declaring openly, "Though I was thousands of miles away, the responsibility still lay on my shoulders."[18] As for Amundsen, while his trek to the pole went off without a hitch, and it seems a stretch to pin Johansen's later suicide directly on him, his last botched voyage to rescue Nobile in the Arctic seems to me the epitome of the act of "worthless heroism" that Huntford consistently rails against Scott for on his pole expedition. Nobile had already made radio contact providing his location, and with at least twenty other search parties already enlisted to pick him up, it was only Amundsen's ego and perceived slight that impelled him to fly under weather conditions that the other parties had deemed too dangerous. Huntford acknowledges this at the end of *The Last Place on Earth*, though it appears his outrage over a leader's fatal shortsightedness is reserved solely for the British—"To go on was foolhardy, but they had gone too far to turn back. . . . Amundsen had thrown away his life. But he would only have been unhappy if he had gone on."[19] A sort of just-as-well shrug as a last comment on the life of this explorer, that does little to address the needless deaths of the other five men who perished in the crash.

Turning back to Fiennes's book, which was published in 2003, one finds it offers an important corrective to some of Huntford's more haphazard scholarship. While the vast majority of polar historians (Huntford being a notable exception) have at least traveled to the Antarctic, no scholar has as much direct experience with polar exploration and Antarctic travel as has Fiennes, who has crossed the continent multiple times on foot and on ski and successfully man-hauled the Beardmore Glacier. This gives him a unique authority to refute claims from Huntford on matters such as the inadequacy of Scott's clothing—"Scott is castigated for his use of man-made clothing materials, not furs, even though polar experts know that man-haulers would be unable to move in furs. . . . For man-hauling, even at −50 C, it is best if you wear lightweight cotton clothes, otherwise your sweat is trapped and freezes on your skin as your body cools."[20] Likewise, Fiennes takes Huntford to task for his claims that the British team's lack of skill on skis was a contributing factor in their deaths—"With loads, the entire business of technique and skill becomes superfluous."[21] The crux of the issue, then, is mode of transport—man-hauling versus dogs. While we can certainly question the merits of Scott's decision in this, the choice to man-haul largely made ski expertise a moot point.

Such criticisms of Huntford's views are important, not simply because they correct some of the needless character assassinations of his work, but because they improve our understanding of tragic historical events. With this in mind, I want to turn now to discuss four instances of Huntford's scholarship that seem particularly guilty of muddling an accurate portrayal of Scott's fatal trip to the South Pole.

1. THE SKI DEPOT

On the last day of 1911, as the two remaining teams of Scott's expedition continued their push to the pole, Scott ordered Lt. Evans's four-man sledge team to depot their skis—shaving one hundred pounds off their total load—while his own team kept theirs. Scott's reasoning behind this is never fully explained in the journals, leading Huntford to come up with his own unsubstantiated theory—"He [Scott] had patently decided by then to take his own team on to the Pole, and wanted to break Evans so as to ease the task of sending him back."[22] The idea, according to Huntford, "was clearly to wear Evans out by depriving him of skis and forcing him to struggle along through the snow on foot. That would, in turn, allow Scott to send him back on grounds of fitness without any public hint of rancour."[23] A damning charge, if this were true, as Scott would essentially be risking the health and fitness of some of his men unnecessarily, and at a stage in the journey when their safe return to base was far from certain.

Yet this theory is largely contradicted by the details of the journals, and the truth is much simpler and less nefarious than this. Quite simply, Scott was unsure whether it was worth bringing skis along. While the British were not near as well trained on skis as their Norwegian counterparts, they had found them to be a great help when sledging on certain surfaces, and a hindrance in areas that were heavily sloped or broken up by sastrugi. As a result, some days they pulled with skis on and other days they added them to their loads. The question of using skis is openly debated by members of the party, and Scott repeatedly comes back to the issue in his journals, such as on December 16, when he records, "We began on ski as usual. . . . Decided to take to our feet, and thus made better progress."[24] When Scott decided to have Lt. Evans's team depot their skis on December 31, Scott knew (or thought he knew) that after another few marches four men would be turning back, and he could only guess at what surfaces awaited them in the days ahead. On their following march, Scott remarks on how he expected to have more trouble on ski than they did, and then again on January 6 (after the support team has turned back) he decided to depot their own skis as they entered an area with heavy pressure—though after a few miles of foot sledging the surface rapidly improves, and he determined that they must go back for them, costing an hour and a half in delay. It was only then that Scott considered the matter settled: "I must stick to the ski after this."[25] This last entry alone is enough to refute Huntford's theory, for the only way that Scott can have purposely sabotaged the other sledging party through depriving them of their skis is if there is no question in his mind that skis are the best option.

One can certainly point to this waffling back and forth on the matter of skis as being revealing of Scott's indecisive character and leadership, but to use it to hint at some evil plot to carelessly risk the lives of several of his men is absurd.

2. THE FIFTH PARTY MEMBER

I have already addressed this matter to some extent in chapter 8, but I want to return to it here. On January 4, 1912, Scott sent the last support party back shorthanded, adding Birdie Bowers as a fifth member to the party continuing to the pole. Again, Scott's reasons for this decision are not made explicit in any of the journals, opening up the door for another unsupported Huntford theory. "In Scott's party, Wilson, Oates and P.O. Evans could not navigate, while Scott himself was out of practice. He needed someone else.... As it turned out, he had a lucky escape. Bowers was a qualified navigator so now, at the last moment, Scott seized on him instead to fill the gap."[26] Again, this is preposterous. Scott had been planning the details of this expedition for years, attending to an infinite number of logistics along the way. Yet in order to go along with Huntford's theory we have to believe not only that Scott had ceased to be a capable navigator (for which there is no supporting evidence), but also that it was only at the last possible moment that Scott remembered that he had long since forgotten how to do it.

Beyond this straining of the imagination, Huntford's theory also does nothing to explain the real crux of the issue—*why Scott chose to take five to the pole*. After all, Scott was in full control of the party, deciding who turns back and who goes on; his determinations in this regard (as can be shown from all previous return parties) were final and not open to debate. If Scott had decided that he needed Bowers to cover for his own navigational shortcomings, there was nothing to stop him from sending one of the other men back in Bowers's place. So not only is Huntford's theory farfetched; it is also almost entirely beside the point.

3. THE BARRIER WEATHER

This is a simple matter to clear up and has been alluded to briefly already. As Scott's team made their way north across the Barrier in March, the temperatures regularly dipped down into the negative thirties and forties. These low temperatures played a tragic role in the fate of Scott's party, resulting in crippling frostbite for Oates (and later Scott) while also having a grave impact on the quality of the snow surface. Clearly, such extreme temperatures came as a surprise to Scott, who wrote on March 14, "No idea there could be temperatures like this at this time of year with such winds."[27] Huntford uses such remarks—and the whole subject of the weather—as another opportunity to highlight Scott's shortsightedness and failure as a leader, arguing, "In fact, the temperatures, between –30 and –40 C, were not exceptionally low for the season of the year."[28] This opinion is at odds with Scott's chief meteorologist, George Simpson, who—after analyzing all the data available to him—deemed 1911 to be "an abnormal year," adding, "There can be no doubt that the weather played a predominating part in the disaster, and . . . was the immediate cause of the final catastrophe."[29] Cherry-Garrard also quoted Simpson as saying that "the polar party would probably have survived in nine years out of ten."[30] So, who is correct: the professional meteorologist or Roland Huntford? Were the extreme temperatures that Scott's men recorded on the Barrier in March 1911 abnormal or not?

Acclaimed Antarctic climatologist Susan Solomon—who is one of the scientists responsible for identifying the hole in the ozone layer—analyzed over thirty years of data, compiled by multiple automated weather stations that have been set up along the Barrier, to help determine the answer. Her book entitled (spoiler alert) *The Coldest March* concludes that only one year on record (1988) comes close to averaging the severity of temperatures that Scott's party records in March 1911, with all the other years of data pointing to average temperatures that are between ten and twenty degrees warmer. As Solomon argues, "the weather stations demonstrate that Scott and his party were fighting for their lives under rare conditions that were surely very much colder than normal," going so far as to add that the cold spell the Pole Team faced, which Simpson hypothesized to occur only once a decade, may actually be less frequent than even that.[31]

4. REVISED ORDERS FOR THE DOGS

The issues surrounding Scott's orders for the dogs will be discussed more fully in appendix 2, but as a way of prefacing that—and dispensing with the meddlesome Huntford component beforehand—I want to address it here. According to Huntford, when Scott sent the last support team back to base on January 4, he gave Lt. Evans revised orders for the dogs: "Meares now was to come out and meet Scott between 82 and 83 S., some time towards the middle of February. . . . This was the furthest Scott had yet wanted the dogs brought out. It was in any case a vital alteration to his plans. It was verbal. It bore the stamp, once more of last-minute improvisation. Scott assumed that Evans would deliver it in time."[32] Another damning charge against Scott, yet oddly there is no mention of these last-minute verbal instructions in either Scott's or Lt. Evans's journals, nor in Lt. Evans's subsequent book *South with Scott*, nor in Cherry-Garrard's book. Even more surprisingly, no historian before Huntford had ever mentioned this "vital alteration" in Scott's plans for the dogs. As Karen May, a researcher writing for *Polar Record*, uncovers in her 2013 article "Could Captain Scott Have Been Saved? Revisiting Scott's Last Expedition," this is because Huntford has made this all up. Or, to put it more charitably, he has mistaken detailed written instructions that Scott left with Cecil Meares at base back in October for last-minute verbal instructions to be relayed by Lt. Evans. Evans includes these written orders in *South with Scott*, and several other members of the expedition allude to them, but somehow Huntford got this all muddled up in his research and wildly recast the story into something else entirely. As May declares, "the story of Scott's last minute change of mind is an error on Huntford's part. It is no minor error, as we shall see."[33]

The far-reaching implications of these fictitious orders are laid bare in Huntford's book: when Lt. Evans broke down with scurvy, in the supposed turmoil of being at death's door, he failed to transmit this crucial information. "In that crisis," Huntford writes, "Scott's vital message that the dogs were to meet him between 82 and 83, casually mentioned just before parting with Evans, was forgotten."[34] As if it wasn't enough simply to make up the existence of a last-minute order, Huntford also offers a condemning editorializing of the tone with which it was never delivered. This issue also shows very clearly the problematic reverberations that Huntford's careless scholarship has had in later historical accounts, as claims of this illusionary additional order have been repeated in countless historical texts over the past forty years.

===

History, of course, is a work in progress, and there is every reason to hope that through the recent scholarship of writers like May, Fiennes, and Solomon, Roland Huntford's biased depiction of Scott's last expedition will be cast aside. In truth, for most anyone who is well read in such matters, the majority of these issues have probably already been dispensed with. Nonetheless, only one book on the Heroic Age of Antarctica has been reprinted in the Modern Library's Exploration Series, or turned into a seven-part miniseries, and that is Huntford's. In fact, along with Alfred Lansing's *Endurance*—a straightforward adventure narrative about Shackleton's most famous voyage—I would wager that *The Last Place on Earth* is still the most widely read book on Antarctic exploration, and so it will take some time to fully right the "popular truth" in such matters. All the more so because Huntford is both a good writer and more than willing to engage in the type of slanderous revelations and open conspiracy theories that are likely to appeal to the general public. In place of objectivity and detailed scholarship, Huntford bombards us with accusations, severe judgments, and a highly charged polemic tone—much like the one I am employing myself in this essay, purposely, as a means for getting my points across. To make use of such a tone while arguing with a contemporary scholar is much different from using it to recast historical figures and events, though, and with this in mind I want to address one last distortion in Huntford's revisionist work.

The most distasteful characterization in *The Last Place on Earth*, at least to me, lies not with Captain Scott, but with the disparagement of Edward Wilson in the last days of his life. Wilson, of course, was held in the highest regard by both Scott and Shackleton (even after their bitter falling-out with each other), and his character was praised by virtually everyone who ever sailed with him. Huntford, however, ridicules the man mercilessly at the end of his book, when Wilson is writing his final letters alongside Scott in their tent. "The paradox," as Huntford writes, "was that Wilson, who for so long had nursed morbid death-wishes, now had regrets. . . . He was a born loser, that he understood. But his life had been thrown away—for nothing."[35]

I have written at some length about Wilson's ascetic views on suffering, and on how he believed that God had watched over his three-man party on the Winter Journey, but I would not characterize any of this as a "morbid death-wish." The only other potential piece of evidence that Huntford puts forth to back up this claim is a thoughtful passage from Wilson's journal that discusses Tennyson's great poem "In Memoriam" that Cherry-Garrard had lent him for the journey to the pole—"What a perfect piece of faith and hope! Makes me feel that if the end comes to me here or hereabouts there will be no great time for Ory to sorrow. All will be as it was meant to be, and her faith and hope and trust will be to her what Tennyson's was to him."[36] Again, to characterize this as a morbid death wish feels wildly off base; he is writing this down while on a dangerous journey far into the Antarctic interior, so some consideration of his own mortality, along with thoughts for loved ones left behind, seems quite natural. As for the juvenile name-calling, I will let the "born loser," stricken with remorse, answer for himself—placing the focus where I ultimately think it belongs—not on a historian's skewed interpretation but on the firsthand accounts—the words and works of art left behind—of those who lived it.

Here, then, is Wilson's last letter:

To my Most Beloved Wife.
God be with you in your trouble, dear, when I have gone. I have written another short letter to you. . . .

I leave this life in absolute faith and happy belief that if God wishes you to wait long without me it will be to some good purpose. All is for the best to those that love God, and oh, my Ory, we have both loved Him with all our lives. All is well. . . .

We have struggled to the end and we have nothing to regret. Our whole journey record is clean, and Scott's diary gives the account. . . . The Barrier has beaten us—though we got to the Pole.

My beloved wife, these are small things, life itself is a small thing to me now, but my love for you is for ever and a part of our love for God. . . . I do not cease to pray for you and to desire that you may be filled with the knowledge of His will. (Later.) God knows I am sorry to be the cause of sorrow to anyone in the world, but everyone must die—and at every death there must be some sorrow. . . . All the things I had hoped to do with you after this Expedition are as nothing now, but there are greater things for us to do in the world to come. . . . My only regret is leaving you to struggle through your life alone, but I may be coming to you by a quicker way. I feel so happy now in having got time to write to you. One of my notes will surely reach you. . . . Dad's little compass and Mother's little comb and looking-glass are in my pocket. Your little testament and prayer book will be in my hand or in my breast pocket when the end comes. All is well.[37]

ON THE QUESTIONS AND
CONTROVERSIES SURROUNDING
SCOTT'S ORDERS FOR THE DOGS

"Three cheers for the dogs!" RGS president Lord Curzon called out, as he took center stage after Amundsen had finished his guest lecture at the Queen's Hall in London, in the year after his conquest of the South Pole.[1] This was, of course, a thinly veiled insult—a not-so-subtle hint about whom Curzon took the real heroes of the Norwegian expedition to be— and Amundsen understood it as such. This was before word of Scott's death had reached the world, yet already his rival venture to the pole was being cast in the light of purity and noble ideals.

Scott had long since laid the groundwork for just that, going back as far as his *Discovery* voyage: "To say that they [dogs] do not greatly increase the radius of action is absurd; to pretend that they can be worked to this end without pain, suffering and death is equally futile. The question is whether the latter can be justified by the gain, and I think that logically it may be; but the introduction of such sordid necessity must and does rob sledge-travelling of much of its glory."[2] Historians are quick to chalk this up to Edwardian ideals of masculinity and British exceptionalism, and certainly the Brits had cultivated these views in their early exploits into the Arctic. Still, there is a wider appeal to such a stance that extends beyond the historic milieu, as is shown in the contemporary outdoor-recreationalist focus on free climbing, unaided ascents, and other unsupported wilderness ventures.

204 / APPENDIX 2

All of this, however, feels at least a little out of place when considering Scott's actual trip to the pole, which set out from Cape Evans with every intention of getting as much assistance as it could, and not just from ponies and dogs, but also from motorized sledges. Scott—it should be mentioned—never placed much faith in the latter, which broke down after a mere fifty miles, eliciting a wry note in his journal entry for the day, "So the dream of great help from the machines is at an end!"[3] The dog teams would wind up faring far better, convincing Scott to take them 345 miles further than he had originally planned. At that point, they would have to navigate the Beardmore Glacier, and Scott was relying, in large part, on Shackleton's determination that the crevasse-ridden nature of that steep glacier was too great an obstacle for dogs or ponies.

Scott's own limited experience with dogs corroborated such a view, as they had almost lost a dog team the previous season, when they slipped down a deep crevasse while returning from the Depot Journey, and Scott himself had to rope up and descend into the blue depths to haul them out. Yet there is also evidence of Scott second-guessing himself, and thereby Shackleton, as the man-hauling teams made their slow way up the lower reaches of the Beardmore, and Scott writes, "Certainly dogs could have come up as far as this."[4] The real controversy surrounding Scott's use of the dogs, however, is centered not on the outbound trip, but rather on the return, and it is these matters that I would like to focus on now.

ORDERS FOR THE DOGS:
LEFT AT BASE AND ALTERED ON THE MARCH

Scott's bid for the pole involved an intricate web of moving parts, including sixteen men split up into various teams defined by their mode of transport.* Perhaps the easiest way to understand this elaborate setup is through the image of a pyramid—with the huge necessitated weight of the expedition divvied up across a host of transport teams with the end goal of supporting the final group (the tip of the pyramid) across the finish line. The logistics and various calculations—both of mileage and of stores—that were required to make this arrangement work were immense, and Scott left detailed instructions back at Cape Evans for the tasks that needed to

*For a full breakdown of the *Terra Nova* expedition's journeys, parties, and teams, see appendix 3.

be completed to ensure the safe return of all parties. The most important duties fell to Cecil Meares, the man in charge of the dogs, and these duties entailed three separate journeys to the south:

> Dear Meares,—In order that there may be no mistake concerning the important help which it is hoped the dog teams will give to the South- ern Party, I have thought it best to set down my wishes. . . . The date of your return [from the southern journey] must be arranged accord- ing to circumstances. Under favourable conditions you should be back at Hut Point by December 19 at latest. . . . At some point during this month or early in January you should make your second journey to One Ton Camp and leave there: 5 units X.S. ration. 3 cases of biscuit. 5 gallons of oil. As much dog food as you can conveniently carry (for third journey). . . . About the first week of February I should like you to start your third journey to the South, the object being to hasten the return of the third Southern unit and give it a chance to catch the ship. The date of your departure must depend on news received from re- turning units, the extent of the depot of dog food you have been able to leave at One Ton Camp, the state of the dogs, etc. . . . It looks at present as though you should aim at meeting the returning party about March 1 in Latitude 82 or 82.30. . . .[5]

These orders were also shared with the chief meteorologist, Dr. George Simpson, who would be acting as the head of base until the other officers returned. One thing to note here is that even before the Southern Jour- ney departs, the elaborate pyramid setup already has a structural prob- lem—that is, the southern parties will deplete the stores already left at the One Ton Depot to such an extent on the outbound journey that they will need to be replenished for the returning parties in order to save it from collapsing. Scott stresses this very point at the end of his written orders to Meares—"You will of course understand that whilst the object of your third journey is important, that of the second is vital. . . . If the dogs are unable to perform this service, a man party must be organized."[6]

As should be clear, before Scott departs on the Southern Journey, he is trying to foresee and advise on possible contingency plans given the in- herent uncertainties of the voyage at hand—these include the unknown return dates of the various parties and the potential loss of animals, among other things. And, in fact, within the first three weeks of the Southern Journey, after the motorized sledges break down, Scott decides to make an adjustment, sending the following written message back with the Motor Party:

> We are making fair progress and the ponies doing fairly well—I hope we shall get through to the Glacier without difficulty but to make sure I am carrying the dog teams farther than I intended at first—the teams may be late returning, unfit for further work or non existent—so don't forget that the 3 XS ration units must be got to One Ton Camp.[7]

An "XS ration unit" was a week's supply of food for a four-man team, so the three weeks of rations referenced here were seen as the bare minimum that the returning parties would require to get through, with the original order's additional two rations, along with the store of dog food, meant for the dog teams' third journey south to meet the Pole Team. The reason for the switch from five to three ration units here is twofold: one, if the dog teams wound up being "unfit for further work or non existent" there would obviously not be a third journey; and two, because a man-hauling unit would be much more restricted by weight, and could not be expected to carry the full resupply. Simpson duly sent out a man-hauling team and the stores at One Ton were replenished. This, however, did not absolve Meares from holding up his end of the bargain (i.e., laying the additional stores upon his return), as the dog teams' third journey to meet the Pole Team would rely on it. This is quite complicated, though—as will soon be shown—Meares clearly understood Scott's intentions for him.

One other potential wrench in the plans involves the expected arrival of the *Terra Nova* at the end of the summer. The ship would be bringing in supplies and a new batch of dogs and horses, and would also be taking an undetermined number of the crew members home. Scott was well aware that Meares was considering leaving on the ship, as Scott addressed instructions to the skipper of the *Terra Nova*, Lieutenant Harry Pennell, regarding this back in October—"Meares may possibly return; it depends on letters from home."[8] Of course, if Meares decided to head home on the *Terra Nova*, then someone else would have to lead the dogs, along with Dimitri (the assistant dog handler), on the third journey. This is exactly what Scott tells Dr. Atkinson as the First Return Party is sent back on December 21, as reported by Cherry-Garrard: "Before we left Scott at the top of the Beardmore he gave him [Atkinson] orders to take the two dog-teams South in the event of Meares having to return home . . . with the depot [of dog food] which has been laid come as far as you can."[9]

The expected rendezvous point with the dogs has become less definite here, likely owing to the fact that the dogs have been brought so much extra distance and the possibility of unforeseen hardships, but clearly Scott is still expecting the dog teams to come out and meet the Pole Team. And it isn't just Scott who is expecting this, but virtually everyone else involved— we know this because the expected rendezvous is spoken of in the journals, letters, and orders of others, including Wilson, Bowers, Oates, Lt. Evans, Cherry-Garrard, Atkinson, Lashly, Meares, and Simpson. In *The Worst Journey in the World*, Cherry-Garrard stresses the fact that this additional trip with the dogs was never intended to serve as a "relief journey," that their job was simply to hasten the Pole Team back to bring news for the ship.[10] But the *intention* of the dog teams seems much less important than its anticipated rendezvous. After all, even if the initial function of the dog teams was something else, their third voyage to the south always had the potential of *becoming* a relief journey, if the need arose. Scott alludes to this very possibility himself on the outbound journey, writing that "the dogs are reported to be doing very well. They are going to be a great standby, no doubt."[11] It is with this in mind that the Pole Team began to talk so persistently about the dogs' arrival once they approached the eighty-second parallel, as shown in Scott's entry from February 27: "We are naturally always discussing possibility of meeting dogs, where and when, &c. It is a critical position."[12] For anyone who has ever felt themselves tiring after a long day on the trail, impatiently awaiting the next camp or summit or parking lot and peering out after each bend or small rise in hopes that the promised relief has arrived, then you have the faintest idea of what that must have been like for them—mile after exhausting mile, day after increasingly desperate day.

If this was the case, however, then why isn't there more direct mention of the dogs in Scott's last entries, more disappointment expressed at their failure to arrive? The simplest reason is that there are so many unknowns. Did the dogs falter on their way back to base? Did Meares and Dimitri, who were returning on reduced rations, have to sacrifice some of the dogs to make it through? Did a dog team fall into another crevasse on the Barrier and have to be abandoned? Did one of the other return parties run into trouble? Had lives been lost? Unknown sacrifices made? There is just so much that could have gone wrong that it makes sense for Scott to couch most of his statements on the dogs with uncertainty, and to repeatedly give the men back at base the benefit of the doubt, to assume that they would have followed through with his orders if at all possible—"I don't know that anyone is to blame. The dogs which would have been our salvation have evidently failed. Meares had a bad trip home I suppose."[13] Yet if the Pole Team knew the full story, that the dogs were not only alive but in good health, that even while all of the return parties faced difficulties, and Lt. Evans had broken down with scurvy, all of the men made it back safely to base, then I think they would have felt betrayed.

By whom? Upon the expedition's return to Britain, certain newspapers singled out Cherry-Garrard as a target, given that he turned back to base at the One Ton Depot instead of continuing further across the Barrier, where the last remaining members of the Pole Team were marching to their deaths. I would argue, however, that of the principal people involved, Cherry-Garrard was perhaps the least culpable individual in the tragedy that was to unfold.

BREAKDOWN OF COMMAND AND FAILURE TO FOLLOW SCOTT'S ORDERS

I should start this section off by saying how indebted this entire essay is to the scholarship of Karen May for her thorough and well-reasoned article "Could Captain Scott Have Been Saved? Revisiting Scott's Last Expedition" and her follow-up article with Sarah Airriess, "Could Captain Scott Have Been Saved? Cecil Meares and the 'Second Journey' That Failed." As the title of the latter foreshadows, May and Airriess feel that Cecil Meares's negligence in following Scott's orders for the second dog journey played a large role in the tragedy—a conclusion that I agree with.

Meares was a shadowy figure among the *Terra Nova* crew, with many unanswered questions regarding his background and how he found his way to sailing south. Scott was a leader who tried to learn from past mistakes, and he was quick to seek out advice from experts in the field. After the failure of the dogs during the *Discovery* expedition, he recognized the advantages of enlisting a trained dog driver, and this job vacancy led him to the far regions of the world. Meares was an adventurer and a loner, who had learned to drive dogs while working in the fur trade in Siberia. He had many exciting tales about his travels throughout central Asia and was somehow recommended to Scott through the Admiralty. "The spirit of the wanderer is in Meares' blood," Scott wrote in his journals. "He has no happiness but in the wild places of the earth."[14] There is a clear thread of awe woven into this statement, yet the two men butted heads on multiple occasions throughout the expedition, most notably, perhaps, when Meares's dog team fell into a crevasse on the Depot Journey. Scott ordered Meares to rope up and descend into the crevasse to haul them out, but Meares refused. Cherry-Garrard volunteered to go in his place, while Wilson was of the opinion that this was too dangerous, and no one should go. In the end, as I have already referenced, Scott himself headed down and the dog team was saved.

Moving on to the more important juncture of the expedition, we see that Meares arrived back at base from the Southern Journey with Dimitri and the dogs on January 5—a little over two weeks later than expected given Scott's decision to have them continue further to the south. Assuming, then, that the dog teams were essentially two weeks behind schedule, Meares should have planned to restock the One Ton Depot in the second half of January. And, in fact, that appears to have been his plan all along, as Simpson records in the journal he was keeping back at base: "On the 17th of January Meares had his sledges packed with the idea of starting that evening."[15] Meares's preparations for departure show clearly that he understood his responsibility to follow through with the second journey, and Simpson is obviously well aware of this plan. Yet on that same day there was a report that the *Terra Nova* had been spotted, and Simpson adds, "Naturally when the ship was seen Meares delayed his departure in the hope of being able to take home news with him."[16] *Naturally* perhaps, but certainly not *necessarily*. Running out news from home would be a welcome surprise to the last returning parties, though hardly something to postpone a vital mission for. In the least, after it became clear that the ship was not landing at Cape Evans (she sailed further up the coast with the intention of picking up Campbell and his men first and did not arrive at Cape Evans until February 7), Meares should have continued on with his initial plan. But for some reason he didn't, and for some reason Simpson did not order him to, and it was at that point that the whole idea of completing the second dog journey was abandoned, meaning the depot was to remain unstocked with dog food.

It appears that Meares became worried that he would miss the ship, that it would depart before he could get back from his second journey, forcing him to spend another winter in the Antarctic. Meares might also have reasoned that if the ship's departure was imminent (which, by the way, it wasn't—it did not leave Cape Evans until March 4), then the dog teams' third journey to the south was pointless, since the dogs would never return with news from the Pole Team in time. All of this seems poorly reasoned and guided by self-interest, though no one seems to have called Meares out on this.

This is where the breakdown in the chain of command came into play, as those left in charge appear to have been largely unfit for the task. Dr. Simpson was an intelligent man and a dedicated scientist, but he had no experience with overseeing a large operation. Dr. Atkinson, who—as the only active officer at base—overtook Simpson in the chain of command upon his return on January 26, also may have been out of his depth, as his services in the Royal Navy were all centered on medicine. As May explains in her article, "The navy expected its medical officers to care for invalids; it did not expect them to hold positions of command, and provided no specific training in this regard."[17] In the least, it is a valid question whether a seasoned military officer such as Bowers or Campbell or Lt. Evans, if left in charge, would have insisted on Meares fulfilling his duties with the second journey.

Nonetheless, after assuming command, Atkinson showed every intention of following Scott's orders, in place of Meares, to head south with the dogs and rendezvous with the Pole Team. He and Dimitri were behind schedule, after getting delayed with unloading all the stores and animals from the *Terra Nova* (another inessential activity, at least in regard to the dog teams), but they traveled out to Hut Point on February 15 in preparation for their imminent departure. This was two weeks behind the schedule that Scott had left in his written orders, though this alone would not result in a tragedy. On the evening before they had planned to leave Hut Point, however, Tom Crean arrived in total exhaustion with the news that Lt. Evans was in the late throes of scurvy over thirty miles away out on the Barrier. As soon as the weather permitted, Atkinson and Dimitri set off with the dogs and managed to bring Lt. Evans safely back to Hut Point on the twenty-second. At that point in time, Atkinson rightly felt that, as a doctor, his duty was to stay with the sick man, and he sent Dimitri back to Cape Evans with a team of dogs and written orders for Charles Wright, the expedition's physicist, to take his place: "I have just brought in Teddy Evans from beyond Corner Camp with a hellish go of scurvy. I want you please to take my team south to meet the last party. If you cannot possibly do so ask Cherry."[18] Atkinson also sent a note to Simpson, making clear his preference that Wright should be the one to "go south to meet Captain Scott."[19]

This stated preference for Wright over Cherry-Garrard makes a great deal of sense, as Atkinson knew them both well, having returned with them on the man-hauling team that had turned back near the top of the Beardmore. While Cherry-Garrard was a strong sledger and an eager volunteer for all tasks, he had no experience with navigation, and cripplingly poor eyesight. Wright, on the other hand, had managed most of the navigation himself on their return journey of nearly five hundred miles. Unfortunately, Simpson was opposed to Wright heading south. News brought from the *Terra Nova* had included notice that Simpson had unexpectedly been recalled to India for work, and he had appointed Wright to serve as the head of the scientific operations in his absence until Wilson's return. Simpson's first priority clearly lay with the scientific component of the expedition, and this may have clouded his judgment in this regard. Still, Simpson sent both Wright and Cherry-Garrard out to Hut Point, making his own strong preference known, but leaving the final decision with Atkinson.

Atkinson did not want to go against Simpson's wishes, nor did he want to compromise the expedition's scientific agenda, but he was also well aware of Cherry-Garrard's shortcomings. In the end, Atkinson decided to send Cherry-Garrard south, along with Dimitri, with verbal orders to supplement the existing stores out at the One Ton Depot, and, if Scott had not arrived then, to judge for himself what to do. Atkinson also is said to have stressed that Scott "was not in any way dependent on the dogs for his return," and that Scott had left explicit instructions that "the dogs were not to be risked."[20] These orders are written out in Cherry-Garrard's *The Worst Journey in the World*, and must have been corroborated with Atkinson, who remained one of his close friends after they returned to Britain. The orders are surprising in at least two regards: (1) the intention of this third journey has been downgraded considerably, with no mention of the eighty-second parallel or even necessarily meeting Scott; and (2) for the first time there is mention of Scott having ordered that the dogs were not to be risked. What seems likely is that Atkinson has revised the plan to meet the abilities of the person entrusted with the task.

To my mind, this was a totally reasonable decision. While May and Airriess make a strong argument in their article for why Atkinson should have overruled Simpson and sent Wright on the third journey instead, once Atkinson has decided on sending Cherry-Garrard he has every reason to worry that he is putting the young man's life at great risk. Even if the dogs were led by a competent navigator, there was a very real possibility of missing a return party over the vast expanse of the interior. Ultimately, it appears that Atkinson placed his faith in the five seasoned polar explorers who were returning together from the pole, as opposed to placing it with the two young and overmatched subalterns under his personal charge. At-kinson also had reason to hope that the scaled-back journey out to One Ton would suffice, for given the rate of travel for all other returning parties, the Pole Team's arrival at One Ton seemed imminent.

Cherry-Garrard's journal entry from the day of his arrival at the One Ton Depot also makes clear this expectation of the Pole Team's arrival: "There is no sign of Scott here, and so perhaps he will get in soon and all will be well. I have decided to wait 2 days and then settle what we will do."[21] And in *The Worst Journey in the World*, Cherry-Garrard also de-tails the missing dog-food rations. "The depot of dog-food spoken of by Scott [at the top of the Beardmore] did not exist," he writes, which makes it sound as though Scott was confused or mistaken, when really Scott is just trusting that his full orders have been carried out.[22] Without the extra dog food, the only recourse available to Cherry-Garrard is to push on to the south, killing dogs as necessary until he, hopefully, crosses paths with the Pole Team. Atkinson's verbal orders to "not risk the dogs," along with Dimitri's failing condition, are enough to render that option unadvisable at best.

Thirty-six years later, near the end of his life, when Cherry-Garrard is discussing the matter over, yet again, with George Bernard Shaw—who has become his closest confidant—Shaw asks him whether he would have proceeded further south if the depot of dog food had been laid. Given all the variables involved, this was not an easy question. Would Dimitri's con-dition continue to deteriorate, and, if it did, how would they ever manage to find their way back to base? Cherry's own stress and exhaustion from leading the team, his dreadful eyesight, his lack of navigational skills, and the lateness of the season all had to be weighed. All the same, Cherry an-swers, without hesitation, "Of course."[23]

None of this is to say that the remaining members of the Pole Team would have been assured a safe return if Cherry-Garrard (or anyone else) had led the dogs further south, though certainly their chances of survival would have greatly increased. A closer look at the rescue of the Second Return Party proves insightful here. On February 18, Lashly and Crean were forced to give up their pursuit of transporting the incapacitated Lt. Evans themselves, after poor ice conditions on the Barrier had reduced their sledging speed to less than a mile an hour. Four days later, however, the two dog teams, led by Atkinson and Dimitri, managed to traverse the thirty-five miles back to Hut Point, with Lashly and Lt. Evans in tow, over the span of just twenty-four hours. This was with Dimitri and Lt. Evans (the latter carried inside his sleeping bag) riding on one sledge, and Atkinson and Lashly sharing the other. Granted, the distance between the site of the Pole Team's last camp and Hut Point was nearly four times this distance, which would have made for a Herculean task for both dogs and men, though the possibility of a full rescue was certainly within reach. Each member of the Pole Team was well aware of what the dogs were capable of, having traveled over four hundred miles with them on the outbound journey, and no doubt the faint hope of their arrival was what kept them pressing on to the north right till the end. Some of the more calloused historians have gone so far as to question why Oates did not sacrifice himself sooner, after it became apparent to all that he could no longer travel the full distance on foot. The clear answer, I would argue, is that he hadn't fully given up on the dogs. And in telling passages from Scott's increasingly desperate journal we see that his last hopes lay not with the men back at base, but rather with the beasts: "We can expect little from man now. . . . We might have a dog's chance, but no more."[24]

HOW HISTORY WOULD COME
TO VIEW ALL THIS

"We took risks," Scott writes in his "Message to the Public" that was discovered among his papers inside their tent. "We knew we took them; things have come out against us, and therefore we have no cause for complaint. . . . These rough notes and our dead bodies must tell the tale."[25] In truth, we might reason that they took rather appalling risks, though certainly not ones that exceeded those of many of the other polar expeditions of the day. Both Shackleton in his bid for the pole and Wilson on his Winter Journey arguably took greater risks, though they are mostly given a free pass, seeing as how they lived. This is by no means a minor distinction, but it hardly seems valid to mark Shackleton a genius and Scott a fool, when the relative outcomes of both could so easily have been reversed. After all, Shackleton also relied on his men back at base coming out to the Barrier to replenish a depot, and if those men had, like Meares, failed to follow orders, Shackleton's team would not have made it back either.

On February 14, 1913, four days after news of the Pole Team's death had arrived in Britain, Scott's "Message to the Public" was read to one and a half million British schoolchildren to coincide with a memorial service being held at Saint Paul's cathedral. When Kathleen Scott died in 1947, among her papers was discovered a bundle of letters she had received from soldiers serving on the front lines, telling her that her late husband's words had helped them to face their hardships. But a reputation, much like an iceberg, is always in some state of transformation or decay.

In truth, historical revisionism started almost at once with Scott, as the surviving members of the expedition closed ranks and shored up their stories upon their return to civilization. It seems likely, for instance, that Atkinson gave false testimony upon discovering the bodies, when he declared that they showed no signs of scurvy. Likewise, Lt. Evans's statement in an interview from February 1913 that "Captain Scott left instructions that no search parties should leave the base to look for him" is patently untrue.[26] Five men were dead, and it may simply have seemed best to those involved to downplay any hint of a scandal. Over time there even emerged a widely held theory that Meares was forced to return home on the ship because his father had passed away, though as May and Airriess uncovered in 2014, genealogical records show that Henry John Meares did not die until 1919— seven years after Meares's return from Antarctica. Eventually, with the meddlesome assistance of some shoddy historian work (see appendix 1), Scott was largely recast into a bumbling failure, a leader who left "confused and contradictory instructions" for the dogs that were directly responsible for his party's death.[27]

As a result, Scott's place in the pantheon of Antarctic explorers has largely been usurped by the likes of Shackleton and Amundsen. Shackleton's reputation, in particular, has been elevated to legendary proportions over the past few decades, with the tales of his voyages recounted in numerous books and films. But this reveals far more about ourselves—our own willful myths and blind spots—than it does about the respective merits of these explorers.

In one particularly ironic twist, Shackleton has recently been rebranded as an American business school model, with talk of achievable benchmarks and entrepreneurship. This of a man who died over £40,000 in debt, who failed miserably at virtually every business venture he undertook in life, and who reneged on promised wages to a number of members of his crew. Truly, if there was one single issue that could be trusted to unite all three of these rival explorers, it would be a shared loathing of the financial world. A necessary evil, perhaps, but also only a temporary one, far removed from the lyric center of life, and meant to be sailed away from at the earliest possible convenience. But if the essence of the Heroic Age of

Antarctic exploration cannot be codified in CEO jargon and PowerPoint presentations on consumer trends, where is it to be found?

Historians and sociologists alike often theorize that today's fascination with Antarctic explorers "fills a heroism void" that our society is faced with today.[28] Though to me this is largely antithetical to what these men really have to teach us. After all, the British explorers who headed down to the Antarctic in the first years of the twentieth century also lived in decadent times, in an era when the needle of the moral compass of their society seemed to have gone astray, and the old ideals were felt surely to be dying out. To my mind, then, what these explorers most demonstrate is a stubborn insistence to not relegate things like heroism and bold discoveries to the distant past. They teach us to recognize that such dreams are still obtainable to us, through our own stories and art, among our own strange companions, and in our own flawed but irreplaceable lives. *Far away in my own white south*, indeed. And not a one of us can call on someone else to haul that dragging sledge.

APPENDIX 3

LIST OF THE TERRA NOVA EXPEDITION'S JOURNEYS, PARTIES, AND TEAMS

THE DEPOT JOURNEY. January to March 1911. Composed of thirteen men, eight ponies, and two dog teams. Established One Ton Depot thirty miles short of the eightieth parallel to aid in the Southern Journey.

THE WINTER JOURNEY. June and July 1911. Composed of Edward Wilson, Henry "Birdie" Bowers, and Apsley Cherry-Garrard. Man-hauled sixty miles out to Cape Crozier in an attempt to examine the live embryos of nesting emperor penguins.

THE SOUTHERN JOURNEY. October 1911 to March 1912. Composed of sixteen men, ten ponies, two dog teams, and two motorized sledges. The end goal of this journey was to allow a final Pole Team to claim the South Pole, with supporting units turning back to Cape Evans at various junctures of the outbound trip.

THE SEARCH JOURNEY. October to November 1912. Composed of eleven men, a team of mules, and two dog teams. Set out from Cape Evans with the goal of learning the fate of the Pole Team; discovered the bodies of Scott, Wilson, and Bowers on November 12.

THE SHORE PARTY. Composed of thirty-four men, nineteen ponies, and two dog teams. Established a base at Cape Evans from which they could conduct research and launch a series of exploratory journeys into the interior.

THE EASTERN/NORTHERN PARTY. A six-man party led by Scott's first officer, Victor Campbell. Operated independently of the rest of the Shore Party, traveling first to the east of McMurdo Sound on board the *Terra Nova*, where they stumbled upon Amundsen's party at the Bay of Whales, then proceeding north to Cape Adare, where they were forced to spend a second winter in an ice cave on Inexpressible Island.

THE MOTOR PARTY. Composed of Lt. Edward Evans, William Lashly, Bernard Day, and Frederick Hooper. Broke down only fifty miles from Cape Evans, after which the party continued south as a man-hauling unit. Day and Hooper turned back on November 24, two hundred miles from base, while Lashly and Lt. Evans continued on with the Southern Journey.

THE DOG TEAMS. Led by Cecil Meares and his assistant Dimitri Gerof. Turned back from the Southern Journey on December 11, 1911, near the bottom of the Beardmore Glacier. The dog teams were intended by Scott to make two additional voyages south in support of the returning parties, though the second was never carried out, and the third (led by Cherry-Garrard) fell well short of its original goals.

THE FIRST RETURN PARTY. Also referred to as the first support team. Composed of Edward Atkinson, Apsley Cherry-Garrard, Charles Wright, and Patrick Keohane. Turned back from the Southern Journey on December 22, 1911, near the top of the Beardmore Glacier. All members returned safely back to base the following January.

THE SECOND RETURN PARTY. Also referred to as the last support team. Composed of Lt. Edward Evans, William Lashly, and Thomas Crean. Turned back shorthanded from the Southern Journey on January 4, 1912, 150 miles short of the South Pole. All members returned safely back to base that February.

THE POLE TEAM. Composed of Robert Falcon Scott, Edward Wilson, Henry "Birdie" Bowers, Edgar "Taff" Evans, and Lawrence "Titus" Oates. Reached the South Pole on January 17, 1912. All members died during their failed return to Cape Evans.

APPENDIX 4

LIST OF EXPLORERS

AMUNDSEN, ROALD (1872–1928). *Belgica, Fram.* Norwegian adventurer. Member of first expedition to winter south of the Antarctic Circle; first to navigate Northwest Passage; first to South Pole; died during a rescue attempt of his former partner, Umberto Nobile.

ATKINSON, EDWARD (1881–1929). Known as "Atch." *Terra Nova.* English surgeon; awarded Albert Medal for rescue work in World War I.

BANKS, JOSEPH (1743–1820). *Endeavour.* English naturalist, botanist. Over eighty species of plants bear his name.

BELLINGSHAUSEN, THADDEUS (1778–1852). *Vostok.* Russian admiral. Discoverer of Peter I Island, Alexander Island, and most likely Antarctica.

BLACKBORROW, PERCE (1896–1949). *Endurance.* Welsh sailor and stowaway. First to set foot on Elephant Island.

BOWERS, HENRY (1883–1912). Known as "Birdie." *Terra Nova.* Scottish lieutenant. Member of the Winter Journey Party to Cape Crozier, as well as Scott's South Pole Party.

BRANSFIELD, EDWARD (1795–1852). *Williams.* Irish officer. Discoverer (along with William Smith) of South Shetland Islands; has disputed claim of discovering Antarctica.

CAMPBELL, VICTOR (1875–1956). Known as "The Wicked Mate." *Terra Nova*. English lieutenant, first officer. Leader of the Eastern/Northern Party that spent seven months in an ice cave on "Inexpressible Island."

CHERRY-GARRARD, APSLEY (1886–1959). Known as "Cherry." *Terra Nova*. English zoologist/classicist. Member of the Winter Journey Party to Cape Crozier; author of *The Worst Journey in the World*.

CLEMENTS, MARKHAM (1830–1916). English explorer, Royal Geographical Society president. Helped lead the revival of British exploration in the Antarctic.

COOK, FREDERICK (1865–1940). *Belgica*. American explorer, physician. Member of first expedition to winter south of the Antarctic Circle; falsely claimed to have reached both the North Pole and the summit of Denali.

COOK, JAMES (1728–1779). *Endeavour, Resolution*. English captain. First circumnavigation of the world in a high southern latitude; first to cross Antarctic Circle (among many other firsts).

CREAN, TOM (1877–1932). *Discovery, Terra Nova, Endurance*. Irish seaman. Member of Second Return Party on Scott's journey to the South Pole, for efforts on which—saving the life of Edward Evans—he was awarded the Albert Medal; participated in the open-boat journey across the Southern Ocean, as well as the first overland crossing of South Georgia.

DRAKE, FRANCIS (1540–1596). *Golden Hind*. English captain, slave trader, privateer. Discoverer of the Drake Passage; first Englishman to circumnavigate the world.

EVANS, EDGAR (1876–1912). Known as "Taff." *Discovery, Terra Nova*. Welsh seaman. Member of Scott's South Pole Party.

EVANS, EDWARD (1881–1957). Known as "Teddy." *Morning, Terra Nova*. English lieutenant. Member of Second Return Party on Scott's journey to the South Pole.

FRANKLIN, JOHN (1786–1847). *HMS Erebus*. English rear-admiral. Commander of an ill-fated expedition attempting to first navigate the Northwest Passage (the entire party, comprising 129 men, perished).

GERLACHE, BARON ADRIEN DE (1866–1934). *Belgica*. Belgian commander. Led the first expedition to winter south of the Antarctic Circle.

GEROF, DIMITRI (1888–1932?). *Terra Nova*. Russian dog-driver.

HANSSEN, HELMER (1870–1956). *Fram*. Norwegian adventurer. Member of Amundsen's South Pole Party, as well as his Northwest Passage crew.

HURLEY, FRANK (1885–1962). Known as "the Prince." *Aurora, Endurance*. Australian photographer, adventurer, film director. Served as a war photographer in both world wars.

HUSSEY, LEONARD (1891–1964). *Endurance, Quest*. English meteorologist/banjo player. Served in both world wars.

JAMES, REGINALD (1891–1964). *Endurance*. English physicist, naturalist. Served in World War I; participated in Mawson's later BANZARE Antarctic expedition.

JOHANSEN, HJALMAR (1867–1913). *Fram*. Norwegian explorer. Established famous Farthest North record with Nansen; sent home in disgrace from Amundsen's *Fram* expedition.

LASHLY, WILLIAM (1867–1940). *Discovery, Terra Nova*. English stoker and seaman. Member of Second Return Party on Scott's journey to the South Pole; awarded the Albert medal for saving the life of Edward Evans; served in World War I.

MACKINTOSH, AENEAS (1879–1916). *Nimrod, Aurora*. English officer. Commander of the ill-fated Ross Sea Party that was enlisted to help in Shackleton's continental crossing.

MAWSON, DOUGLAS (1882–1958). *Nimrod, Aurora*. Australian geologist and explorer. Member of first party to summit Mount Erebus and to trek to the South Magnetic Pole; led first exploratory expedition to King George V Land and Adelie Land; served in World War I; organized and led later BANZARE Antarctic expedition.

MCLEOD, TOM (1869–1960). *Terra Nova, Endurance, Quest*. Scottish seaman and Bible-retriever.

MCNISH, HENRY (1874–1930). Known as "Chippy." *Endurance*. Scottish seaman, carpenter. Participated in the open-boat journey across the Southern Ocean.

MEARES, CECIL (1877–1937). *Terra Nova*. Irish dog-handler, adventurer. Served in World War I.

NANSEN, FRIDTJOF (1861–1930). Norwegian scientist, renowned Arctic explorer. First interior crossing of Greenland; winner of the Nobel Prize.

NOBILE, UMBERTO (1885–1978). *Norse* [airship]. Italian aviator. Piloted
the first aircraft to reach the North Pole; survived a later crash landing
onto Arctic pack ice that launched a rescue effort that claimed the life of
his former flight partner Roald Amundsen.

OATES, LAWRENCE (1880–1912). Known as "Titus" or "the Soldier." *Terra
Nova*. English army captain. In charge of pony transport; member of
Scott's Pole Party.

PALMER, NATHANIEL (1799–1877). *Hero*. American sealer and adventurer.
Discoverer of South Orkney Islands; disputed claim of discovering
Antarctica.

PEARY, ROBERT (1856–1920). American explorer, captain. Disputed claim
of being first to reach the North Pole.

ROSS, JAMES CLARK (1800–1862). *Erebus*. English captain. First to travel
to North Magnetic Pole; discoverer of Ross Ice Shelf and McMurdo Sound
(among many other discoveries).

SCOTT, ROBERT FALCON (1868–1912). Sometimes known as "the Owner."
Discovery, Terra Nova. English captain. Discoverer of Dry Valleys; leader
of the British South Pole Party.

SHACKLETON, ERNEST (1874–1922). Known as "Shackles" and later
"the Boss." *Discovery, Nimrod, Endurance, Quest*. Anglo-Irish explorer.
Discoverer of Beardmore Glacier; leader of the open-boat journey across
the Southern Ocean, as well as the first overland crossing of South
Georgia.

SMITH, WILLIAM (1790–1847). *Williams*. English captain. Discoverer
(along with Edward Bransfield) of the South Shetland Islands.

SIMPSON, GEORGE (1878–1965). *Terra Nova*. English meteorologist.
Served in World War I and II.

WEDDELL, JAMES (1787–1834). *Jane*. English sealer, explorer. Discoverer
of Weddell Sea.

WILD, FRANK (1873–1939). *Discovery, Nimrod, Endurance, Quest*. English
lieutenant. Placed in charge of twenty-one shipwrecked men for five
months on Elephant Island; served in World War I.

WILSON, EDWARD (1872–1912). Known as "Uncle Bill." *Discovery, Terra
Nova*. English doctor, naturalist, artist. Leader of the Winter Journey to
Cape Crozier, and member of Scott's South Pole Party.

WORSLEY, FRANK (1872–1943). Known as "Wuzzles" or "Skipper." *Endurance, Quest.* New Zealand sailor. Served as navigator on the open-boat journey across the Southern Ocean, and participated in the first overland crossing of South Georgia; awarded the Distinguished Service Order in World War I.

ACKNOWLEDGMENTS

A book such as this would have never existed without the writings of those who preceded me. This holds true not just for the historical accounts of early explorers, but also for the contemporary writers who have furthered our understanding of—and fascination with—all things Antarctic. A handful of books that I feel particularly indebted to include the following: Caroline Alexander's *The Endurance*, David Campbell's *The Crystal Desert*, Edward Larson's *An Empire of Ice*, and Sarah Wheeler's *Terra Incognita*. From start to finish, these books are not only chock-full of useful information, but also a genuine pleasure to read. And while this book wound up being a work of prose, it was originally conceived as a small batch of poems, so I also want to credit Elizabeth Bradfield's wonderful collection of poetry *Approaching Ice*, which first opened my eyes into the wealth of Antarctic stories and their metaphoric potential.

My deepest thanks to Walter Biggins for believing in this book, and to Melissa Bugbee Buchanan and all the people associated with the University of Georgia Press for seeing it through the stages of production. I first began work on this manuscript during the winter of 2012–13, when I was snowed in at the Dutch Henry Homestead in southern Oregon, after having been awarded the Margery Davis Boyden Wilderness Writing Fellowship. For that, I will always be grateful to Bradley and Frank Boyden. I also would have never been able to afford that winter without the generous support of the Warren Wilson MFA Program's Larry Levis Stipend. (You may have awarded me those funds to complete a different book, but some-how this one found its way into the world first.)

For purposes of anonymity, some of the names of the passengers and crew from the cruise narrative have been changed. That being said, I've got only kind words to say about all the fine people I met associated with Lindblad Expeditions, with Stefan Lundgren and Kendra Bee deserving special mention. Along with, of course, Eric Guth, who—in addition to ev-erything else—offered much-needed feedback on an earlier draft of this manuscript. As did my wife, Rose McLarney: thanks.

NOTES

CHAPTER 1. *RESOLUTION* (1772–1775)

1. Beaglehole, *Journals*, 1:cclxxxii.
2. Cook, *Voyage towards the South Pole*, 2:124–25.
3. Cook, *Voyage towards the South Pole*, 1:16.
4. O'Sullivan, *In Search*, 165.
5. Cook to Walker, in Beaglehole, *Journals*, 2:689.
6. Beaglehole, *Journals*, 1:881, "Ships' Companies," entry for Daniel Clark, 32, from Essex. The only other accompanying information is that a shipmate calls him "Writer."
7. Cook, *Voyage towards the South Pole*, 2:124.
8. A sensible though incorrect theory, as salt gets precipitated out of seawater as it freezes.
9. Cook, *Voyage towards the South Pole*, 1:150.
10. On the website Goodreads, for instance, the quote is attributed to both "Cook" and "Crook."
11. Cook, *First Voyage*, 53.
12. Beatus of Liebana, quoted in Chapman, *Loneliest Continent*, 5.
13. Quoted in O'Sullivan, *In Search*, 17.
14. Quoted in Chapman, *Loneliest Continent*, 21.
15. Beaglehole, *Journals*, 3:479–80.
16. Beaglehole, *Journals*, 2:13 (adapted from chart).
17. Cook, *Voyage towards the South Pole*, 1:14.
18. Cook, *Voyage towards the South Pole*, 154.
19. Joseph Addison, quoted in Smithers, *Life*, 75.
20. Cook, *Voyage towards the South Pole*, 2:118–19.
21. Beaglehole, *Journals*, 2:960.
22. Quoted in Horwitz, *Blue Latitudes*, 405.

CHAPTER 2. *VOSTOK* (1819–1821)

1. Bellingshausen, *Voyage*, 33–34.
2. Bellingshausen, *Voyage*, 136.
3. Bellingshausen, *Voyage*, 152.
4. Bellingshausen, *Voyage*, 359.
5. Bellingshausen, *Voyage*, 120.
6. Campbell, *Crystal Desert*, 130.
7. Bellingshausen, *Voyage*, 410.
8. Bellingshausen, *Voyage*, 425.
9. Bellingshausen, *Voyage*, 425.
10. Quoted in Chapman, *Loneliest Continent*, 45.
11. Nunatak is an Inuit word commonly used in Antarctica. It means "a hill or mountain completely surrounded by glacial ice."
12. Bellingshausen, *Voyage*, 465.
13. Quoted in Montaigne, *Fraser's Penguins*, 81.

CHAPTER 3. *BELGICA* (1897–1899)

1. Cook, *Through the First Antarctic Night*, 48.
2. Cook, *Through the First Antarctic Night*, 172–73.
3. Cook, *Through the First Antarctic Night*, 132.
4. Cook, *Through the First Antarctic Night*, 200.
5. Cook, *Through the First Antarctic Night*, xiii.
6. Quoted in Lord, *Green Alaska*, xvii.
7. Cook, *Through the First Antarctic Night*, 213.
8. Amundsen, *My Life*, 28.
9. Cook, *Through the First Antarctic Night*, 319.
10. Cook, *Through the First Antarctic Night*, 310.
11. Carver, from "Locking Yourself Out, Then Trying to Get Back In," in *Where Water*, 33.
12. Cook, *Through the First Antarctic Night*, 326.
13. Cook, *Through the First Antarctic Night*, 339.
14. Quoted in D'Ambrosio, *Orphans*, 40.
15. Cook, *Through the First Antarctic Night*, 398.
16. Cook, *Through the First Antarctic Night*, 400.
17. Chauncey Depew, quoted in Bryce, *Cook & Peary*, 473.

CHAPTER 4. *DISCOVERY* (1901–1904)

1. Cherry-Garrard, *Worst Journey*, 207.
2. Quoted in Seaver, *Edward Wilson*, 75.
3. Wilson, *Diary of the Discovery Expedition*, 31.
4. Quoted in Seaver, *Edward Wilson*, 124.
5. Hemingway, *Nick Adams Stories*, 238.
6. Wilson, *Diary of the Discovery Expedition*, 48.
7. Wilson, *Diary of the Discovery Expedition*, 77.

8. Wilson, *Diary of the Discovery Expedition*, 77.

9. Wilson, *Diary of the Discovery Expedition*, 100.

10. Scott, *Voyage*, 1:110.

11. This story relayed in Fiennes, *Race*, 17.

12. Quoted in Montaigne, *Fraser's Penguins*, 1.

13. Cherry-Garrard, introduction to Seaver, *Edward Wilson*, xxii.

14. J. M. W. Turner was a great English landscape painter of the nineteenth century. He is reported to have once had himself tied to the mast of a ship during a storm to draw inspiration for his paintings.

15. Wilson, *Diary of the Terra Nova Expedition*, 92.

16. Frederic Kanoute, quoted in Hunter, "Sorry, Premier League."

17. Quoted in Crace, "Captain Scott."

18. Wilson, *Diary of the Discovery Expedition*, 171.

19. Wilson, *Diary of the Discovery Expedition*, 121.

20. Yeats, from "Adam's Curse," in *Collected Poems*, 80.

21. Wilson, *Diary of the Discovery Expedition*, 207.

22. "Hoosh" was the name for their daily stew, comprising an ever-changing host of ingredients, including biscuits, pemmican, raisins, curry paste, and cocoa powder.

23. Wilson, *Diary of the Discovery Expedition*, 288–89.

24. Wilson to his wife, quoted in Seaver, *Edward Wilson*, 60–61.

25. Scott, *Voyage*, 1:347.

26. Quoted in Seaver, *Edward Wilson*, 271.

27. Wilson, *Diary of the Discovery Expedition*, 216.

28. Wilson to his wife, quoted in Seaver, *Edward Wilson*, 106.

29. Wilson, *Diary of the Discovery Expedition*, 223.

30. Wilson, *Diary of the Discovery Expedition*, 229.

31. Wilson, *Diary of the Discovery Expedition*, 227.

32. Wilson, *Diary of the Discovery Expedition*, 238.

33. Quoted in Larson, *Empire*, 87.

34. Wilson, *Diary of the Discovery Expedition*, 243.

35. Quoted in Cherry-Garrard, *Worst Journey*, xxxiii.

36. Quoted in Cherry-Garrard, *Worst Journey*, xxxiv.

CHAPTER 5. *TERRA NOVA* (1910–1912),
WINTER JOURNEY

1. Cherry-Garrard, *Worst Journey*, vii.

2. Cherry-Garrard, *Worst Journey* (with preface to 1923 ed.), 3.

3. Cherry-Garrard, *Worst Journey* (with preface to 1923 ed.), 3.

4. Cherry-Garrard, *Worst Journey* (with preface to 1923 ed.), 3.

5. Quoted in Wheeler, *Cherry*, 64.

6. Quoted in Seaver, foreword to Wheeler, *Cherry*, lxi.

7. Cherry-Garrard, *Worst Journey*, 204–6.

8. Cherry-Garrard, *Worst Journey*, 180–81.

9. Cherry-Garrard, *Worst Journey*, 191.

10. Quoted in Wheeler, *Terra Incognita*, 170.

11. Cherry-Garrard, *Worst Journey*, 307.

12. Wilson to his wife, quoted in Cherry-Garrard, *Worst Journey*, lxiv.

13. Wheeler, *Cherry*, 69.

14. Cherry-Garrard, *Worst Journey*, 69.

15. Quoted in Wheeler, *Cherry*, 69.

16. Cherry-Garrard, *Worst Journey*, 214.

17. Cherry-Garrard, *Worst Journey*, 160.

18. Quoted in Cherry-Garrard, *Worst Journey*, 147–48.

19. Cherry-Garrard, *Worst Journey*, 232.

20. Wheeler, *Cherry*, 3.

21. Quoted in Wheeler, *Cherry*, 3.

22. Cherry-Garrard, *Worst Journey*, 254.

23. Cherry-Garrard, *Worst Journey*, 242.

24. Cherry-Garrard, *Worst Journey*, 242, 245.

25. Cherry-Garrard, *Worst Journey*, 274.

26. Cherry-Garrard, *Worst Journey*, 279.

27. Cherry-Garrard, *Worst Journey*, 278.

28. Wilson, *Diary of the Terra Nova Expedition*, 156.

29. Cherry-Garrard, *Worst Journey*, 284.

30. Cherry-Garrard, *Worst Journey*, 289.

31. Cherry-Garrard, *Worst Journey*, 302.

32. Cherry-Garrard, *Worst Journey*, 304.

33. Cherry-Garrard, *Worst Journey*, 597–98.

34. Parsons, quoted in McKie, "How a Heroic Hunt."

CHAPTER 6. *FRAM* (1910–1912)

1. Quoted in Montaigne, *Fraser's Penguins*, 88.

2. Amundsen, *My Life*, 2.

3. Quoted in Amundsen, *South Pole*, 1:42.

4. Amundsen, *South Pole*, 1:179.

5. Amundsen, *South Pole*, 1:1.

6. Amundsen, *South Pole*, 1:54, 67, 95.

7. Quoted in Solomon, *Coldest March*, 64.

8. Amundsen, *South Pole*, 1:44.

9. Crane, *Scott*, 383.

10. Amundsen, *South Pole*, 1:129.

11. Amundsen, *My Life*, 237.

12. Amundsen, *South Pole*, 1:137.

13. Fiennes, *Race*, 61.

14. Amundsen, *South Pole*, 1:44.

15. Campbell, *Crystal Desert*, 9.

16. Shapley, *Seventh Continent*, 15.

17. Abbey, *Journey*, 87.

18. Wheeler, *Terra Incognita*, 308.

19. Scott to Kinsey, quoted in Solomon, *Coldest March*, 170.

20. Amundsen, *My Life*, 258.

21. Amundsen, *South Pole*, 1:384.

22. Quoted in Alexander, "Man," 125.

23. Amundsen, *South Pole*, 1:389.

24. Quoted in Huntford, Race, 42.

25. Amundsen, *South Pole*, 2:2.

26. Amundsen, *South Pole*, 2:62.

27. Scott, *Voyage*, 1:343.

28. Amundsen, *South Pole*, 2:65.

29. Senator Dodd, quoted in Day, *Antarctica*, 493.

30. For their part, the Soviet Union had to settle for establishing their largest base far into the barren interior of East Antarctica. The *Vostok* station records an annual mean temperature of negative sixty-seven degrees—ten degrees colder than the South Pole.

31. Quoted in Huntford, *Last Place*, 469.

32. Hanssen, *Voyages*, 113–14.

33. Quoted in Alexander, "Man," 134.

CHAPTER 7. *ENDURANCE* (1914–1917)

1. 38:29, KJV.

2. Quoted in Larson, *Empire*, 53.

3. Quoted in Alexander, *Endurance*, 193.

4. Quoted in Huntford, *Shackleton*, 652.

5. Lopez, *About This Life*, 72.

6. Quoted in Lansing, *Endurance*, 11.

7. Quoted in Huntford, *Shackleton*, 364.

8. Quoted in Wheeler, *Cherry*, 187.

9. Quoted in Huntford, *Shackleton*, 365.

10. Reginald Ford, quoted in Huntford, *Shackleton*, 75.

11. Worsley, *Endurance*, 14–15.

12. Quoted in Hurley, *South*, 233.

13. Quoted in Huntford, *Shackleton*, 384.

14. Quoted in Alexander, *Endurance*, 13.

15. Alexander, *Endurance*, 54.

16. Shackleton, *South*, 71.

17. Hurley, *Argonauts*, 187.

18. Quoted in Alexander, *Endurance*, 88.

19. Quoted in Huntford, *Shackleton*, 455.

20. Quoted in Huntford, *Shackleton*, 463.

21. Quoted in Alexander, *Endurance*, 99.

22. Shackleton, *South*, 96.

23. Shackleton, *South*, 96.

24. Quoted in Lansing, *Endurance*, 96.

25. Quoted in Alexander, *Endurance*, 115.

26. Hurley, *Argonauts*, 166.

27. Shackleton, *South*, 119.

28. Shackleton, *South*, 120.

29. Quoted in Alexander, *Endurance*, 125.

30. Shackleton, *South*, 139.

31. Shackleton, *South*, 140.

32. Wordie, quoted in Alexander, *Endurance*, 127.

33. Quoted in Alexander, *Endurance*, 125.

34. Cherry-Garrard, *Worst Journey*, 580.

35. Taking all the poetry out of the process, the three lifeboats were simply named after the expedition's chief benefactors.

36. Wheeler, *Terra Incognita*, 81.

37. Quoted in Alexander, *Endurance*, 139–41.

38. Shackleton, South, 169.

39. Campbell, *Crystal Desert*, 206.

40. Quoted in Huntford, *Shackleton*, 547.

41. Shackleton, *South*, 168.

42. Emily Shackleton to H. R. Mill, quoted in Huntford, *Shackleton*, 154.

43. Le Guin, *Compass Rose*, 257.

44. Le Guin, *Compass Rose*, 259.

45. Le Guin, *Compass Rose*, 272.

46. Campbell, *Crystal Desert*, 34.

47. Shackleton, *South*, 173.

48. Worsley, *Shackleton's Boat Journey*, 144.

49. Le Guin, *Compass Rose*, 270.

50. Le Guin, *Compass Rose*, 263. Implicit in this is also a clear literary critique, disputing the level of merit in a canon made up almost exclusively of white males.

51. Some of the dialogue in this section is adapted from a *National Geographic* article, "First Conquest of Antarctica's Highest Peaks" (Clinch), and from an interview and profile of John Evans (Knapp, "Meet John Evans").

52. Shackleton, *South*, 187–88.

53. Shackleton, *South*, 201.

54. Worsley, *Shackleton's Boat Journey*, 216.

55. Quoted in Wheeler, *Terra Incognita*, 81.

56. Quoted in Williams, *With Scott*, 191.

57. Shackleton, *South*, 204.

58. Eliot, "The Waste Land," in *Waste Land*, 67.

59. Quoted in Alexander, *Endurance*, 171.

60. Alexander, *Endurance*, 174.

61. Alexander, *Endurance*, 181.

62. Alexander, *Endurance*, 202.

63. Hurley, *Argonauts*, 290.

64. Shackleton, *South*, xvii.

65. Shackleton, *South*, xxvi.

66. Sara Wheeler puts forth this very claim, in relation to Cherry-Garrard, in the opening pages of her biography *Cherry*, so I am really just expanding it here through a comparison with Shackleton.

67. Quoted in Wheeler, *Terra Incognita*, 88.

68. Shackleton to Janet Stancomb-Wills, quoted in Huntford, *Shackleton*, 685.

69. Alexander, *Endurance*, 193.

CHAPTER 8. *TERRA NOVA* (1910–1912), POLE JOURNEY

1. Scott, *Scott's Last Expedition*, 423.
2. Scott, *Scott's Last Expedition*, 418.
3. Scott, *Scott's Last Expedition*, 423–24.
4. Scott, *Scott's Last Expedition*, 424.
5. Scott, *Scott's Last Expedition*, 424.
6. Huntford, *Race*, 248.
7. Scott, *Scott's Last Expedition*, 424–25.
8. Scott, *Scott's Last Expedition*, 426.
9. Quoted in Bainbridge, *Birthday Boys*, 181.
10. Amundsen, *South Pole*, 2:133.
11. Scott, *Scott's Last Expedition*, 428.
12. Cherry-Garrard, *Worst Journey*, 512.
13. Cherry-Garrard, *Worst Journey*, 513.
14. Scott, *Scott's Last Expedition*, 428.
15. Quoted in Wheeler, *Terra Incognita*, 155.
16. Scott, *Scott's Last Expedition*, 429–30.
17. Scott, *Scott's Last Expedition*, 430.
18. Scott, *Scott's Last Expedition*, 416.
19. Scott, *Scott's Last Expedition*, 430–31.
20. Scott, *Scott's Last Expedition*, 422.
21. Cherry-Garrard, *Worst Journey*, 222.
22. Scott, *Scott's Last Expedition*, 431.
23. Scott, *Scott's Last Expedition*, 431.
24. Wilson, *Diary of the Terra Nova Expedition*, 95.
25. Quoted in Cherry-Garrard, *Worst Journey*, 514.
26. Wilson, *Diary of the Terra Nova Expedition*, 232.
27. Scott, *Scott's Last Expedition*, 432–33.
28. Scott, *Scott's Last Expedition*, 434.
29. Scott, *Scott's Last Expedition*, 412–13.
30. Scott, *Scott's Last Expedition*, 434–35.
31. Wilson, *Diary of the Terra Nova Expedition*, 238.
32. Scott, *Scott's Last Expedition*, 435–36.
33. Quoted in Cherry-Garrard, *Worst Journey*, 382.
34. Scott, *Scott's Last Expedition*, 436.
35. Scott, *Scott's Last Expedition*, 437.
36. Scott, *Scott's Last Expedition*, 438; quoted in Huntford, *Race*, 271, 277.
37. Scott, *Scott's Last Expedition*, 439.
38. Scott, *Scott's Last Expedition*, 396.
39. Scott, *Scott's Last Expedition*, 439.
40. Scott, *Scott's Last Expedition*, 440.
41. Scott, *Scott's Last Expedition*, 396–97.
42. Scott, *Scott's Last Expedition*, 440–41.
43. Wilson, *Diary of the Terra Nova Expedition*, 241.
44. Scott, *Scott's Last Expedition*, 442–43.

45. Wilson, *Diary of the Terra Nova Expedition*, 242.
46. Scott, *Scott's Last Expedition*, 444.
47. Scott, *Scott's Last Expedition*, 446.
48. Wilson, *Diary of the Terra Nova Expedition*, 243.
49. Scott, *Scott's Last Expedition*, 446–47.
50. Wilson, *Diary of the Terra Nova Expedition*, 212.
51. Quoted in Cherry-Garrard, *Worst Journey*, 407.
52. Wheeler, *Cherry*, 132.
53. Scott, *Scott's Last Expedition*, 451.
54. Scott, *Scott's Last Expedition*, 453.
55. Wilson, *Diary of the Terra Nova*, 245.
56. Quoted in Wheeler, *Terra Incognita*, 154.
57. Scott, *Scott's Last Expedition*, 455.
58. Scott, *Scott's Last Expedition*, 455–56.
59. Scott, *Scott's Last Expedition*, 456–57.
60. Scott, *Scott's Last Expedition*, 458–59.
61. Scott, *Scott's Last Expedition*, 459.
62. Wheeler, *Cherry*, 134.
63. Scott, *Scott's Last Expedition*, 460.
64. Scott, *Scott's Last Expedition*, 461.
65. Scott, *Scott's Last Expedition*, 461–64.
66. Cherry-Garrard, *Worst Journey*, 501.
67. Scott, *Scott's Last Expedition*, 470–71.
68. Scott, *Scott's Last Expedition*, 470.
69. Quoted in Seaver, *Edward Wilson*, 293.
70. Quoted in Larson, *Empire*, 284–85.
71. Scott, *Scott's Last Expedition*, 475; quoted in Fiennes, *Race*, 339.

APPENDIX 1. ON HISTORIAN ROLAND HUNTFORD AND CONTROVERSIES SURROUNDING SCOTT AND AMUNDSEN

1. See Fiennes, *Race*, 386.
2. Young, "On the Debunking of Captain Scott," in *Encounter*, 9.
3. Quoted in Huntford, *Last Place*, 45.
4. Huntford, *Last Place*, 229.
5. Quoted in Wheeler, *Terra Incognita*, 57.
6. Huntford, *Race*, 35.
7. Huntford, *Last Place*, 539.
8. Huntford, *Last Place*, 403.
9. Oates to his mother, quoted in Solomon, *Coldest March*, 267.
10. Quoted in Huntford, *Shackleton*, 264.
11. Quoted in Fiennes, *Race*, 379.
12. Huntford, *Last Place*, 456.
13. Oates to his mother, quoted in Solomon, *Coldest March*, 212.
14. Translated in Huntford, *Last Place*, 546.
15. Solomon, *Coldest March*, xvi.

16. Huntford, *Race*, 307.
17. Fiennes, *Race*, xiii.
18. Shackleton to Joyce, Huntford, *Shackleton*, 641.
19. Huntford, *Last Place*, 561–62.
20. Fiennes, *Race*, 375.
21. Fiennes, *Race*, 61.
22. Huntford, *Last Place*, 452.
23. Huntford, *Race*, 215.
24. Scott, *Scott's Last Expedition*, 394.
25. Scott, *Scott's Last Expedition*, 415.
26. Huntford, *Race*, 221.
27. Scott, *Scott's Last Expedition*, 461.
28. Huntford, *Last Place*, 516.
29. Quoted in Solomon, *Coldest March*, 295.
30. Quoted in Solomon, *Coldest March*, 295.
31. Solomon, *Coldest March*, 297.
32. Huntford, *Last Place*, 457.
33. May, "Could Captain Scott," 79.
34. Huntford, *Last Place*, 520.
35. Huntford, *Last Place*, 525.
36. Wilson, *Diary of the Terra Nova Expedition*, 212.
37. Quoted in Seaver, *Edward Wilson*, 294.

APPENDIX 2. ON THE QUESTIONS AND CONTROVERSIES SURROUNDING SCOTT'S ORDERS FOR THE DOGS

1. Quoted in Amundsen, *My Life*, 72.
2. Scott, *Voyage*, 1:343.
3. Scott, *Scott's Last Expedition*, 352.
4. Scott, *Scott's Last Expedition*, 394.
5. Quoted in Evans, *South*, 160–62.
6. Evans, *South*, 162–63.
7. Quoted in May and Airriess, "Could Captain Scott," 261.
8. Quoted in Evans, *South*, 153.
9. Cherry-Garrard, *Worst Journey*, 424–26.
10. Cherry-Garrard, *Worst Journey*, 424.
11. Scott, *Scott's Last Expedition*, 374.
12. Scott, *Scott's Last Expedition*, 453.
13. Scott, *Scott's Last Expedition*, 459.
14. Scott, *Scott's Last Expedition*, 309–10.
15. Quoted in May and Airriess, "Could Captain Scott," 264.
16. Quoted in May and Airriess, "Could Captain Scott," 264.
17. May, "Could Captain Scott," 81.
18. May, "Could Captain Scott," 73.
19. May, "Could Captain Scott," 80.
20. Cherry-Garrard, *Worst Journey*, 430.
21. Quoted in May and Airriess, "Could Captain Scott," 270.

22. Cherry-Garrard, *Worst Journey*, 427.
23. Wheeler, *Cherry*, 135.
24. Scott, *Scott's Last Expedition*, 456, 459.
25. Scott, *Scott's Last Expedition*, 477.
26. Quoted in Fiennes, *Race*, 351.
27. Huntford, *Race*, 293.
28. Potier, "Shackleton in Business School," *Harvard Gazette*.

SELECTED BIBLIOGRAPHY

Abbey, Edward. *The Journey Home*. New York: Penguin: 1991.

Alexander, Caroline. *The Endurance*. New York: Knopf, 1998.

———. "The Man Who Took the Prize." *National Geographic*, Sep. 2011.

Amundsen, Roald. *My Life as an Explorer*. New York: Doubleday, 1928.

———. *The South Pole: An Account of the Norwegian Antarctic Expedition in the "Fram," 1910–1912*. Trans. A. G. Chater. 2 vols. London: John Murray, 1913.

Bainbridge, Beryl. *The Birthday Boys*. New York: Carroll & Graf, 1994.

Baughmann, T. S. *Before the Heroes Came*. Lincoln: University of Nebraska Press, 1994.

Beaglehole, J. C., ed. *The Journals of Captain James Cook*. 4 vols. Cambridge: Cambridge University Press, 1961.

Bellingshausen, Thaddeus von. *The Voyage of Captain Bellingshausen to the Antarctic Seas, 1819–1821*. Ed. Frank Debernham. 2 vols. London: Hakluyt Society, 1945.

Bradfield, Elizabeth. *Approaching Ice*. New York: Persea Books, 2010.

Bryce, Robert M. *Cook & Peary: The Polar Controversy, Resolved*. Mechanicsburg, Pa.: Stackpole Books, 1997.

Campbell, David. *The Crystal Desert*. New York: Houghton Mifflin, 1992.

Carver, Ray. *Where Water Comes Together with Other Water*. New York: Random House, 1985.

Chapman, Walker. *The Loneliest Continent*. Greenwich, Conn.: New York Graphic Society Publishers, 1964.

Cherry-Garrard, Apsley. *The Worst Journey in the World*. New York: Carrol & Graf, 2003.

——. *The Worst Journey in the World*. With preface to 1923 ed. Washington, D.C.: National Geographic Society, 2002.

Clinch, Nicholas. "First Conquests of Antarctica's Highest Peaks." *National Geographic*, June 1967.

Cook, Frederick. *Through the First Antarctic Night*. Centennial ed. Pittsburgh: Polar Publishing, 1998.

Cook, James. *First Voyage round the World*. Bremen, Germany: Salzwasser Verlag, 2009.

——. *A Voyage towards the South Pole and round the World*. 2 vols. Columbia, S.C.: Jefferson Publication, 2016.

Crace, John. "Captain Scott: A Second-Rate Hero?" *Guardian*, Sep. 27, 2010.

Crane, David. *Scott of the Antarctic: A Biography*. New York: Vintage Books, 2007.

D'Ambrosio, Charles. *Orphans*. Astoria, Ore.: Clear Cut Press, 2004.

Day, David. *Antarctica: A Biography*. New York: Oxford University Press, 2013.

Dodds, Klaus. *The Antarctic: A Very Short Introduction*. New York: Oxford University Press, 2012.

Eliot, T. S. *The Waste Land and Other Poems*. New York: Penguin, 1998.

Evans, Edward. *South with Scott*. London: Collins Sons, 1958.

Fiennes, Ranulph. *Race to the Pole*. New York: Hyperion, 2004.

Franzen, Jonathan. "The End of the End of the World." *New Yorker*, May 2016.

Glasberg, Elena. *Antarctica as Cultural Critique*. New York: Palgrave Macmillan, 2012.

Green, Bill. *Water, Ice & Stone: Science and Memory on the Antarctic Lakes*. New York: Bellevue Literary Press, 2008.

Gurney, Alan. *Below the Convergence: Voyages toward Antarctica*. New York: Norton, 1997.

Hanssen, Helmer Julius. *Voyages of a Modern Viking*. London: George Routledge & Sons, 1936.

Hass, Robert. *Human Wishes*. New York: Ecco, 1989.

Hemingway, Ernest. *The Nick Adams Stories*. New York: Scribner, 1972.

Horwitz, Tony. *Blue Latitudes*. New York: Henry Holt, 2002.

Hunter, Graham. "Sorry, Premier League." ESPN Football website, Jan. 17, 2017. http://www.espn.com/soccer/spanish-primeradivision/15/blog/post/3040734/spanish-liga-still-beats-the-premier-league-and-here-is-why.

Huntford, Roland. *The Last Place on Earth* (published in the UK as *Scott and Amundsen*). New York: Modern Library, 1999.

——. *Race for the South Pole*. London: Continuum International, 2010.

——. *Shackleton*. New York: Athenum, 1986.

Hurley, Frank. *Argonauts of the South*. New York: G.P. Putnam's Sons, 1925.

——. *South with Endurance*. New York: Simon & Schuster, 2001.

Knapp, Stephen. "Meet John Evans." justaroundhere.com, March 30, 2015. http://justaroundhere.com/index.php/all-sections/names-faces/it-s-nice-to-know-you/1364-meet-john-evans.

Lansing, Alfred. *Endurance*. New York: Carroll & Graf, 2000.

Larson, Edward J. *An Empire of Ice*. New Haven: Yale University Press, 2011.

Le Guin, Ursula K. *The Compass Rose*. New York: Harper & Row, 1982.

Lopez, Barry. *About This Life*. New York: Knopf, 1998.

Lord, Nancy. *Green Alaska: Dreams from the Far Coast*. New York: Counter Point, 1999.

May, Karen. "Could Captain Scott Have Been Saved? Revisiting Scott's Last Expedition." *Polar Record* 49, no. 1 (January 2013), 72–90.

May, Karen, and Sarah Airriess. "Could Captain Scott Have Been Saved? Cecil Meares and the 'Second Journey' That Failed." *Polar Record* 51, no. 1 (January 2015), 260–73.

McKie, Robin. "How a Heroic Hunt for Penguin Eggs Became 'The Worst Journey in the World.'" *Guardian*, Jan. 14, 2012.

McLynn, Frank. *Captain Cook*. New Haven: Yale University Press, 2011.

Montaigne, Fen. *Fraser's Penguins*. New York: Henry Holt, 2010.

O'Sullivan, Daniel. *In Search of Captain Cook: Exploring the Man through His Own Words*. New York: St. Martin's, 2008.

Potier, Beth. "Shackleton in Business School." *Harvard Gazette*, Jan. 29, 2012. https://news.harvard.edu/gazette/story/2004/01/shackleton-in-business -school/.

Richie, Tom. "The Antarctica Primer" (informational booklet). New York: Lindblad Expeditions, 1990.

Scott, Robert F. *Scott's Last Expedition*. New York: Dodd, Mead, 1929.

———. *The Voyage of the Discovery*. 2 vols. London: Smith, Elder, 1907.

Seaver, George. *Edward Wilson of the Antarctic*. London: Butler & Tanner, 1936.

Shackleton, Ernest. *The Heart of the Antarctic*. New York: Greenwood, 1969.

———. *South*. New York: Penguin, 2004.

Shapley, Deborah. *The Seventh Continent: Antarctica in a Resource Age*. New York: RFF, 2011.

Smithers, Peter. *The Life of Joseph Addison*. London: Oxford University Press, 1968.

Solomon, Susan. *The Coldest March*. New Haven: Yale University Press, 2001.

Thomas, Nicholas. *Cook: The Extraordinary Voyages of James Cook*. New York: Walker, 2003.

Wheeler, Sara. *Cherry: A Life of Apsley Cherry-Garrard*. New York: Modern Library, 2003.

———. *Terra Incognita*. New York: Modern Library, 1999.

Williams, Isobel. *With Scott in the Antarctic: Edward Wilson*. Gloucestershire: History Press, 2008.

Wilson, Edward. *Diary of the Discovery Expedition*. New York: Humanities Press, 1967.

———. *Diary of the Terra Nova Expedition*. London: Blandford, 1972.

Worsley, Frank. *Endurance*. New York: Norton, 1931.

———. *Shackleton's Boat Journey*. New York: Norton, 1977.

Yeats, William Butler. *The Collected Poems of W. B. Yeats*. Ed Richard J. Finneran. 2nd ed. New York: Scribner, 1996.

Young, Wayland. "On the Debunking of Captain Scott." *Encounter*, 1980, 8–18.